WITHDRAWN
UTSA Libraries

Generating Natural Language Under Pragmatic Constraints

Generating Natural Language Under Pragmatic Constraints

Eduard H. Hovy

Information Sciences Institute
of the University of Southern California

 LAWRENCE ERLBAUM ASSOCIATES, PUBLISHERS

1988   Hillsdale, New Jersey   Hove and London

LIBRARY
The University of Texas
at San Antonio

Copyright © 1988 by Lawrence Erlbaum Associates, Inc.
All rights reserved. No part of this book may be reproduced in
any form, by photostat, microform, retrieval system, or any other
means, without the prior written permission of the publisher.

Lawrence Erlbaum Associates, Inc., Publishers
365 Broadway
Hillsdale, New Jersey 07642

Library of Congress Cataloging-in-Publication Data

Hovy, Eduard H.
   Generating natural language under pragmatic
constraints.

   Based on the author's thesis (doctoral--Yale Univer-
sity, 1987)
   Bibliography; p
   Includes index.
   1. Artificial intelligence--Data processing.
2. Linguistics--Data processing. I. Title.
Q336.H68 1988   006.3'5   88-3552
ISBN 0-8058-0248-7
ISBN 0-8058-0249-5 (pbk.)

Printed in the United States of America
10 9 8 7 6 5 4 3 2 1

To Beverly

Contents

Appendices   157

Bibliography   187

Name Index   205

Topic Index   209

Preface

This book is based on my doctoral dissertation at Yale University, submitted in February 1987. It includes a few major changes, some updates, and lots of small amendments.

The temptation existed to cut out a large part of chapter 2 because it is rather imprecise — the kind of thing that gives the scruffies in Artificial Intelligence a bad name. But I withstood the temptation, since the book is aimed at a larger audience than just AI people and linguists who happen to be doing generation. I hope anyone interested in understanding how language works in the wider sense — that is, including pragmatics — will get from the book an idea of the numerous issues involved and the marvelous ways they work together for successful communication. I also hope they will be inspired to go ahead and work out all the imprecisions, so that we can slowly make concrete the many pragmatic issues that have remained unexplored during the first thirty years of natural language processing. It is sad that there exist today, to my knowledge, *no* parsers and only two generators that try to take into account more than just factual information!

The Form of this Book

This book mirrors the generation process: first, discussion centers on pragmatic goals (chapter 2), next, on rhetorical goals and strategies for achieving them (chapters 3, 4, and 5), and after that follows a description of the appropriate nature of the lexicon and a walkthrough of the realization process (chapter 6). Chapter 7 contains an overview of the program together with an argument for the way in which text planning and text realization should interleave. Chapter 8, the conclusion, traces the development of AI work in language generation, PAULINE's place in it, and mentions what must come next. Appendix A contains an annotated trace of a PAULINE session and appendix B contains PAULINE's phrasal grammar.

Throughout the book, theory and program description appear in parallel. This is largely due to the fact that no single aspect of text planning, realization, or the lexicon is fully worked through. The topic is simply too large. Rather, each chapter states some problem that arises in generation, develops a pragmatics-based solution, and then describes briefly how the solution is implemented in PAULINE. Thus readers who are not excited by AI programs may comfortably skip the latter third of each chapter, except for chapter 2.

Acknowledgements

When writing this section, your first inclination is to make a list of everyone you know and delete those you don't like. I suspect this has been done. The second inclination is just the opposite: thank you, dear colleagues, and goodbye.

A little too brusque, perhaps.

Oh well, then, switch the formality on high and the verbosity on high and the gratefulness on effusive and let the phrasal lexicon do its stuff...

> In the first place, I wish to express my heartfelt gratitude to my advisor, professor Roger Schank. Acting in loco parentis, as he was not infrequently wont to inform us, to his students, he does a truly excellent job of fostering the creative approach, the wide view, and an energetic and challenging environment.

Stop. Not good. Quit now, or at least try the verbosity on low and the formality on medium!

> I would also like to thank professors Drew McDermott and Bob Abelson, the other two members of my thesis committee, as well as doctor Chris Riesbeck.

Better? Nyaaah... Need less gratefulness and more force.

> For discussion and analysis and occasional healthy doses of cynicism, there's nobody to beat Larry Birnbaum. Thanks, LB.
>
> For working on PAULINE and its predecessors and providing ideas, language skills, and comments, thanks to Gita Ashok, Yang-Dong Lee, Ashwin Ram, Jeff Grossman, Natalie Dehn, Steve Lytinen, Michael Factor, and Chris Owens. Thanks to Rod McGuire for the very first push and to Laurence Danlos for more pushes; and to David McDonald and Tony Jameson for talks and proofreading comments. David Littleboy provided more cynicism (his peculiar flavour, though) and chess, and Bill Bain provided JUDGE and interesting discussions. Thanks to the T people, the secretaries, and the facility staff. And of course to the Advanced Research Projects Agency, monitored by the Office of Naval Research, whose contract N00014-82-K-0149 supported most of this work. Special thanks to Norm Sondheimer and Bill Mann for help when I needed it.

Well, *that's* not too interesting any more. Too much thanks. Cut it short. Haste on high.

> *Thanks to all the other people in the lab and outside it who made life bearable when I got homesick, especially to Rob and Ilana for chamber music and motor mechanics; to Gabriel (on and off the squash court) and Paola (inside and outside the ice-cream store). Most especially to Beverly.*

Final tally: syrupiness unhealthily high. Rewrite? No, that's really a program's job.

Hmmm...

So is writing in the first place...

E.H.H.

Chapter 1

Introduction

1.1 Things People Say

When you compare the language produced by people to the text produced by existing language generation programs, one thing becomes clear immediately: people can say the same thing in various ways to achieve various effects, and generators cannot. The generator described in this book, PAULINE (Planning And Uttering Language In Natural Environments), addresses this shortcoming.

It is straightforward to write a language generation program that produces impressive text by associating a sentence template (or some equivalent general grammatical form) with each representational item and then using a grammar to realize the template into surface form. Such a program, however, is not sensitive to anything but the input items, and therefore produces the same output to all hearers in all circumstances.

When we produce language, we tailor our text to the hearer and to the situation. This enables us to communicate more information than is contained in the literal meanings of our words; indeed, the additional information often has a stronger effect on the hearer than the literal content has. This information is carried by both the content and the form of the text:

> "Old Bill finally kicked the bucket last night!"
> "We are not going to see Uncle Bill any more..."
> "I am very sorry to have to tell you that Bill passed away"

As speakers and hearers, we attach various interpretations of the speaker, his or her goals, the hearer, and the conversational circumstances, to the various ways of

expressing a single underlying representation. These interpretations are governed
by rules. Speakers use the rules to determine how to say what they want to say.
In order to exhibit the same degree of flexibility of expression, generator programs
require such rules too.

What, then, is the additional information that speakers can convey? Consider
the different points of view the speaker communicates in each of the following four
descriptions of an event that happened at Yale University in April 1986:

(a) *On April 4, concerned Yale students constructed a shantytown
on Boesak Plaza as a reminder to those in Woodbridge Hall (and all
over campus and the community) that Yale is complicit (sic) with the
system of apartheid that creates shantytowns where thousands of blacks
are forced to live in squalor and fear. The shantytown, Winnie Mandela
City, served as a focal point of education concerning South Africa and
Yale's investments there. At 5:30 am on April 14 the Yale Administration had the shantytown torn down and had 76 students and community
members who were defending the shanties arrested. After a huge outcry,
the Administration allowed the shanties to be rebuilt. We will not be
silenced; we will continue to challenge the University on their moral failure.* (From: protester literature; the protesters renamed the plaza after
the South African churchman Allan Boesak)

(b) *On April 4, a small group of students took over Beinecke Plaza
and built some shanties; they wanted to force Yale to sell its stocks in
companies with branches located in South Africa. The university asked
the students to move the shanties to another location, but the students
refused. The university then granted them permission to occupy the
plaza until the end of the week, so that they could be there to be seen
by the university's trustees, the Yale Corporation, at their meeting. But
even after the meeting, the students refused to leave the plaza, and police
had to clear the shanties. Later, the university relented, and gave them
permission to rebuild the shanties. It also announced that it would send
a fact-finding mission to South Africa.* (Speaker: anti-divestment Yale
student)

(c) *On April 4, students at Yale built a symbolic shantytown to
protest their school's investments in companies doing business in South
Africa. The college ordered the shanties destroyed. The police arrested
76 protesters when the shantytown was torn down. Local politicians and
more than 100 faculty members criticized the action. A week after it had
ordered the removal of the shantytown – named Winnie Mandela City,
after the South African foe of apartheid – the shantytown was recon-
structed and the administration agreed to allow it to remain standing.*

Concurrently, Yale announced that its trustees, the Yale Corporation, would soon send a fact-finding mission to South Africa to investigate the actions of corporations in which it owns between $350 million and $400 million of stock. (From: *The New York Times*, Sunday, 27 April 1986, Connecticut section)

(d) *Some students erected a shantytown to protest Yale's investments in companies that have operations in South Africa. The University tore it down and arrested several of them. The students continued to demonstrate and finally the university said they could put up the shantytown again. The university said it would investigate its investments in South Africa.* (Speaker: neutral student)

Clearly the first two speakers incorporate strongly their opinions about the shantytown issue; the second two speakers seem more neutral but differ in level of formality. But how do you "incorporate opinions" and what does it mean to "seem more neutral" and to "be formal"? There is no single item in the texts that can be pinpointed as carrying the opinion or setting the level or formality; rather, each text seems to contain a number of little clues, and these clues cumulatively convey a certain impression to the reader. What are these little clues? Where do they appear in language and how do we decide to use them? How do they interact? What other impressions — information such as the speaker's emotional state, social status relative to the hearer, the ways he or she would like to influence the hearer's future behavior — can be incorporated into language?

Some additional, rather overt, techniques are used in the following two texts. They date from a labor strike at Yale University in 1984. The first is an excerpt from an open letter to Yale President Giamatti from the university's clerical and technical workers' labor union negotiating committee, November 9, 1984:

(e) *It is time, in the best interests of all concerned, to settle the strike. It is our understanding that the University administration, as well as the Union, has received a document entitled 'A Statement of Purpose by the Coalition to End the Strike'. We appreciate the spirit of the document. Clearly, the community earnestly desires and needs a settlement, so that Yale can get back to what it is supposed to be. Our members earnestly want a settlement. You have said that you do, too, and we are prepared to take you at your word. We are willing to compromise significantly to achieve a settlement. Therefore, we propose the immediate resumption of negotiations on a daily basis.*

Style is expressly used to impute blame to the other side: the union "earnestly desires and needs a settlement"; they "are willing to compromise"; they will "take [Yale] at [its] word" that Yale wants a settlement too. Clearly Yale does not *really* want a settlement! Clearly the union has to prod an unwilling Yale into negotiating! In contrast, compare this excerpt from an open letter from President Giamatti to the Yale community, September 26, 1984:

> (f) *I write with great disappointment following Local 34's action in calling a strike against the University. The University negotiating team has made concerted efforts, lately with the help of the Mediator, Eva Robins, to find common ground and to bring about a fair and reasonable settlement of the outstanding issues in a manner satisfactory to both parties. But the agreement has not been achieved.*

Giamatti's response is much calmer, more reasoned: he writes "with great disappointment"; his team has "made concerted efforts"; the agreement "has not been achieved". It is clear that *he* is not to blame! His disappointment casts Giamatti as a reasonable man who hopes others will be reasonable too. He even refrains from blaming the union for the failure of the settlement... Similar techniques appear in the shantytown texts. In example (a), for instance, the protesters say "concerned Yale students"; "constructed a shantytown... as a reminder"; Yale "had 76 students... arrested"; "a huge outcry" — clearly they are a well-meaning, harmless lot with much popular support. But what about the opposing account (b), containing "a small group of students"; "took over Beinecke Plaza"; "they wanted to force Yale to..."; "police had to clear the shanties"? Obviously the university did its best to remain conciliatory even when dealing with a few radicalized students!

1.2   Things PAULINE Says

PAULINE, the computer program described here, uses strategies based on these techniques to produce various texts from underlying representations. In all, it has been tried on three distinct episodes. The first set of examples are generated from a representation of the shantytown episode. From a single representation — a network of about 120 representation elements — PAULINE produces over 100 different texts. For example, as an informal description of the issue, PAULINE says:

> **Example 1.**
> YALE UNIVERSITY PUNISHED A NUMBER OF STUDENTS FOR BUILDING A
> SHANTYTOWN ON BEINECKE PLAZA BY ARRESTING 76 STUDENTS AND
> TEARING IT DOWN ONE MORNING IN EARLY APRIL. THE STUDENTS
> WANTED YALE TO DIVEST FROM COMPANIES DOING BUSINESS IN SOUTH
> AFRICA. FINALLY, THE UNIVERSITY GAVE IN AND ALLOWED THE
> STUDENTS TO REBUILD IT.

This is the kind of description one may hear from a passerby who knows about the issue. Compare this with the following version, in which PAULINE, now being a journalist, uses much more formal language for its newspaper article (including, for example, such conjunctive phrases as "so that" and "concurrently", such verbs as "construct", "request", and "give permission", and the passive mode):

Example 2.
IN EARLY APRIL, A SHANTYTOWN --- NAMED WINNIE MANDELA CITY
--- WAS CONSTRUCTED BY SEVERAL STUDENTS ON BEINECKE PLAZA
SO THAT YALE WOULD DIVEST FROM COMPANIES DOING BUSINESS IN
SOUTH AFRICA. THE LOCAL COMMUNITY SUPPORTED THE ACTION. AT
5:30 AM ON APRIL 14, THE SHANTYTOWN WAS DESTROYED BY
OFFICIALS; ALSO, AT THAT TIME, THE POLICE ARRESTED 76
STUDENTS. THE STUDENTS REQUESTED THAT THE UNIVERSITY GIVE
THEM PERMISSION TO REASSEMBLE THE SHANTYTOWN WHILE SEVERAL
LOCAL POLITICIANS AND FACULTY MEMBERS EXPRESSED CRITICISM
OF YALE'S ACTION. FINALLY, THE UNIVERSITY PERMITTED THE
STUDENTS TO RECONSTRUCT IT AND, CONCURRENTLY, YALE ANNOUNCED
THAT A COMMISSION WOULD GO TO SOUTH AFRICA IN JULY TO
EXAMINE THE SYSTEM OF APARTHEID.

Examples 1 and 2 are fine ways to introduce someone to the topic. They are the kind of thing we would say if we were unbiased informers, such as passersby and reporters. But what if we were protesters and were trying to convince someone of our opinion? When PAULINE is set up to produce text supporting the protesters' cause, i.e., when it is given the goals to slant its description of the episode toward the protesters, it produces:

Example 3.
AS A REMINDER TO YALE UNIVERSITY TO DIVEST FROM COMPANIES
DOING BUSINESS IN SOUTH AFRICA, A LARGE NUMBER OF CONCERNED
STUDENTS ERECTED A SHANTYTOWN --- NAMED WINNIE MANDELA CITY
--- ON BEINECKE PLAZA IN EARLY APRIL. THE LOCAL COMMUNITY
EXPRESSED SUPPORT FOR THE STUDENTS' ACTION. THE UNIVERSITY
TOLD THE STUDENTS TO ERECT THE SHANTYTOWN ELSEWHERE. LATER,
AT 5:30 AM ON APRIL 14, THE SHANTYTOWN WAS DESTROYED BY
OFFICIALS; ALSO, AT THAT TIME, THE POLICE ARRESTED 76
STUDENTS. THE STUDENTS REQUESTED THAT YALE UNIVERSITY GIVE
THEM PERMISSION TO REASSEMBLE IT ON BEINECKE PLAZA AND AT
THE SAME TIME SEVERAL LOCAL POLITICIANS AND FACULTY MEMBERS
EXPRESSED CRITICISM OF YALE'S ACTIONS. FINALLY, YALE PERMITTED
THE STUDENTS TO RECONSTRUCT THE SHANTYTOWN AND, CONCURRENTLY,
THE UNIVERSITY ANNOUNCED THAT A COMMISSION WOULD GO TO SOUTH
AFRICA IN JULY TO EXAMINE THE SYSTEM OF APARTHEID.

In contrast, when PAULINE has to produce the official Yale version, it says:

Example 4.
IN EARLY APRIL, A SMALL NUMBER OF STUDENTS WERE INVOLVED IN
A CONFRONTATION WITH YALE UNIVERSITY OVER YALE'S INVESTMENT
IN COMPANIES DOING BUSINESS IN SOUTH AFRICA. THE STUDENTS
CONSTRUCTED A SHANTYTOWN --- NAMED WINNIE MANDELA CITY ---
ON BEINECKE PLAZA IN ORDER TO FORCE THE UNIVERSITY TO DIVEST
FROM THOSE COMPANIES. YALE REQUESTED THAT THE STUDENTS ERECT
IT ELSEWHERE, BUT THEY REFUSED TO LEAVE. THE UNIVERSITY
INTENDED TO BE REASONABLE. THE UNIVERSITY GAVE IT PERMISSION
TO EXIST UNTIL THE MEETING OF THE YALE CORPORATION, BUT EVEN
AFTER THAT THE STUDENTS STILL REFUSED TO MOVE. AT 5:30 AM ON
APRIL 14, OFFICIALS HAD TO DISASSEMBLE THE SHANTYTOWN. FINALLY,
YALE, BEING CONCILIATORY TOWARD THE STUDENTS, NOT ONLY PERMITTED
THEM TO RECONSTRUCT IT, BUT ALSO ANNOUNCED THAT A COMMISSION
WOULD GO TO SOUTH AFRICA IN JULY TO EXAMINE THE SYSTEM OF APARTHEID.

Of course, this is not the way a protester or Yale official would tell you the story in person. For one thing, they may cut it a little shorter, and for another, they will be less formal and more openly opinionated. PAULINE illustrates:

Example 5.
I AM ANGRY ABOUT YALE'S ACTIONS. THE UNIVERSITY HAD
OFFICIALS DESTROY A SHANTYTOWN CALLED WINNIE MANDELA CITY ON
BEINECKE PLAZA AT 5:30 AM ON APRIL 14. A LOT OF CONCERNED
STUDENTS BUILT IT IN EARLY APRIL. NOT ONLY DID YALE HAVE
OFFICIALS DESTROY IT, BUT THE POLICE ARRESTED 76 STUDENTS.
AFTER THE LOCAL COMMUNITY'S HUGE OUTCRY, THE UNIVERSITY
ALLOWED THE STUDENTS TO PUT THE SHANTYTOWN UP THERE AGAIN.

Example 6.
IT PISSES ME OFF THAT A FEW SHIFTLESS STUDENTS WERE OUT TO
MAKE TROUBLE ON BEINECKE PLAZA ONE DAY: THEY BUILT A
SHANTYTOWN, WINNIE MANDELA CITY, BECAUSE THEY WANTED YALE
UNIVERSITY TO PULL THEIR MONEY OUT OF COMPANIES WITH
BUSINESS IN SOUTH AFRICA. I AM HAPPY THAT OFFICIALS REMOVED
THE SHANTYTOWN ONE MORNING. FINALLY, YALE GAVE IN AND LET
THE SHITHEADS PUT IT UP AGAIN, AND YALE SAID THAT A
COMMISSION WOULD GO TO SOUTH AFRICA TO CHECK OUT THE SYSTEM
OF APARTHEID.

The second set of examples PAULINE can talk about concerns a fictitious primary election between politicians Carter and Kennedy during their race for the Democratic nomination for Presidential candidate. The numbers and dates are not to be taken seriously. From a single network of about 80 representation elements, PAULINE can again simply describe the outcome:

Example 7.
ON 20 FEBRUARY, CARTER AND KENNEDY WERE THE CANDIDATES IN A
PRIMARY IN MICHIGAN. CARTER LOST TO KENNEDY BY 1335 VOTES.
AT PRESENT, KENNEDY HAS A BETTER CHANCE OF GETTING THE
NOMINATION THAN HE HAD BEFORE. CARTER IS ALSO CLOSER TO
GETTING THE NOMINATION THAN HE WAS BEFORE. BOTH CARTER AND
KENNEDY WANT TO GET THE NOMINATION.

However, this text is clearly inappropriate if the hearer already knows something about the nature of candidates, nominations, and primaries. If, say, the interlocutors are in a hurry — for example, while making a long-distance phone call — the following is better:

Example 8.
WELL, SO CARTER LOST THE PRIMARY TO KENNEDY BY 1335 VOTES.

Of course, if we had any feelings about the matter, we would not say it this way. Our biases sneak into what we say so easily and so often that producing slanted text seems much more natural than being neutral! Given the goal to support Kennedy, PAULINE says:

Example 9.
KENNEDY NARROWED CARTER'S LEAD BY GETTING ALL OF 21850 VOTES
IN THE PRIMARY IN MICHIGAN. IN A SIMILAR CASE, CARTER
DECREASED UDALL'S LEAD IN A PRIMARY IN 1976, AND HE EASILY
TROUNCED UDALL TO BE NOMINATED BY 2600 DELEGATES. I AM GLAD
THAT PRESENTLY KENNEDY IS CLOSER TO GETTING THE NOMINATION
THAN BEFORE.

This example is obviously spoken by a Kennedy supporter: it focuses on Kennedy's victory and current standing, Carter's loss, and the way in which a front-runner can be overtaken. Note that Kennedy is still behind Carter, so the most the program can claim is that Kennedy is closer than he was. What happens if PAULINE is, instead, a Carter supporter? Of course, it should make the most of the fact that Carter is still ahead in committed delegates, while downplaying his loss:

Example 10.
CARTER HAS GOT MANY DELEGATES AT PRESENT; WHAT'S MORE, HE
HAS GOT MANY DELEGATES MORE THAN IN THE PAST. I THINK IT'S
GREAT THAT HE HAS GOT MANY MORE DELEGATES THAN KENNEDY.

And with the same sympathies, but in a more formal style, while making a speech:

> **Example 11.**
> I AM PLEASED TO INFORM YOU THAT CARTER HAS IMPROVED HIS
> CHANCES OF WINNING THE NOMINATION. AT THE PRESENT TIME,
> CARTER HAS MANY MORE DELEGATES THAN HE HAD IN THE PAST;
> ALSO, CARTER HAS MANY MORE THAN KENNEDY DOES.

But what would happen in an extreme case? — what if you, a Carter supporter, are speaking to your boss, an irascible Kennedy man, under pressure? How would you even bring the topic up? Under these circumstances PAULINE chose to do:

> **Example 12.**

...exactly nothing! (This occurred as a surprise. What happened was the following: Initially, the program didn't find any topics that it liked and the hearer also liked, and it didn't have time to search the story representation for other topics or to find ways of mitigating the unpleasant ones). The program can also be aggressive, if it is speaking to someone it dislikes and wants to anger:

> **Example 13.**
> BUSTER, I THINK IT'S WONDERFUL THAT YOUR HERO, THAT JERK
> CARTER, REALLY GOT JUST 20515 VOTES. SO CARTER GOT AS MANY
> AS 1335 VOTES FEWER THAN THAT WONDERFUL KENNEDY DID IN THE
> PRIMARY. FORTUNATELY, KENNEDY SUCCEEDED IN GETTING ALL OF
> 21850 VOTES; ALSO, HE HAS GOT MANY DELEGATES AT THE PRESENT
> TIME. THAT MEANS THAT HE HAS GOT SEVERAL DELEGATES MORE THAN
> HE DID IN THE PAST.

These are some of the variations that PAULINE can produce, from a single under-lying representation, under different circumstance settings.

The third set of examples derives as output from the JUDGE program that models the sentencing behavior of a judge (see Bain (1985, 1986)). In a neutral setting, when just describing a typical case, PAULINE says:

> **Example 14.**
> AFTER JIM BUMPED MIKE ONCE, THEY FOUGHT, AND EVENTUALLY HE
> WAS KNOCKED TO THE GROUND BY MIKE. HE SLAPPED HIM A FEW
> TIMES. MIKE STABBED JIM, AND JIM DIED.

The program is given a lot more information about each action of the fight, and is able to select appropriate topics, and group them together. Being concise, it can say:

Example 15.
JIM DIED IN A FIGHT.

Example 16.
AFTER JIM BUMPED MIKE ONCE, THEY FOUGHT, AND EVENTUALLY MIKE
KILLED JIM.

Being more expansive, PAULINE can include information that the JUDGE program inferred and used in sentencing, such as the actors' intents and justifications, in order to slant its description toward the victim or the defendant. For example, when defending Mike, PAULINE says:

Example 17.
FIRST, THAT JERK JIM BUMPED MIKE HARD AND HURT HIM. THEN
MIKE JUST TAPPED JIM ONCE. AFTER THAT, JIM DID NOT EXPECT
THAT MIKE WAS GOING TO HURT HIM ANY LONGER; ALSO; JIM COULD
FORESEE THAT HE WOULD INJURE MIKE IF HE PURPOSELY STRUCK
HIM. HE REALLY SMASHED HIM. THE RESULT WAS THAT HE INJURED
HIM.
etc...
MIKE REALIZED THAT JIM REALLY HURT HIM; ALSO, HE EXPECTED
THAT JIM'S GOAL WAS TO HURT HIM. JIM WAS STABBED. AS A
RESULT, JIM ONLY DIED.

(not taking Jim's death too seriously, there...). And, in contrast, when defending Jim, different aspects are selected from the same representation; in this case the program says:

Example 18.
JIM COULD NOT EXPECT THAT MIKE WOULD BE HURT IF JIM
ACCIDENTALLY BUMPED HIM; ALSO, A REASONABLE PERSON COULD NOT
FORESEE THAT IF HE BUMPED HIM HE WOULD HURT HIM. HE HAD NO
INTENTION TO BOTHER MIKE. MIKE ONLY WAS BUMPED BY JIM ONCE.
THE ACTION WAS AN ACCIDENT. THEN MIKE REALIZED THAT JIM HURT
HIM. IN ADDITION, MIKE DID NOT EXPECT THAT JIM WAS GOING TO
HURT HIM ANY LONGER. MIKE'S GOAL WAS TO INJURE JIM. MIKE
COULD FORESEE THAT HE WOULD INJURE HIM IF HE PURPOSELY HIT
HIM ONCE. HE HIT HIM. THE RESULT WAS THAT HE INJURED HIM. HE
REQUIRED JUSTIFICATION FOR CAUSING HIM TO BE INJURED. THE
ACTION WAS AN ESCALATED RETALIATION.
etc...
MIKE COULD EXPECT THAT IF HE STABBED JIM SEVERAL TIMES HE
WOULD KILL HIM. HE STABBED HIM. THE RESULT WAS THAT HE WOUNDED
HIM. MIKE'S CAUSING JIM TO BE KILLED WAS NOT JUSTIFIED. AS A
RESULT, JIM DIED.

1.3   PAULINE

In order for generator programs to produce varied, appropriate, information-bearing text, they must have some means of representing relevant characteristics of the hearer, the conversation setting, and their own 'interpersonal' goals. These are the *pragmatic* concerns of language. With respect to language generation, the idea is straightforward: since different realizations carry different pragmatic effects, pragmatic goals provide a principled way to guide the generation process. Thus, whenever the generator must choose among two or more ways or expressing something, the goals furnish decision criteria. The choice points that enable the topic to be said in various ways, encountered during the process of sentence realization, include the syntactic issues of language. Some of the more important choice points occur during topic collection, organization and juxtaposition of topics into sentences, selection of aspects of topics to be said, and phrase and word choice.

PAULINE is organized in the following way:

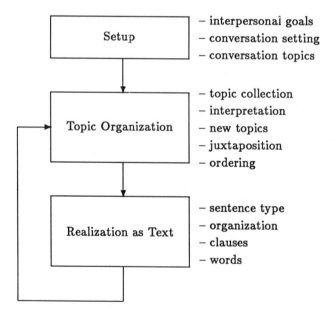

PAULINE uses a number of features to represent the conversational setting. In addition, it uses pragmatic goals to represent its 'desire' to affect the hearer in such respects as: *opinion, knowledge, future behavior, emotional state,* and *interpersonal relationship.* These features and goals are initially given values by the user. In addition, the user provides one or more topics of conversation — usually, some elements central in the story representation network. Then the program repeats the following overall cycle: it collects representation elements associated with the topic as possible additional sentence topics; it orders them, interprets them, and juxtaposes them into multi-predicate sentences; it builds sentences for each topic, choosing appropriate phrases and words to express each element, and determining in what order and which aspects to include (usually as adverbial and adjectival modifiers). After saying the sentence, it continues the search for other, related, topics, and repeats the cycle. (However, under various settings, execution of the cycle can be changed: for example, under a setting corresponding to measured, highly-planned text, the program first collects all the sentence topics it will say, then finishes all the planning, before it produces any text.)

1.4 Conclusion

Current Artificial Intelligence work in natural language processing places far too little emphasis on the role of pragmatics. This is a mistake. Not only does this omission limit the power and capabilities of parsers and generators, but it seems to imply that the problem of language will essentially be solved when semantics has been straightened out (assuming, of course, that we know enough about syntax already!).

The work in this book is based on the recognition that language generation is a goal-driven process, where many of these goals are pragmatic in nature. Nobody has yet attempted to formulate a wide range of pragmatic goals in terms a generator can plan with and otherwise manipulate, and nobody knows how such goals would interact with a generator's syntactic component. The time is ripe to start examining what kinds of goals are relevant, what strategies achieve them, and what planners and realizers must be like to operate under their control. We must face the fact that, in order to have real, flexible text, we simply cannot do without recourse to the airy world of pragmatics. We need to experiment!

Chapter 2

Pragmatics

Since different realizations of a topic convey different pragmatic effects, the pragmatic aspects of communication must help to control the choices facing the generator. But, though there has been much discussion about what pragmatics as a field of inquiry is all about, no generally accepted scheme has yet emerged. After a review of some relevant literature, a classification is presented of the kinds of pragmatic information that text can convey. However, pragmatic goals are invariably too general to support rules that directly control generator decisions. Thus an intermediate level of goals, specifically attuned to the requirements of language production, is postulated; these goals, called rhetorical goals, determine the slant and the style of text.

2.1   What is Pragmatics? — Some Definitions

There has been much discussion about what pragmatics as a field of inquiry is all about in both the philosophy and linguistics literature (see Morris (1938), Gazdar (1979), Carnap (1938, 1956, 1959), Grice (1971), Katz (1977), Gordon and Lakoff (1975), Cole (1978), Searle (1979), McCawley (1978), and Levinson (1983)). However, beyond sketching out a number of areas in which pragmatic considerations play a role, little agreement has been reached on what exactly it encompasses and how it relates to communication in general.

This is not to say that attempts have not been made. Levinson (1983), for example, offers the following definition:

> Pragmatics is the study of those relations between language and context that are grammaticalized. (p. 9)

Unfortunately, as Levinson notes, this definition sidesteps the issue of speaker intent. The slurred speech of a drunk or the accented speech of a non-native speaker can

13

also be "grammaticalized", and these aspects also convey non-literal information, but they can only properly be called pragmatic when the speaker uses them to some definite purpose.

A definition by Carnap (1938) doesn't suffer from this shortcoming:

> If in an investigation explicit reference is made to the speaker, or to put it in more general terms, to the user of the language, then we assign [the investigation] to the field of pragmatics... If we abstract from the user of the language and analyze only the expressions and their designata, we are in the field of semantics. And, finally, if we abstract from the designata also and analyze only the relations between the expressions, we are in (logical) syntax. (p. 2)

In other words,
- syntax = relations between words in a sentence
- semantics = relations between expressions and their designata
- pragmatics = reference to interlocutors and context in communication

Though this provides some idea of what a definition may look like, it lacks a clear enough description of interlocutor and context; what of "oh!" or "phew!"? These two expressions illustrate the difficulty of separating semantic content — the meaning of "phew!" — from pragmatic information — the mutual semi-humorous experiencing of a distasteful sensation, with perhaps a plan to avoid it, and so forth. The same problem appears in a definition suggested by Gazdar (1979):

> Pragmatics has as its topic those aspects of the meaning of utterances which cannot be accounted for by straightforward references to the truth conditions of the sentences uttered. Put crudely:
> PRAGMATICS = MEANING − TRUTH CONDITIONS. (p. 2)

What is to be understood by "truth conditions"? Those aspects of semantics that semanticists have succeeded in formalizing? Leaving all the rest to pragmatics? What, for instance, would the truth conditions of sentences such as "can you pass the salt?" include?

The general problem is that no clear distinction exists between pragmatics and semantics. Though attempts to establish the distinction were made (see Katz (1980)) and were countered (in, say, Jackendoff (1981)), the question is not yet resolved. For example, Jackendoff (1985, p. 105) says:

> ... the distinction between "semantic" rules of linguistic inference and "pragmatic" rules of linguistic interaction with general knowledge is less marked than is often supposed. In a theory with an autonomous semantic level, the two kinds of rules involve different levels of mental representation. Here, however, they both are rules for the manipulation of

conceptual structures; they deal with the same primitives and principles of combination. If there is a distinction between semantic and pragmatic rules, then, it lies only in the formal manipulations the rules perform on conceptual structure. For example, the principles involved in judging a sentence *true* potentially involve extralinguistic information as well as information within the sentence itself; hence "true" is a pragmatic notion. On the other hand, a judgement that a sentence is *analytic* involves only information conveyed by the sentence itself plus rules of (semantic) inference; hence "analytic" is a semantic notion. In either case, though, the information conveyed by the sentence is a conceptual structure.

and elsewhere (ibid.):

> Thus, although a terminological distinction between "semantic" and "pragmatic" notions undoubtedly remains useful, it is an open question whether it is a bifurcation of particular theoretical interest. (p. 106)

This work is based on the belief that the bifurcation is not of particular interest in functional terms (... at least, not until we know a lot more about semantic representations, speakers' goals, and speakers' conceptions of interpersonal relationships). In practice, in any generator written today, no fundamental difference need exist between the nature of processes that make use of so-called pragmatic information and the nature of processes that work with semantic information. Hence no attempt will be made here to provide a definition of pragmatics as a distinct, closed, formalizable field of inquiry.

2.2 Some Pragmatic Aspects of Communication

Not having a definition does not, of course, prohibit one from identifying a certain body of information and a certain class of considerations as typically pragmatic. Most work on pragmatics in the philosophy of language focuses on the ways in which text can convey various types of information. These are:

- *deixis*: references within a discourse to the interlocutors, the time and context, and to the discourse itself. Sentences such as "as long as I'm speaking, you must continue doing that" and "three miles from here, yesterday, a bomb exploded" can only be understood in context.

- *presupposition*: the logical assumptions underlying utterances. Thus after hearing "the king of France is bald" and "flying saucers appeared again last night", the hearer may assume that (as far as the speaker is concerned) there is a king of France and that flying saucers had appeared before.

- *implicature*: the implications (often social, script-based) that can be drawn from utterances, if licensed by certain assumptions. The principal assumptions are called Grice's maxims and cooperative principle (Grice, 1975). For example, after "where is Mary?", the response "well, her car is in front of the supermarket" is not perverse only if the requester can trust that the responder doesn't in fact know where Mary is, but does know that she travels by car, does know that her car is at the supermarket, that Mary is quite likely to visit the supermarket by car, etc.

- *speech acts*: the effects of stages of utterances (the initial act of production by the speaker, the hearer's understanding of the utterance, the hearer's reaction to it — both his preparation and his actions), and the ways utterances can address certain of these stages and (often only ostensibly) not others. The sentence "I promise to do it" refers both to the speaker's intent to do it as well as to his actual making of the utterance. Very often studied are indirect speech acts, in which the speaker mentions a less important part of a standard sequence of actions (while meaning some other part) in order to give the hearer some leeway, as in the request "can you pass the salt?".

In AI research on language generation, most work has been done not on the general *ways* in which pragmatic information can be conveyed, but on *what types* of pragmatic information is used by speakers. Cohen (1978) studied the effect of the hearer's knowledge on the selection of appropriate speech act. Reasoning about the hearer's knowledge in order to plan the inclusion and organization of topics is described by Appelt (1981, 1985); the effect of hearer knowledge on object description is described by Paris (1987) and Paris and McKeown (1987) and on user instruction by Woolf and McDonald (1984); the explanation generator of Swartout (1981) had a switch distinguishing between two types of hearer knowledge (either programmer or medical expert). Jameson (1987) describes a program that selects appropriate utterances in evaluative contexts such as job interview situations, based on what effect each utterance is defined to have on the hearer's belief state. Bienkowski (1986) describes automatic elaboration of basic text. Much related work on the structure of discourse uses some pragmatic information; see, for example, Grosz and Sidner (1985), Grosz (1986), and McCoy (1987). Mann's (1983a, 1983b) systemic generator Penman contains a number of oracles that would be based on pragmatic criteria. Clippinger's (1974) program contains a module that reasons about the pragmatic effects of its generation goals.

In addition, a number of general classifications of speaker intent have been made by AI researchers. A very general discussion of speaker goals is given by Bruce et al. (1978). Johnson and Robertson (1981) use goals to model a speaker having a conversation. Schank et al. (1981) analyze the different "points" or speaker intents underlying a statement. Other goal classifications can be found in Carbonell (1978) and De Beaugrande (1984). Furthermore, much sociological and psycholinguistic work has been done in this regard. Bloomfield (1914) mentions the effects of emotional relations on sentences; Gazdar (1980) lists general pragmatic constraints on sentences; Bühler (1934) names some pragmatic aspects of conversations; Jakobson (1960) extends this list. Both Grimes (1975) and Van Dijk (1985) identify a number of pragmatic features and discuss what roles they play in topic selection, focus, and realization. In the tradition of systemic grammar (see, say, Halliday (1961, 1976, 1978)), interesting recent work can be found in Fawcett (1980) and Gregory (1982). The effects of context on utterances was studied by Clark and Carlson (1981), Clark and Murphy (1982); Gibbs (1979, 1981) discusses the effects of context on the processing of indirect requests. Osgood (1957), Osgood, Mey, and Miron (1975), Osgood and Bock (1977) discuss effects of notions such as 'naturalness' and 'vividness'.

What types of pragmatic information can affect language? What additional information can speakers convey in their text? Based on the work mentioned above, the following high-level categorization will be used here:

- **interlocutors' personal characteristics**: factual knowledge, opinions, emotional states, interpersonal relationship, etc.
- **the speaker's goals with respect to the hearer**: effects on future behavior, opinions, relative status, etc.
- **the conversational atmosphere**: tone, time, physical setting, etc.

These aspects are discussed in the next few sections. Throughout, we enumerate the relevant pragmatic goals, for they underlie PAULINE's pragmatic characterization.

2.2.1　Interlocutors' Factual Knowledge

The most common speaker goal relates to factual knowledge. For example, in

> A: "When does the New Haven train leave?"
> B1: "The train leaves at 4:15"

A and B are concerned with facts. (Frequently, though utterances appear to address factual knowledge, they do so only incidentally; in such cases, this goal is subsidiary if present at all; consider

> B2: "Oh gosh, the train leaves at 4:15!"

in which the point is a sense of pressure and haste, even though the sentence topic is the same as B1's.)

A speaker can address the hearer's knowledge with any of the following goals:

1. *goal: increase knowledge (i.e., instruct, describe, relate)*
2. *goal: access knowledge (i.e., query)*
3. *goal: reorganize knowledge (i.e., reinterpret, explain)*
4. *goal: "decrease" knowledge (i.e., confuse, obfuscate)*

Each of these goals can be achieved in various ways. For example, with the goal to increase knowledge with the general topic of buttermilk:

- **Instruct:** "Combine:
  1 quart 70^0 to 80^0 skim milk
  $\frac{1}{2}$ cup 70^0 cultured buttermilk
  $\frac{1}{8}$ teaspoon salt
  Stir well and cover. Let stand at 70^0 until clabbered. Stir until smooth.
  Refrigerate before serving." (from Rombauer and Becker (1975, p. 533))

- **Describe:** "BUTTERMILK. Originally this was the residue left after butter making. Today it is usually made from pasteurized skim milk and contains about 8.5% milk solids other than fat. A culture is added to develop flavor and to produce a heavier consistency than that of the skim milk from which it is made." (ibid.)

- **Relate:** First, Sue combined some skim milk and some cultured buttermilk. She threw in a dash of salt, stirred it well, and let it stand for a while.

In computer language generation, differences of this kind can be achieved by associating with each knowledge goal a set of explicit instructions to indicate which aspects of the topic are appropriate and in what order to say them. Such script-like instructions have been called *schemata* by McKeown (see McKeown (1982) or Paris (1987)) and *plans* by Allen and others (say, Allen and Perrault (1979)). The preponderance of knowledge-related goals in conversation has sparked much work on recognizing them (Allen and Perrault, 1979; Litman and Allen 1984), expressing them by means of speech acts (Cohen & Perrault, 1979; Cohen 1978), and describing their elements (McKeown, 1982; Rösner, 1986, 1987). Rich (1979) describes a librarian program that builds a stereotype of the user and uses this information to select what to say.

PAULINE's goal to affect the hearer's knowledge can take three of the four above-mentioned values, as described later. The program's topic collection plans are described in chapter 4 and its planning methods in chapter 7.

2.2.2   Interlocutors' Opinions

Almost all spoken and written communication contains the interlocutors' opinions, whether explicit or implicit. In our daily lives, we constantly face a barrage of persuasive text — from blatant advertising to subtle cozening. In fact, our biases sneak into what we say so easily and so often that producing genuinely unslanted text can be quite a problem! However, to make a generator inject opinion into its text, we have to give it explicit goals and strategies that prescribe when and how to slant the topic. For a given topic, assuming the hearer's opinion is known, the goals are:

5. *goal: make the topic seem good or bad, contrary to the hearer's opinion*
6. *goal: make the topic seem good or bad, bolstering the hearer's opinion*

Pursuing opinion goals can serve or hinder other goals. For example, when the speaker's desired opinion opposes that of the hearer, the latter may become angry and even eventually dislike the speaker. To forestall this, the speaker must attempt argument or persuasion. An analysis of the relationships among elements of arguments was done in the context of understanding arguments by Birnbaum (1985), Birnbaum, Flowers, and McGuire (1980), and a study of argumentation in labor-dispute arbitration was done by Sycara-Cyranski (1985a, 1985b, 1987). Jameson (1987) describes a program that selects appropriate utterances in evaluative contexts such as job interview situations. Some strategies to achieve the goal of altering the hearer's opinions are discussed in chapter 4.

2.2.3 Interlocutors' Emotional States

Many utterances spring from the desire to create a given emotion in the hearer. Though any discussion of emotions is beyond the scope of this work, one emotional state — that of anger — can be achieved relatively easily by a generator, by the simple method of inverting certain of its rules of status and respect, as described in chapter 5. Discussions of politeness appear in Goody (1978), R. Lakoff (1977), and Clark and Schunk (1980).

2.2.4 Interlocutors' Goals: Altering Future Actions

Many language interactions occur when a speaker wants to affect the hearer's future actions; for example,

> *Keep off the grass!*

Often, such desires arises in service of the speaker's goals for his or her future. For example, in order to be told the time, the speaker must activate in the hearer the goal to inform him or her; this causes requests such as

> "Excuse me, do you have the time?"

All requests, questions, orders, and warnings attempt somehow to affect the hearer's goals, plans, and actions. They are, in short, the applicable elements of the planbox of the goal D-CONT in Schank and Abelson (1977):

- **Request:** "Where is the station?"

- **Make indirect request:** "You are standing on my foot"

- **Order:** "Go wash the floor!"

- **Bargain:** "If you pay me $25 I'll cross the street on my hands"

- **Threaten:** "If you don't give me some ice-cream I'll rub sand in your hair"

as well as

- **Warn:** "Beware of the quicksand!"

With respect to the hearer's goals, a generator should have at least the following goal:

    7. *goal: activate or deactivate a specific goal in the hearer*

Much philosophical work has been done on the nature and interpretation of requests (see especially Searle (1969, 1975) on indirect speech acts, and Levinson (1983) for an overview). With respect to computer systems, Cohen (1978) describes the selection of an appropriate speech act (REQUEST vs INFORM OF WANT); some criteria that determine the selection of the surface form of a request are studied in Kempen (1977) and Herrmann and Laucht (1978); a discussion of the relation between the degree of directness of a request and the speaker's certainty of its being granted appears in Laucht and Herrmann (1978). Cohen and Levesque (1985) describe a formal theory of rational interaction which is based on four modal operators: BEL (interlocutor believes), GOAL (interlocutor has a goal), BMB (interlocutor believes mutual belief), and AFTER (proposition true after action). Using these and other symbols, they show how the preconditions for the illocutionary act of requesting can be stated and how the difference between serious and nonserious imperatives (such as "go jump in the lake") can be represented.

2.2.5   Interpersonal Relationships

A large amount of psycholinguistic and sociological work studies the way language expresses relationships between interlocutors. Wish, Deutsch, and Kaplan (1976) scaled subjects' responses and found that four dimensions captured most of the distinctions subjects considered important:
- regard: positive – negative
- relative social status: dominant – inferior
- intensity: intense – superficial
- formality: formal – informal

A similar study by Joncas (1972) yielded three distinct dimensions: regard, relative social status, and formality. Schank and Abelson (1977) discuss life themes (the long-term goals people typically have). Of these, interpersonal themes give rise to goals of various levels of specificity that can affect language generation. For example, the speaker's goal CAUSE Y BE MENTAL-STATE (HAPPY) can activate an appropriate generation goal; the goal A-RESPECT (Y) can activate the generator goal to increase Y's social status by using appropriate address forms and expressions. Straker (1980) tested the effects of intimacy, setting, and social status on language dialect and style with 28 students speaking both standard American and Black English. By varying the following three parameters

- Interlocutor status: dominant – equal (instructor – student)
- Topic formality: formal – informal (subject's aspirations – worst experience)
- Setting formality: formal – informal (office – lounge)

she found that the interlocutor and topic significantly determined language style: the subjects used Black English only in intimate conversations when the interlocutor was a student too. Schank *et al.* (1981) analyze the various kinds of "points" a speaker can make with an utterance in a conversation, and Johnson and Robertson (1981) use some of these in a computer model. Brown and Levinson (1978) describe aspects of language use that depend on social relationships.

This discussion will address three ways in which speakers and hearers relate: interpersonal emotion, interpersonal distance, and relative social status.

(a) Hearer's Emotions toward Speaker

Usually, speakers have the goal, at some low level of priority, of making their hearers like them. This goal gives rise to a number of goals that most speakers have active during their conversations and that act as default goals when more specific ones are lacking. Sometimes, however, the goals to affect the hearer's emotions toward the speaker are of primary importance, and determine topic choice and especially topic presentation; one typical result is, of course, flattery. Again, though this is not the place to discuss emotion, some emotional effects can be achieved by relatively straightforward generation techniques. Two typical goals are:

8. *goal: make the hearer like or dislike the speaker*
9. *goal: make the hearer respect (or, perhaps, disrespect) the speaker*

(b) Depth of Acquaintance; Distance

Similar to but distinct from the hearer's feeling toward the speaker is his or her perception of the distance between them. The speaker can have the goal to have the hearer like him, yet not feel very close to him; this is a goal, for example, that many people in positions of authority have with respect to their subordinates. This goal may cause a speaker to be formal yet polite, as is discussed in chapter 5. The generator's pragmatic goal of distance should be:

10. *goal: make the hearer feel closer to or more distant from the speaker*

(c) Relative Social Status

The relative social status of interlocutors has a large effect on their text. For example, after the following interaction, what effects do A's responses 1, 2, and 3 have on B?

A: "How are things?"
B: "Not good"
A: "How come?"
B: "I'd rather not discuss it"

(1) A: "Hey just watch who you are talking to!"
(2) A: "Oh, sorry; please excuse me"
(3) A: "Ok"

Clearly, in (1) A wants to establish his dominance over B, whereas in (2) his apology indicates his subordination to B, and in (3) he signals neither. Typically, a speaker's status-related pragmatic goal affects the way the topic is expressed rather than which aspects of the topic are chosen to be included. In a generator, the status goal takes the following form:

11. *goal: make the hearer feel socially inferior to, equal with, or*
      dominant over the speaker

Studies on the ways in which languages communicate status information abound; for example, see Kuno (1973), Harada (1976), and Gasser and Dyer (1986) on Japanese deictic honorifics. The abovementioned experiments described in Straker (1980) illustrated the effect of social differences on speakers' choice of dialect.

2.2.6   Conversational Atmosphere

Each conversation takes place in a physical and social setting. Every setting has a certain tone (a level of formality and intimacy) by virtue of such factors as privacy, the nature of the conversational topics socially prescribed, and the amount of background disturbance. It is much harder to be formal at a picnic or at a football game than in an office or at a conference; it is much harder to be uninhibited and intimate in a subway car than at home! Still, the speaker can manipulate to some extent the atmosphere of the conversation by selecting appropriate topics and by employing appropriate phrasing; consider, for example, the difference between

(a) "This is Pete's girlfriend Maria."
    "I am very pleased to meet you. Is there any special reason you are
    here in Sydney?"

(b) "This is Pete's girlfriend Maria."
    "Oh hi! So what brings you to Sydney?"

Much work by sociologists, anthropologists, and psycholinguists describes the characteristics of various settings and the corresponding tone of language: see, for example, Irvine (1979) and Atkinson (1982) describe formal events in various cultures; Brown and Levinson (1978) discuss the use of honorifics in formal situations; Levinson (1983) presents an overview of relevant literature; Straker (1980) was mentioned above. In this category a generator should have a pragmatic goal of the following form:

12. *goal: make the tone formal, informal, or intimate*

Tone is not the only factor, however. The background conditions, such noise level and privacy, can affect (say, shorten) a conversation. In addition, the amount of time available for the interaction can have a large effect, for example, on the topics chosen and on the level of detail discussed. Not many studies of this point exist, though it is not particularly abstruse. During generation — especially during planning — a number of generator subtasks can be bypassed, since they are relatively time-consuming and serve only to increase the quality of the text. Two such tasks are interpretation (the task of finding an appropriate level of detail; discussed in chapter 3) and additional topic collection (discussed in chapter 4); the effects of more or less hasty generation on these two tasks is illustrated at the end of chapter 5. A time-related generator goal is:

13. *goal: be hasty, normal, or effusive*

2.3 Pragmatics in PAULINE

2.3.1 Pragmatic Settings and Goals

The above discussion is very vague. Each individual aspect mentioned, and its relation to the generation process, is a large and complex field of study; certainly nobody is in a position today to formulate the pragmatic aspects of language concretely enough to model in a computer program. Nonetheless, if we want to generate flexible and appropriate language by computer, we have to take into account pragmatic considerations in some form or other. As a first approximation to characterizing the pragmatics of conversations, consider again the thirteen goals assembled in the discussion above:

1. **goal:** access knowledge (i.e., query)

2. **goal:** increase knowledge (i.e., inform, teach)

3. **goal:** reorganize knowledge (i.e., reinterpret, explain, teach)

4. **goal:** "decrease" knowledge (i.e., confuse, obfuscate)

5. **goal:** make the topic seem good or bad, contrary to the hearer's opinion

6. **goal:** make the topic seem good or bad, bolstering the hearer's opinion

7. **goal:** activate or deactivate a specific goal in the hearer

8. **goal:** make the hearer like or dislike the speaker

9. **goal:** make the hearer respect (or, perhaps, disrespect) the speaker

10. **goal:** make the hearer feel closer to or more distant from the speaker

11. **goal:** make the hearer feel inferior to, equal with, or dominant over the speaker

12. **goal:** make the tone formal, informal, or intimate

13. **goal:** be hasty, normal, or effusive

This list characterizes the pragmatics of an interaction and provides some of the goals speakers have. As its starting point, PAULINE was given a corresponding list of features and goals. The (pragmatic!) justification of these features is that they are the kinds of features necessary to make a generator produce these types of text. No additional claims are made about the completeness or adequacy of this categorization.

When activating the program, the user selects a value for each feature. In most cases, the defined values lie on some intuitive scale; sometimes, two or more scales are conflated and the result is merely given as a set of distinct values; this can eventually be refined. Default values are the middle settings. PAULINE has the following interpersonal goals (items 1 and 2) and conversation setting (items 3 to 6):

1. With respect to the Hearer:

   - **affect hearer's knowledge** — *teach, inform, confuse*
   - **affect hearer's opinions of topic** — *switch, no effect, reinforce*
   - **involve hearer in the conversation** — *involve, no effect, repel*
   - **affect hearer's emotional state** — *anger, no effect, calm down*
   - **affect hearer's goals** — *activate, no effect, deactivate*

2. Speaker-Hearer Relationship:

   - **affect hearer's emotion toward speaker** — *make respect, like, dislike*
   - **affect relative status** — *make feel dominant, equal, subordinate*
   - **affect interpersonal distance** — *make intimate, close, distant*

3. Conversational Atmosphere (setting):

   - **time** — *much, some, little*
   - **tone** — *formal, informal, festive*
   - **conditions** — *good, normal, noisy*

4. Speaker (i.e., PAULINE):

   - **knowledge of the topic** — *expert, student, novice*
   - **interest in the topic** — *high, normal, low*
   - **opinions of the topic** — *good, neutral, bad*
   - **emotional state** — *happy, angry, calm*

5. Hearer:

   - **knowledge of the topic** — *expert, student, novice*
   - **interest in the topic** — *high, normal, low*
   - **opinions of the topic** — *good, neutral, bad*
   - **language ability** — *high, normal, low*
   - **emotional state** — *happy, angry, calm*

6. Speaker-Hearer Relationship:

   - **depth of acquaintance** — *friends, acquaintances, strangers*
   - **relative social status** — *dominant, equal, subordinate*
   - **emotion** — *like, neutral, dislike*

2.3.2 Rhetorical Goals and Generator Decisions

Though the pragmatic aspects of the conversation help determine the speaker's text, most do not do so directly, since they are too general to be attuned to the requirements of language production. As a result, attempts to write down rules that relate pragmatic aspects to the details of generator production decisions are doomed to failure; inevitably, such attempts quickly become bogged down in minutiae and produce rules with little credibility. For example, what is the effect on sentence length if the speaker is socially dominant over the hearer? If the speaker is antagonistic toward the hearer, should he or she make active or passive sentences? Is it right to say that if the speaker wants to impress the hearer he or she should select formal words?

Yet, of course, pragmatic aspects do influence text production. Therefore, rules must exist that relate these aspects to the generation process. These rules must depend on the pragmatic aspects (on the one hand) and must interact with the generation process in order to produce text that serves the speaker's goals (on the other). Since the interpersonal goals are too far removed from the syntactic concerns of language to provide such rules, *there must exist a number of intermediate goals expressly designed for this purpose.*

These goals will be called *rhetorical goals*. They act as intermediaries between, on the one hand, the speaker's interpersonal goals and other pragmatic aspects of the conversation, and, on the other, the syntactic decisions a text producer has to make. These entities are called here goals rather than strategies specifically to emphasize their independence from the system's interpersonal goals. After all, any identifiably distinct collection of information that is activated to guide the behavior of the system toward a desired specific final state can be called a goal; in practice, we dignify those collections that we consider somehow "natural" starting points by calling them goals, and the rest we simply call strategies or plans. In PAULINE, rhetorical strategies are only applied in decisions if the rhetorical goal controlling them has been activated.

The production of a sentence involves a large number of decisions (in the form of selecting from a set of alternatives); a typical sentence, such as this one, can require about 50 decisions (pretend you are a generator and count the the number of ways you can say this!). Consider, for example, generating a sentence such as "Mary bought the book from John yesterday" from the following simple representation elements (ATRANS represents the transfer of control of the OBJECT; this is part of Conceptual Dependency Theory, a system for representing semantic information, developed by Schank (1972, 1975, 1982) and Schank and Abelson (1977):

```
ATRANS                          ATRANS
    ACTOR John                      ACTOR Mary
    OBJECT book                     OBJECT money
    TO Mary                         TO John
    FROM John                       FROM Mary
    LOCATION store                  LOCATION store
    TIME yesterday at T1            TIME yesterday at T1
```

Any reasonably powerful generator must make at least the following six types of decision:

- **topic choice:** ("Mary bought the book"; "John sold the book yesterday"; "John sold the book to Mary"; etc.) — collect and decide which representation elements to say

- **topic organization:** ("John gave Mary the book and she gave him the money"; "John sold Mary the book"; "Mary got the book from John, to whom she gave the money"; etc.) — find appropriate groupings and interpretations of candidate topics (use "sell" instead of two "give"s); find appropriate ways to juxtapose candidates in multi-predicate phrases (use "and", or relative clause subordination "to whom...")

- **sentence inclusion:** ("John sold something yesterday"; "The book was sold yesterday in the store"; etc.) — select appropriate aspects of each sentence topic

- **sentence organization:** ("John sold Mary the book"; "Mary was sold the book in the store yesterday"; "In the store yesterday, John sold Mary the book"; etc.) — select appropriate subject, pre-sentence adverbial clauses, verb, predicate clauses, etc., and order them. Also determine the position and order of the adverbial clauses

- **clause/noun group inclusion and organization:** ("the book"; "the big blue book"; "the blue big book"; etc.) — determine which aspects of each clause topic to include and determine their order

- **word choice:** ("book"; "tome"; "novel"; "store"; "boutique"; "emporium"; etc.) — select appropriate words and phrases

The simplest existing generators, of course, perform these decisions by having only one available option. However, as soon as the generator is given the ability to realize the topic in more than one way, it has to be able to make its choice in a principled manner. Since different realizations convey different pragmatic effects, the pragmatic aspects of conversations *must* help determine the choices. Rhetorical goals supply the criteria by which these decisions are made; if the final text communicates any additional information at all, it is due to the control exercised over the generator by the set of active rhetorical goals.

2.3.3 Rhetorical Goals and Pragmatics

On the other hand, the relationship between the rhetorical goals and the pragmatic aspects of the conversation is not so clear-cut. Pragmatic-based language generation would be simple if each rhetorical goal reflected one and only one interpersonal goal or conversational aspect. In this case, each rhetorical goal would simply be a repository for the generator-specific knowledge required to express its pragmatic partner. But the pragmatic aspects of conversations are not independent; they influence each other. This fact makes the rhetorical goals more complex. To see why, note that a single rhetorical goal can express opposite pragmatic aspects under different conditions. For example, if the speaker has the goal to make the hearer feel close, he or she may activate the rhetorical goal to be humorous (say, by choosing funny words and by selecting funny topics). Usually this will work well, but it will backfire if the hearer has just lost both legs in an accident. In this case, an appropriate rhetorical goal is the goal to be serious and slightly formal — which, under normal circumstances, would tend to alienate them. Thus different rhetorical solutions can achieve the same pragmatic goal under different circumstances.

As it is, a pragmatic effect is seldom the result of a single rhetorical goal; combinations of rhetorical goals act in concert to produce pragmatic results. For example, low **formality**, high **force**, and high **partiality** together have an effect on the text that is distinctly pragmatic and can be characterized as *no-nonsense*. (Similarly, *blather* is the result of high **formality**, low **force**, and low **partiality**...) Therefore, rhetorical goals cannot simply be paired one-to-one with pragmatic aspects, unless a distinct goal is defined for each possible combination of aspects. Rhetorical goals have to be independent goals in their own right.

A second reason for defining rhetorical goals as independent carriers of pragmatic information is more practical. At this time, the field of pragmatics contains a number of very complex unsolved issues. In order to generate language with pragmatic effects today, we can use rhetorical goals as a starting point. Whatever form the eventual pragmatic solutions take, they will be able to interface with a pragmatics-sensitive generator through a set of rhetorical goals. These intermediate goals then are a reasonable level to which both generator builders and researchers in pragmatic issues can relate in order to find common ground.

Furthermore, the notion of rhetorical goals as independent entities is useful from an AI/programming/engineering point of view: they provide a useful level of organization for certain types of criterial information. In practice, the generator builder sometimes finds that when a number of generator decisions vary together, the text has an unexpected pragmatic import. He or she can then assemble the relevant information and define a new rhetorical goal to take care of the issue. For example, consider the honesty of a generator that says "tap" when its input representation is ACTION HIT with aspect DEGREE HARD. If the generator is slanting its text in order to support the hitter, and its verb choice strategies prescribe the use of "tap" — is it lying or not? Must the generator stick to the 'letter of the representation'? Furthermore, what should it do about the use of adjectives and adverbs: may it say "hit lightly"? And what about sentence topics as a whole: may it suppress topics that hinder its goals? In some conversations, the generator must be scrupulously honest; in others, it may have more leeway. The generator designer can then group together the relevant decision strategies and activation criteria and define a new rhetorical goal called **honesty**.

The advantages of identifying and using a set of intermediate goals should be obvious. Not only do they seem intuitively plausible, but they furnish a place to make explicit, collect, and organize many generator decisions and design characteristics that most generators have left implicit or avoided altogether.

Each rhetorical goal causes characteristic effects in the text. Different combinations of rhetorical goals result in differences in textual content and form. Some rhetorical goals are achieved by slanting the text; others find their expression as the style of the language. Through slant and style, the speaker can communicate additional information which the hearer can interpret and respond to. The rhetorical goals of opinion are described in the next section and discussed in chapters 3 and 4; following them, some rhetorical goals of style are listed. They are discussed in more detail in chapter 5.

2.4 Rhetorical Goals of Opinion

A very common speaker goal is to alter the hearer's opinion about a topic. This is the goal, for example, in all advertising, one of the primary goals in biased reporting, and one of the goals in soliciting money or help. Usually, at least two opinions exist — for the topic (sympathetic) and against it. Often two parties are involved — "our side" and "the opponent". People use a number of techniques for slanting the topic one way or the other; we list some from the Yale-Union texts quoted in chapter 1:

> *It is time, in the best interests of all concerned, to settle the strike. It is our understanding that the University administration, as well as the Union, has received a document entitled 'A Statement of Purpose by the Coalition to End the Strike'. We appreciate the spirit of the document. Clearly, the community earnestly desires and needs a settlement, so that Yale can get back to what it is supposed to be. Our members earnestly want a settlement. You have said that you do, too, and we are prepared to take you at your word. We are willing to compromise significantly to achieve a settlement. Therefore, we propose the immediate resumption of negotiations on a daily basis.*
> (From: open letter from Yale university's clerical and technical workers' labor union negotiating committee, November 9, 1984)

> *I write with great disappointment following Local 34's action in calling a strike against the University. The University negotiating team has made concerted efforts, lately with the help of the Mediator, Eva Robins, to find common ground and to bring about a fair and reasonable settlement of the outstanding issues in a manner satisfactory to both parties. But the agreement has not been achieved.*
> (From: open letter from Yale president Giamatti to the university community, September 26, 1984)

Some slanting techniques the speakers used caused them to say the following:

- "in the best interests of all concerned" — they care about the university's goals

- the union "earnestly want[s] a settlement" — they want to settle

- they "are willing to compromise significantly" — they want to settle

- they will "take [Yale] at [its] word" — they are trusting

- they "propose an immediate resumption of negotiations" — they want to talk

- Giamatti writes "with disappointment" — he is reasonable; the union is not

- his team has "made concerted efforts" — they tried to negotiate

- "in a manner satisfactory to both parties" — he cares about the union's goals

- the agreement "has not been achieved" — the union won't settle

Next, let us list the techniques used in the slanted shantytown texts:

> On April 4, concerned Yale students constructed a shantytown on
> Boesak Plaza as a reminder to those in Woodbridge Hall (and all over
> campus and the community) that Yale is complicit (sic) with the sys-
> tem of apartheid that creates shantytowns where thousands of blacks are
> forced to live in squalor and fear. The shantytown, Winnie Mandela City,
> served as a focal point of education concerning South Africa and Yale's
> investments there. At 5:30 am on April 14 the Yale Administration had
> the shantytown torn down and had 76 students and community members
> who were defending the shanties arrested. After a huge outcry, the Ad-
> ministration allowed the shanties to be rebuilt. We will not be silenced;
> we will continue to challenge the University on their moral failure.
> (From: protester literature; the protesters renamed the plaza after the
> South African churchman Allan Boesak)

> On April 4, a small group of students took over Beinecke Plaza and
> built some shanties; they wanted to force Yale to sell its stocks in com-
> panies with branches located in South Africa. The university asked the
> students to move the shanties to another location, but the students re-
> fused. The university then granted them permission to occupy the plaza
> until the end of the week, so that they could be there to be seen by the
> university's trustees, the Yale Corporation, at their meeting. But even
> after the meeting, the students refused to leave the plaza, and police had
> to clear the shanties. Later, the university relented, and gave them per-
> mission to rebuild the shanties. It also announced that it would send a
> fact-finding mission to South Africa.
> (Speaker: anti-divestment Yale student)

Some slanting techniques used:

- "concerned Yale students" — the students care about others

- "constructed a shantytown...as a reminder" — they are not aggressive

- Yale "had 76 students... arrested" — Yale is aggressive and nasty

- "a huge outcry" — the students have much popular support

- "a small group of students" — the students have little support

- "took over Beinecke Plaza" — they overstep the bounds of propriety

- "they wanted to force Yale..." — they are aggressive, coercive

- "asked the students to move" — Yale is not aggressive

- "granted them permission... to be seen" — Yale cares about students' goals

- "police had to clear the shanties" — the police were forced into action

- "the university relented" — it wants to settle

In every case, the speaker had the central goal to create support for his or her point of view. This goal found expression in a number of ways, using *rhetorical goals of opinion* that control slanting techniques. The techniques to make "our side" look good are:

- **Our goals:** Show how our side has good goals, by describing how (a) we help other people; (b) we want a solution to the conflict; and (c) our goals are good according to accepted standards

- **Our actions:** Explain how our side does good actions to achieve the goals: (a) the actions are not unreasonable or nasty; (b) they are good according to accepted standards; and (c) they are performed in the open. In addition, describe (d) our side's response to the opponent: which negotiations that have taken place and how we have moderated our demands

- **Our claim:** State outright that our side is good

- **Our reactions:** Show our reasonable reaction to their actions, such as that we were (a) disappointed; (b) hurt; or (c) outraged; or else (d) satirize their actions

- **Our support:** Show how other people believe that we are good, by describing (a) their active support and (b) their statements and recommendations to that effect

The goal to show how bad the opponent's side is can be similarly subclassified:

- **Their goals:** Show how their side has bad goals, by describing how (a) they are only in it for their own benefit; (b) they don't really want a solution to the conflict; (c) their demands are beyond reasonable expectations; and (d) their goals are immoral and unfair according to accepted standards

- **Their actions:** Explain how their side does bad actions to achieve their goals: (a) they started the whole affair; (b) their actions are ugly, distasteful and overstep the bounds of propriety; (c) the actions are aggressive and inciting;

(d) they coerce other people into doing things for them; (e) they disseminate false or misleading information; and (f) they have a hidden agenda. In addition, describe their response to our overtures: (g) they won't negotiate; and (h) they won't moderate their demands

- **Our claim:** State outright that their side is bad

- **Their reactions:** Show their unreasonable reactions by saying that they are (a) nasty and spiteful; (b) gleeful at our misfortune and suffering; and (c) intransigent and unconciliatory

- **Their support:** Show how nobody likes them — (a) their events are not well-attended; (b) people attack them publicly; and (c) they claim to have more support than they really have

These subgoals activate strategies that suggest to the generator where and how, in relation to a given topic, appropriately slanted material can be found and used. Clearly, however, not all these subgoals are appropriate in every conversation about which opinion differs! Thus each subgoal must be associated with conditions for its activation; and therefore they can be thought of as inferences. The inference process by which given topics are interpreted as other concepts is described in chapter 3, and the process by which additional topics are introduced is described in chapter 7.

2.5   Rhetorical Goals of Style

In addition to opinions, text can convey a lot of other information. Consider the following example: When, in Wodehouse (1979, p. 37), the butler Jeeves says to his master Wooster

> *The scheme I would suggest cannot fail of success, but it has what may seem to you a drawback, sir, in that it requires a certain financial outlay.*

and Wooster paraphrases this to a friend as

> *He means... that he has got a pippin of an idea, but it's going to cost.*

we understand that the former is urbane and formal, while the latter is young and trendy. By varying the style — by making Jeeves's text highfalutin and Wooster's slangy — the author has communicated far more to us than the literal content of the forty-six words.

In order to produce pragmatic-based, goal-directed language, then, we have to understand style: what it is, what effects various styles have on the hearer, and what information various styles convey.

Classifying all possible styles of text is an impossible task, since one can imagine text characteristics that fit almost any adjective (for example: *heated* text: short, explosive sentences, full of opinions, forceful language; *greasy* text: devious, subtle presentation, dishonest flattery. And clearly, without a well-defined set of stylistic primitives, such circular definitions are worthless). In order that generators be able to produce pragmatically varied text, we require a theory of style that provides components that can be used in programs and from which we can build various styles (even heated and greasy ones).

A study of some of the major handbooks of good writing (such as Weathers and Winchester (1978), Birk and Birk (1965), Payne (1969), Hill (1892), Loomis, Hull, and Robinson (1936), Baker (1966), Cowan and McPherson (1977), Strunk and White (1959), Willis (1969)) indicates that the authorities agree on a few such common broad-based features in their discussions of style. For example, some of the more complete categorizations are:

- formality, texture, emphasis (Weathers and Winchester)

- coherence, concreteness, economy, emphasis, formality, tone, unity, variety (Birk and Birk)

- clearness, force, ease, unity (Hill)

These features they describe in terms of characteristics of complete paragraphs of text. Unfortunately, this descriptive approach is of very little use in a theory of language production, since it never makes clear why and how each style is formed; nor does it indicate any systematicity behind the feature classification.

In contrast to such descriptions, a functional approach is to describe styles in terms of the decisions a generator has to make. The decision-based approach enables a more concrete description of each style and its relation to other styles.

Just as the rhetorical goals of opinion determine the slant of text by controlling generator decisions, the *rhetorical goals of style* determine the style. These goals control such traditional notions as formality, force, and respect. Having been discovered during the construction of PAULINE (rather than through abstract reasoning or psycholinguistic experimentation), these goals are motivated empirically: when you vary the decisions you make during generation, certain types of decision group together and form stylistically coherent text, and other types, when grouped, produce text that is incoherent or odd. The coherent groupings conform to traditional stylistic concepts. The classification of stylistic goals presented here is not the only possible one; many groupings are open to reorganization and reformulation. It is not complete or completely consistent. The claims made here are about: the function of style — the expression of rhetorical goals in order to achieve pragmatic goals in the text; and the method of definition of style — constraints on the generator's decisions.

In this book, all PAULINE's rhetorical goals will be prefixed by **RG:**. Thus, for example, **RG:formality** refers to the collection of strategies that control the generation of formal or informal text. PAULINE's rhetorical goals of style are contained in the following list (names are somewhat whimsical; this is to suggest their function without identifying them too closely with traditional stylistic terms). This list does not contain all possible rhetorical goals, since such a list is impossible to make: every speaker has an idiosyncratic set of goals and techniques for manipulating language. However, this list contains of the common rhetorical styles; most other rhetorical goals are refinements and extensions of them. Anybody is welcome to define his own particular *heated* and *greasy* text styles in this manner, either in terms of generator decisions or in terms of the styles described here. The goals are:

- **RG:formality** (*highfalutin, normal, colloquial*): Highfalutin language is used for speeches and toasts

- **RG:simplicity** (*simple, normal, complex*): Simple text has short sentences and easy words

- **RG:timidity** (*timid, normal, reckless*): Willingness to include opinions

- **RG:partiality** (*impartial, implicit, explicit*): How explicitly opinions are stated

- **RG:detail** (*details only, interpretations, both*): Too many details can be boring to non-experts

- **RG:haste** (*pressured, unplanned, somewhat planned, planned*): When there's little time, you speak fast...

- **RG:force** (*forceful, normal, quiet*): Forceful text is energetic and driving

- **RG:floridity** (*dry, neutral, flowery*): Flowery text contains unusual words

- **RG:color** (*facts only, with color*): Colorful text includes examples and idioms

- **RG:personal reference** (*much, normal, none* — two ranges, for speaker and hearer): Amount of direct reference to the interlocutors

- **RG:openmindedness** (*narrow-minded, openminded*): Willingness to consider new topics

- **RG:respect** (*arrogant, respectful, neutral, cajoling*): Communicating relative social status

Each of the rhetorical goals mentioned above is implemented in PAULINE. Each goal is activated by criteria that depend on the program's initial set of pragmatic values and goals; in turn, each goal activates a number of strategies that guide the generator during the planning and realization of text. This guidance takes the form of suggestions at choice points, whenever the generator encounters more than one topic-related, phrasal, or syntactic option. The rhetorical goals **RG:detail** and **RG:color** are discussed in chapter 3; **RG:partiality** and **RG:timidity** appear in chapter 4; and **RG:formality**, **RG:haste**, and **RG:force** in chapter 5.

2.6 Conclusion

In order to begin to study how pragmatics is used in generation, a number of rather crude assumptions must be made about plausible types of goals of speakers and about the relevant characteristics of hearers and of conversational settings. The specific pragmatic features used by PAULINE are but a first step. They are the types of factors that play a role in conversation; no claims are made about their literal veracity. Similarly, the strategies PAULINE uses to link its pragmatic features to the actual generator decisions, being dependent on the definitions of the features, are equally primitive; again, no strong claims are made about their existence in people in exactly the form shown. However, in even such a simple theory as this, certain constraints emerge, and these constraints, I believe, hold true no matter how sophisticated the eventual theory is. The constraints pertain primarily to the organization of pragmatic information in a generator: (a) the fact that pragmatic and interpersonal information is too general to be of immediate use; (b) the resulting fact that intermediate strategies, here called rhetorical strategies, are required to run a generator; (c) the fact that, as described in chapter 7, in a model of generation that incorporates these goals, rhetorical planning and realization are interleaved processes, where the interleaving takes place at the choice points. This view supports the standard top-down planning-to-realization approach, as well as a bottom-up approach, in which partially realized syntactic options present themselves as opportunities to the rhetorical criteria, at which point further planning can occur. Pragmatic/stylistic strategies thus exist as active criteria throughout the generation process. This design can be called a limited-commitment planner that satisfies its pragmatic goals opportunistically.

Chapter 3

Interpretation in Generation

The computer maxim *garbage in, garbage out* is especially true of generation. When a generator slavishly follows its input topics it usually produces bad text. One remedy is to give the generator the ability to decide what topics to include and at what level of specificity — that is, the ability to interpret its input as instances of other representation elements. Since interpretation requires inference, generators must be able to exercise some control over the inference process. Some general strategies of control and some specific techniques, geared toward achieving pragmatic goals, are described in this chapter.

3.1 The Problem

The following example is one of the JUDGE texts from chapter 1 (see Bain (1985, 1986)). In this example, the generator's input consists of a list of topics, where each topic describes some episode in a fight between two people:

(a) FIRST, JIM BUMPED MIKE ONCE, HURTING HIM. THEN MIKE HIT JIM, HURTING HIM. THEN JIM HIT MIKE ONCE, KNOCKING HIM DOWN. THEN MIKE HIT JIM SEVERAL TIMES, KNOCKING HIM DOWN. THEN JIM SLAPPED MIKE SEVERAL TIMES, HURTING HIM. THEN MIKE STABBED JIM. AS A RESULT, JIM DIED.

Simply put, the generator's task, for a given sentence topic, is to find a form of expression — either a syntactic rule or a phrase — that will enable it to select and to order aspects of the topic in order to build a sentence. The straightforward approach is to define a fixed correspondence between topic representation types on the one hand and grammatical rules and lexical elements on the other. As is apparent from the example, this approach has a flaw: the results are invariably bad or boring.

How bad, of course, depends on the representation, but anything detailed enough to be useful for other purposes, such as learning or diagnosing, simply does not make great prose in practice.

This example is an extreme case because it contains only two main representation types, ACTION and STATE, which can relate in only one way, RESULT. When the generator knows only one way to express this combination, what more can we hope for? Even in stories that contain more representation types (and hence a larger variety of sentence patterns, which makes the problem less apparent), it still is a problem.

Correcting this inflexibility seems straightforward. Though there is nothing wrong with the sentence form used above, namely

[SAY-TIME #TIME] [SAY-SENTENCE #ACTION] , [SAY-PARTICIPLE #STATE]

one can add to the grammar a few more sentence forms expressing actions and their resulting states, as well as some more time words and verbs, and then make the generator cycle through its options whenever it encounters a choice point:

> (b) FIRST, JIM BUMPED MIKE ONCE AND HURT HIM. THEN MIKE
> SMACKED JIM, HURTING HIM. NEXT, JIM HIT MIKE ONCE. THE
> RESULT WAS THAT HE KNOCKED HIM DOWN. AFTER THAT, MIKE
> SMACKED JIM SEVERAL TIMES AND KNOCKED HIM DOWN. JIM SLAPPED
> MIKE SEVERAL TIMES, HURTING HIM. AFTER THAT, MIKE STABBED
> JIM. AS A RESULT, JIM DIED.

Yet this produces no real improvement! Clearly, simply extending the number of phrase patterns for each representation type does not solve the problem. When we speak, we do a lot more than simply cast input topics in various forms; we might say, for example, the following:

> (c) JIM DIED IN A FIGHT WITH MIKE.

> (d) AFTER JIM BUMPED MIKE ONCE, THEY FOUGHT, AND EVENTUALLY
> MIKE KILLED JIM.

> (e) AFTER JIM BUMPED MIKE ONCE, THEY FOUGHT, AND EVENTUALLY
> HE WAS KNOCKED TO THE GROUND BY MIKE. HE SLAPPED MIKE A FEW
> TIMES. THEN MIKE STABBED JIM, AND JIM DIED.

Illustrated this way, the problem seems rather simple. Obviously, the solution is to group together similar enough topics, where the similarity criterion can be varied depending on external factors, and then to generate the groupings instead of the individual actions. Grouping together contiguous actions of similar force, PAULINE produced variants (c), (d), and (e). (In the first variant, all actions were grouped together; in the second, all actions more violent than bumping but less violent than killing; and in the third, the grouping resulted from defining four levels of violence : bumping, hitting and slapping, knocking to the ground, and killing.)

Clearly, though it improves the JUDGE examples, the technique of grouping actions by levels of force is very specific and not very useful. However, when "group" is used in a wider sense to mean "interpret", this technique becomes both difficult and interesting, and provides a very powerful way to increase the expressive flexibility and text quality of a generator. So the questions are: what interpretation/grouping criteria are general and still useful? When and how should the generator interpret input topics? How should it find appropriate grouping criteria?

3.2 An Example of Interpretation

Consider again the fictitious primary between Carter and Kennedy from chapter 1. In straightforward generation of the outcome for each candidate, PAULINE says:

> (f) IN THE PRIMARY ON 20 FEBRUARY, CARTER GOT 20515 VOTES.
> KENNEDY GOT 21850.

However, PAULINE can notice that the two outcomes relate to the same primary, and can say instead:

> (g) IN THE PRIMARY ON 20 FEBRUARY, KENNEDY BEAT CARTER BY
> 1335 VOTES.

> (h) IN THE PRIMARY ON 20 FEBRUARY, CARTER LOST TO KENNEDY BY
> 1335 VOTES.

(or any of a number of similar sentences using "beat", "win", and "lose"). But why stop there? If PAULINE examines the input further, it can notice that Carter's current delegate count is greater than Kennedy's, that this was also the case before the primary, and that the primary is part of a series that culminates in another election, the nomination. In other words, PAULINE can recognize that what happened in this primary was

> (i) IN THE PRIMARY ON 20 FEBRUARY, KENNEDY NARROWED CARTER'S
> LEAD BY GETTING 21850 VOTES TO HIS 20515.

Or if, hypothetically, Carter's current delegate count were now smaller than Kennedy's, the program should have inferred that

> (j) IN THE PRIMARY ON 20 FEBRUARY, KENNEDY OVERTOOK CARTER BY
> GETTING 21850 VOTES TO HIS 20515.

instead. If we want good text from our generators, we have to give them the ability to recognize that "beat" or "lose" or "narrow lead" can be used instead of only the straightforward sentences (f).

This ability is more than a simple grouping together of the two outcomes. It is an act of generator-directed inference, of interpretation, forming out of the two topics a new topic, perhaps one that does not even exist in memory yet. And the new topic is not simply a generator construct, but is a valid concept in memory. The act of determining that "beat" is appropriate *is* the act of interpreting the input as an instance of the concept BEAT — denying this is to imply that "beat" can logically be used where BEAT is not appropriate, which is a contradiction[1]. This is not an obvious point; one could hold that the task of finding "beat" to satisfy a syntactic or pragmatic goal is a legitimate generator function, whereas the task of instantiating it as a concept and incorporating it into memory is not. However, it is clearly inefficient for the generator to interpret its input, say the interpretation, and then simply to forget it again! — especially when there is no principled reason why generator inferences should be distinct from other memory processes. Instead, after interpretation, the newly-built instance of the concept should be added to the system's representation of the story, where it can also be used by other processes, or by the generator itself the next time it tells the story. In this way the content of memory can change as a result of generation. This is consistent with the fact that you often understand a topic better after you have told someone about it: the act of casting concepts and their interrelationships into coherent sentences has caused you to make explicit and remember some information you didn't have explicit before. In other words, not only does thinking influence talking, but also talking influences thinking.

Immediately, this view poses the question: *which process is responsible for making these inferences?*. The possible positions on this issue reflect the amount of work one expects the generator to do. According to the strict minimalist position — a position held by most, if not all, generator builders today —, the generator's responsibility is to produce text that faithfully mirrors the input topics with minimal deviation: each sentence-level input topic produces a distinct output sentence (though perhaps conjoined with or subordinated to another).

This minimalist position derives from a (presumably) unconscious reliance on linguistic arguments made by grammarians two decades ago. The arguments assumed (tacitly or otherwise; see for example Chomsky (1965, pp. 148-163)) a separation between the processes that perform syntactic and semantic tasks. This separation

---

[1]We make the assumption that lexical entities — words and phrases — can be accessed only via conceptual entities. (This may not be completely true, since analyses of certain kinds of slips of the tongue indicate that lexical items can also be accessed purely phonologically. However, phonological processes are not germane here, since they (presumably) occur only at a later stage, and in the generation of spoken language.) It is not clear how lexical entities would have to be organized to enable non-conceptual access. What other factors could possibly facilitate such access? How would one get "beat" from Carter's and Kennedy's outcomes, if not via semantics?

is the antecedent of the belief of today's generator builders that tasks such as inference toward appropriate interpretations, being "semantic", are not properly the concern of a generator. By separating out any tasks that operate upon or alter the semantic content of the domain, these grammarians and generator builders relegate the generator to its traditional position: that of passive back end, a more or less standalone module that can be given representation elements and then forgotten. This view cripples generators. Such inflexible minimalist attitudes give rise to text like the JUDGE examples (a) and (b). To circumvent this problem, in practice, most generator builders employ in their programs a number of special-purpose techniques, such as sophisticated sentence specialists that are sensitive to the subsequent input topics. Of course, this is a tacit acknowledgement that the minimalist position is not tenable.

3.3   Unfortunate Practical Realities

Properly, generators should be fully integrated with the encapsulating main processing system, should have full access to the system's inferential capability, and should be able to activate processing goals and control the expansion of plans where appropriate. With this architecture, the above question doesn't arise; in the main system, the generator's inferential needs are indistinguishable from those of any other subprocess. In practice, unfortunately, generator programs are always back ends for other systems. And, since generators can hardly expect these other systems to care about rhetorical and stylistic concerns, they have to perform interpretive inference under their own power. Thus, on renouncing the hard-line "no-inference" position, but not having access to the resources of the parent system, one is forced to face the question *how much inference must the generator do?*

I do not believe that a simple answer can be given to this question. The issue here is the same as that faced by planners in general: how much time can be spent developing alternative plans, checking their trustworthiness, and determining the likely costs and the likely benefits? In generator terms: a tradeoff exists between the time and effort required to make alternative formulations of the topic (which includes finding candidate interpretations, making them, and deciding on one) on the one hand, and the importance of flowing, good text on the other. Greater expense in time and effort produces better text. But, of course, the expenditure of these resources is controlled by the speaker's goals and other pragmatic (i.e., interpersonal and situational) concerns. Thus such pragmatic criteria are appropriate for treating this question.

What are the likely benefits of running interpretation inferences? If they are successful, they may produce interpretations that:

- contain *fewer details* than the original topic(s) (as PAULINE's example (c) "Jim died in a fight" contains no details about individual blows). The relevant pragmatic questions are: does the hearer know (some of) the details already? Is he or she able to infer them? Even if he or she were able to infer them, should they be said explicitly in order to lend them importance? These questions relate to Grice's maxim of manner (Grice, 1975), and are discussed below.

- are *appropriately slanted*. Interpretations often add new facets or aspects to the topic; both the inclusion of new information and the exclusion of old details may slant the text. Here, relevant questions are: Can interpretations be found that state or imply the desired slant? Can interpretations be found that drop details working against the slant? These questions relate to Grice's maxim of quality; a discussion of strategies controlling opinion appears in chapter 4.

- contain some *additional information*. The inferences required to uncover new interpretations can, of course, provide additional information, even if it is only conjectural or default. For example, in a memory organized as PAULINE's is, interpretations can provide indices to similar instances as remindings. The information contained in these instances may play a pragmatic role as well, as discussed later in this chapter.

Balancing this, of course, is the fact that running inferences takes time. Thus the generator must compare the importance of its goal to keep the conversation going against the importance of its other pragmatic goals. PAULINE's answer to the question is: *given the underlying pragmatic goal to express myself appropriately and well, I'll do as much inference as I can do, taking into account the available time, how much and what I want the hearer to know, and the richness of my memory and my lexicon.* No doubt this answer offends people who like systems with well-defined boundaries; however, they must decide if they are happy with simple-minded JUDGE-like texts, and if not, they must provide an alternative without in any way doing interpretive inference, tacit or otherwise.

3.4   Determining the Appropriate Level of Detail

Of the three factors (the available time, how much the hearer should know, and the richness of the concept definition network and lexicon), the most difficult is clearly the pragmatic constraints on what the hearer should be told. When does the hearer need to know the details of the topic? What is the effect of telling him or her only interpretations? Or of telling both details and interpretations? The answer can be summarized as: if you can trust the hearer to make the high-level interpretations, then all you need say are the details. To repeat the two relevant sentences from the Carter-Kennedy example:

(f) IN THE PRIMARY ON 20 FEBRUARY, CARTER GOT 20515 VOTES. KENNEDY GOT 21850.

(i) IN THE PRIMARY ON 20 FEBRUARY, KENNEDY NARROWED CARTER'S LEAD BY 1335 VOTES.

If the hearer is a political pundit who is following the nomination race with interest, then clearly (f) is better, since he or she can draw the conclusion without difficulty, and has, in addition, the precise numerical information. If, in contrast, the hearer has only minimal knowledge about or interest in the nomination procedure, then (i) is better, since it relieves the burden of details and the task of interpretation. What must you say, however, if the hearer is interested and has just a limited amount of knowledge — say, he or she is a student of the political process —, or is knowledgable but unlikely to make the right interpretation — say, he or she is a strong Kennedy supporter, whereas you are pro-Carter? In both these cases you must ensure that the hearer understands how you expect the facts to be interpreted. So you say the details *and* the interpretations:

(m) KENNEDY NARROWED CARTER'S LEAD IN THE PRIMARY ON 20 FEBRUARY. HE GOT 21850 VOTES AND CARTER GOT 20515.

These considerations can be stated as the following rules (using the terms defined in chapter 2 to characterize the pragmatic aspects of conversations and goals of speakers), which PAULINE uses to activate the rhetorical goal **RG:detail**. This goal controls the level of detail of topics generated. It takes one of the values *details*, *interpretations*, *all* (both details and interpretations):

1. set **RG:detail** to *details* if the hearer is likely to understand the details or wants to hear the details. This rule bears on his or her background knowledge, and in PAULINE, it is decided by referring to its user-supplied information: is the **hearer's knowledge level** marked *expert* (does he or she know enough about the topic to be able to understand the details and their significance?); or is the **hearer's interest level** marked *high* (does he or she care enough about the answer to want to hear more than an interpretation?)

2. otherwise, set **RG:detail** to *all* if the hearer is likely to make the wrong interpretations. This rule depends on various factors: is the **hearer's knowledge level** marked *student novice* (does he or she have too little knowledge to be able to make the interpretation?); or is the **atmosphere (time)** not marked *little*; and finally, will different sympathies cause him or her to make a different interpretation? (check the hearer's sympathies and antipathies for the central topic of the conversation)

3. otherwise, set **RG:detail** to *interpretations*

4. In addition to these considerations, the value of the goal can be affected by the desire not to upset the hearer's sympathies; therefore, set **RG:detail** to *interpretations* if painful aspects (the details, the interpretation, or the inferences used to make it) can simply be left out. This rule translates as follows: is **speaker-hearer depth of acquaintance** marked *strangers*, or is **speaker-hearer relative social status** marked *subordinate*, or is **desired effect on hearer's emotion toward speaker** marked *like*, or is **desired effect on interpersonal distance** marked *close*, or is **desired effect on hearer's emotional state** marked *calm*?

In summary, you must be as specific as the hearer's knowledge of the topic allows: if you are too specific the hearer won't understand, and if you are too general you run the risk of seeming to hide things, or of being uncooperative. In the first case, you violate the default speaker goal to be intelligible, and in the second, you violate the goal to avoid unacceptable implications. In either case, you violate Grice's (1975) maxim of quantity to say neither more nor less than is required.

3.5   Where do Interpretations Come From?

The problem in interpretive inference is to find valid interpretation inferences easily and quickly. One solution to this problem is to try inferences directly on the input topics. This bottom-up method uses the structure of the memory network itself. Another solution is run only inferences that are likely to produce useful results. Such top-down inferences are associated with the generator's goals.

3.5.1   Bottom-Up Inference

In PAULINE, bottom-up interpretation inferences reside in memory and the lexicon as part of the definitions of concept types. In order to enable bottom-up inferences, links are defined from concepts types to the interpretations in which they could take part (rather than have the pattern-matcher check all patterns in memory). This scheme forms a concept representation network slightly different from the usual multi-parent schemes such as in, say, Stefik and Bobrow (1986), Charniak, Riesbeck, and McDermott (1980), Brachman (1978), and Bobrow and Winograd (1977). Links are not defined to the interpreted concepts themselves, but to configurations (patterns) describing them, which are then used by a pattern-matcher to check the characteristics of the input topics. Note that the configurations exist separately from the concepts they describe, because some configurations could be made underspecific in order to furnish more than one concept depending on other (say, pragmatic) criteria; for example, BEAT and LOSE could share a configuration, where the specific interpretation concept chosen may depend on the sympathies of the generator, thus on whom it wants to highlight.

Even with such links, the program may have to run a large number of fruitless inferences in a highly interlinked network. In order to limit further the number of configurations PAULINE has to check, only some concepts are linked to the configurations of which they are part. Typically, these are more central (that is, linked to the most other concepts); they are called *pivot concepts*. For example, PAULINE can access the configuration for NARROW-LEAD from an outcome or from the main primary election, but not directly from the current delegate counts or from the relations between concepts. This strategy cuts down on the search time considerably; but it also means that PAULINE is unable to find an interpretation for which it has all but the pivots as input topics. For this reason, when it has enough time (that is, when the rhetorical goals that control the level of detail and the amount of time permit), the program uses the aspects of its current input topics as well, since they might be pivots even when the topics themselves are not. Still, for a large set of input topics containing many pivots, collecting all configurations can be a daunting task.

Of course, this is not a wonderful inference system — it depends on the right links being defined beforehand — but it is an acceptable solution for limited domains. The implementation of a full-blown inferencing scheme is not a generation problem. Whether you define links from concepts to possible configurations or associate with concepts appropriate inferences, you are simply simulating the action of a mechanism that provides you with a number of (hopefully appropriate) candidate interpretations in a reasonably short time.

3.5.2 Top-Down Inference

Another solution is to run only inferences that are likely to produce useful results. But where can such inferences be found? One source is the plans that serve the generator's goals. Potentially useful interpretation inferences can be explicitly included in these plans, in such as way that running a plan causes appropriate inferences to be applied to the collected candidate sentence topics. Since interpretation is such a powerful way of slanting the text, the generator's rhetorical goals of opinion are an eminently suitable source of guidance. Indeed, many of these goals can *only* be achieved through finding appropriate interpretations of the input topics.

In the shantytown examples, a number of top-down inferences were used. These inferences are obtained from the rhetorical goals of opinion described in chapter 2. In the program, they are defined as patterns (described below); these are English equivalents:

- **Present as confrontation:** state that the actor you oppose (B) did some action (ACT) as a confrontation with some actor you support (A). In more detail, this rule can be represented as:

  ```
  IF B has the goal that some actor X must do some action Z
  ```

```
      AND A has goal that X must do Z'
      AND Z' conflicts with Z
      AND B's action ACT forces X to do Z' (disregarding A)
   THEN interpret and present ACT as a confrontation with A
```

- **Present as conciliation:** state that the actor you support (A) did some action (ACT) in the spirit of conciliation. Represented as:

```
   IF A has some goal G
      AND B has some opposing goal G'
      AND ACT serves some other goal H
      AND H does not conflict with G'
      AND H is (or serves) a goal of the opponent B
   THEN interpret and present ACT as an act of conciliation
```

- **Present as coercion:** state that the actor you oppose (B) forced someone else (X) to do some action (ACT). Represented as:

```
   IF ACT serves one of B's goals G
      AND G opposes the goal(s) of the actor you support
      AND X, the actor, is not directly an agent of B
      AND B has had interactions with X
   THEN interpret and present B's action as coercing X into
        doing ACT (and use ''force'' and additional verbs
        such as ''have do'', ''cause'')
```

- **Present as appropriation:** state that the actor you oppose (B) took over something by force (ACT). Represented as:

```
   IF ACT serves one of B's goals
      AND and instrumental to ACT,
         the actor used some thing INSTR
      AND INSTR does not belong to the actor or to B,
         but to someone else
   THEN interpret and present the use of INSTR as an
        appropriation (and use ''take over'', ''grab'')
```

These are a few of the top-down interpretation rules implemented in PAULINE. By using them PAULINE is able to generate the same input topics differently depending on its goals of opinion in order to help slant the text. In the following texts,

PAULINE inferred the interpretations *confrontation* (a), *appropriation* (b) and (e), *coercion* (c), and *conciliation* (d) and (f), none of which were represented in the input story:

> (k) IN EARLY APRIL, A SMALL NUMBER OF STUDENTS [WERE INVOLVED IN A CONFRONTATION] $_{(a)}$ WITH YALE UNIVERSITY OVER YALE'S INVESTMENT IN COMPANIES DOING BUSINESS IN SOUTH AFRICA. THE STUDENTS [TOOK OVER] $_{(b)}$ BEINECKE PLAZA AND CONSTRUCTED A SHANTYTOWN NAMED WINNIE MANDELA CITY [IN ORDER TO FORCE] $_{(c)}$ THE UNIVERSITY TO DIVEST FROM THOSE COMPANIES. YALE REQUESTED THAT THE STUDENTS ERECT IT ELSEWHERE, BUT THEY REFUSED TO LEAVE. LATER, AT 5:30 AM ON APRIL 14, OFFICIALS HAD TO DISASSEMBLE THE SHANTYTOWN. FINALLY, YALE, [BEING CONCILIATORY] $_{(d)}$ TOWARD THE STUDENTS, NOT ONLY PERMITTED THEM TO RECONSTRUCT IT, BUT ALSO ANNOUNCED THAT A COMMISSION WOULD GO TO SOUTH AFRICA IN JULY TO EXAMINE THE SYSTEM OF APARTHEID.

> (l) I AM SAD TO SAY THAT A FEW STUDENTS [TOOK OVER] $_{(e)}$ BEINECKE PLAZA IN EARLY APRIL AND BUILT A SHANTYTOWN CALLED WINNIE MANDELA CITY. THEY WANT YALE UNIVERSITY TO DIVEST FROM COMPANIES DOING BUSINESS IN SOUTH AFRICA. OFFICIALS HAD TO TEAR IT DOWN, BECAUSE YALE WANTED THINGS TO BE ORDERLY. FINALLY, THE UNIVERSITY [COMPROMISED] $_{(f)}$ AND ALLOWED THE STUDENTS TO PUT IT UP AGAIN. YALE'S DESIRE TO BE REASONABLE WAS A GOOD THING.

3.6 How PAULINE Does It

In order to interpret the input topics as instances of some concept, the interpretation process must recognize when the topics (or some of them) conform to the definition (or part of the definition) of the concept. Thus, either concepts must be defined in such a way as to allow a general process to read their definitions, or inferences must exist that fire when a definition is matched — in other words, the antecedent of the inference is the definition and the consequent asserts the existence of the new instance of the concept.

PAULINE was implemented with the second approach, using patterns called configurations. A configuration is the description of the way in which a collection of concepts must relate to one another to form a legitimate instance of another concept. Therefore each configuration contains three types of information: placeholders for concepts; type requirements on concepts; and relations between concepts. Accordingly, each configuration pattern takes the form of a list of triplets (*type ?var pattern*), where:

- *type* is either the type (in the property inheritance memory network) of the concept currently to be matched, or a variable *?var* which must have been encountered before

- *?var* is either (), or a variable *?var* by which the current concept will be identified later in the match, or a number of such variables that must be bound to different concepts for a match

- *pattern* is a list of (*aspect config*) pairs, where the filler of each *aspect* must recursively match the *config*, which is itself a pattern

The interpretation mechanism matches potentially useful configurations against the collected topics, and, if matched, creates a new instance of the interpretation and adds it to the memory network. The program can then generate text from the interpretation instead.

Obviously, configuration patterns depend on the representation language used. For example, the configuration for the concept BEAT is:

```
(VOTE-OUTCOME ?X                          ; ?X is a VOTE-OUTCOME
   (instance (ELECTION ?Y))               ; in some primary ?Y,
   (relations (REL-GREATER ()             ; and it is greater
               (conc1 (?X))               ; than
               (conc2 (VOTE-OUTCOME ()    ; another VOTE-OUTCOME
                      (instance (?Y)))))))); in primary ?Y
```

which means: some concept is of type VOTE-OUTCOME; its aspect RELATIONS contains a GREATER relation, of which the greater part is that same concept and the smaller part is another VOTE-OUTCOME in the same primary. Thus, since Kennedy's outcome is the outcome of a primary and it is greater than Carter's outcome, the two form an instance of BEATing. Most configurations are considerably more complex; consider, for example, CONCILIATION:

```
(T ()                                     ; The input is any concept (say,
                                          ; the permission to reconstruct)
    (actor (AGENT ?X))                    ; and its actor is ?X (Yale).
    (relations                            ; This concept
      (REL-SUBGOAL-TO ()                  ; serves a goal (the goal that
        (conc2                            ; the students be orderly)
          (HAVE-GOAL ()                   ; held by ?X.
            (actor (?X))))))))
```

```
(relations                  ; Also,
  (REL-SUBGOAL-TO ()        ; this concept serves a goal
    (conc2                  ; (maintenance of the shanties)
      (HAVE-GOAL ()
        (actor
          (AGENT ?P         ; held by ?P (the students)
            (opposites      ; who is not the same
              (?P ?X))))    ; person as ?X.
      ; which opposes another goal that ?X has
      (relations
        (REL-OPPOSING ()    ; Furthermore, this goal opposes
          (conc2            ; another goal held by ?X
            (HAVE-GOAL ()   ; (the removal of the shanties).
              (actor (AGENT ?X)))))))))))))))))
```

During the topic organization stage, PAULINE gathers likely interpretation inferences (both top-down and bottom-up) and, using a simple pattern-matcher, applies their configurations to the candidate topics and collects all the matched occurrences. With a partial match — partial in the sense that the remaining concepts are not among the candidate topics — the program can either accept or reject the interpretation. In the latter case, it can use the relationships contained in the configuration definition to search the concept network for the additional concepts, although they may not originally have been included as topics. (At present, PAULINE does not do this (it simply rejects partial matches); adding this capability to the program would be a simple extension, requiring in addition a pragmatic-based decision that could be characterized as, say, **thoroughness**, and perhaps be implemented as a rhetorical goal with the possible values *pedantic, neutral, lax*.)

When a number of configurations have been matched, through either top-down control or bottom-up methods, the generator must select which one(s) to say. Three pragmatic factors play a role: interest, slant, and reminding.

(a) **Interest:** This relates to the number of concepts contained in a configuration. With respect to interest, interpretations provide a way to compress many concepts and say them briefly so as not to bore the hearer. (However, the process of finding a suitable interpretation can take some time and is not even guaranteed to work, so as a time-saving strategy the use of interpretations is not reliable.) Appropriate strategies depend on the value of the rhetorical goal **RG:detail**:

- if *interpretations*, select the largest configuration (i.e., be most concise)
- if *detailed*, say no configuration (i.e., say all the details)
- otherwise select an intermediate configuration

(b) **Slant:** This relates to the number of affectively sensitive concepts in a configuration. With respect to affect, interpretations provide a way of including topics into the conversation without actually saying them explicitly, thereby satisfying both the speaker's need to say them and the hearer's need not to hear them. For instance, in the Carter-Kennedy example, by choosing to say

> (i) IN THE PRIMARY ON 20 FEBRUARY, KENNEDY NARROWED CARTER'S
> LEAD BY 1335 VOTES.

the speaker avoids explicitly mentioning Carter's defeat. These strategies are independent from those of interest, since a large configuration may contain fewer or more sensitive concepts than its smaller alternatives (sets of small configurations seldom span the same concepts as large ones). The strategies depend on the value of RG:partiality (which is discussed in chapter 4):

- if *partial*, select the configuration with most sensitive concepts
- if *impartial*, select the configuration with fewest sensitive concepts
- otherwise, select a configuration with some intermediate number

(c) **Remindings:** This relates to the presence of other instances in memory similar to the interpretations, and is discussed later in this chapter.

When a group of concepts matches a configuration, the interpretation can be formed and placed in the memory network. Following the memory organization principles described by Schank (1982), PAULINE creates a new instance of the interpretation and indexes it as an instance of the interpretation. It also links the pivot concept(s) to the configuration that matched. For example, when PAULINE first generates a Carter-Kennedy story, it creates the new interpretations BEAT and NARROW-LEAD and adds them to the concept network, associated with the story representation. The next time PAULINE generates the story, it finds the two new interpretations immediately, using links from one of the pivot concepts, thereby avoiding the search and matching process. (Of course, at this point, the program tries to make further interpretations off these, but finds no appropriate concepts in its limited memory.) Thus, as a result of having said this once, memory has been extended, and PAULINE can be said to "understand" the topic better.

Finally, the interpretation can be said. Of course, the interpretation replaces the topics it subsumes; for example, after deciding to say BEAT or NARROW-LEAD, the two input topics (Carter's and Kennedy's outcomes) become redundant.

3.7   Color: The Inclusion of Remindings

3.7.1   Adding Color to the Text

Color means any reference to personal experience to illustrate general statements: specific instances (as remindings), idioms and frozen phrases (as interpretations of the situation), and descriptions of occurrences of personal evaluation.

When and why do speakers include examples and idioms? When used appropriately, a well-chosen example makes abstract points clear and gives dull text life. Nobody can forget the agony of suffering through a textbook containing few or no examples. Also, the speaker can strengthen the force of his or her argument by citing an appropriate example. In addition, since instances and statements of personal evaluation are in some sense interjections, they are the perfect way of repairing goals that are in danger of being thwarted by the text, or even simply reviving goals that have been ignored for too long. For example, in the following real example, why else would the speaker refer to his French:

> "You don't speak proper English — it's better than my French, but it's still not good — ..."

thereby doubling the length of the sentence? Clearly, the speaker had active both the goal to express his evaluation of the hearer's English and the goal to have the hearer like him. The former goal gave rise to the first part of the sentence. After it was said, some goal tracking mechanism inferred that that part of the sentence could be taken as an insult, which conflicted with the latter goal; so it had to be repaired. This conflict gave rise to the goal to mitigate the effects of the sentence. Any of the following strategies could have been used:

- say something good about the hearer: "— but at least you write tolerably well"

- say something bad about the speaker: "— but it's better than my French"

- say how nobody else is any better: "— though second languages are hard"

- help the hearer to improve: "— so how about attending a writing class?"

Two shades of color are implemented in PAULINE: colorful phrases and remindings. Based on these considerations, it uses the following rules to establish a value (one of *with examples, normal, no examples*) for its rhetorical goal **RG:color**:

1. set **RG:color** to *with color* if the following goals are present: **desired effect on hearer's knowledge** is marked *teach* (since a paragraph explaining something is usually more effective if it contains an example; or if **desired effect on hearer's goals** is marked *activate* (for example, if the speaker has the goal to suggest to the hearer possible future plans and actions, since concrete examples are more direct and effective than simple injunctions; compare
   - "If you want to become rich, try the lottery"
   - "If you want to become rich, try the lottery. Last week a woman won 10 million when she used her family's birthdates").
   Also, if **desired effect on hearer's emotion toward speaker** is marked *respect* or *like* and the speaker's and hearer's affects for the topic differ (since explaining his or her reasoning or reactions can help to make the speaker be

better understood); or if **topic collection goal** is marked *convince* (since when the speaker wants to present support for his or her interpretation or opinion; for example, in
- "Stalin, a ruthless man, was a charmer"
- "Stalin, a man who killed 15 thousand people, was a charmer"

the latter underscores the speaker's antipathy. Almost any concrete facts that can be mustered in support of an argument lend it force)

2. set **RG:color** to *facts only* if the following goals are present (since an example can aid most goals, it is perhaps best to note when they should *not* be included): **desired effect on interpersonal distance** is marked *distant*; or if **atmosphere (tone)** is marked *formal* (especially, for example, if the topic itself is embarrassing or intimate — one does not describe your dental problems in a conference address, even if appropriate); or if **desired effect on hearer's emotion toward speaker** is marked *dislike*; or if **desired effect on hearer's knowledge** is marked *confuse* (that is, when the speaker doesn't want to be understood)

Color can be injected into text by selecting appropriate options at the following decision points:

- **topic selection and inclusion:** include, as examples, other instances similar to the topic, such as those found off interpretations

- **topic inclusion:** summarize an argument or a point by including an appropriate idiom rather than general statements, for example by adding "So don't count your chickens before they're hatched!" to texts (n) or (o) (PAULINE cannot add such phrases, though it clearly has some of the requisite information and goals)

- **topic inclusion:** include sentences describing personal evaluations

- **clause inclusion:** make adjectival clauses of appropriate instances, for example the Stalin example above

- **phrase/word selection:** select metaphoric and idiomatic phrases and words, such as "crowned with the nomination" rather than "got the nomination"

3.7.2   Remindings

Schank (1982) describes how memory is organized so that specific instances are indexed off general concepts to aid argumentation, generalization, and explanation. These specific instances come up during processing as remindings. Since a generator's interpretations are themselves concepts, they can furnish remindings; these remindings can be used as examples in the text. That is to say, if the generator has the goal to say a number of concepts, and it finds an interpretation which neatly expresses the concepts and their relations, and the interpretation can furnish a specific instance of itself, this instance will be relevant and can be used to strengthen the argument. This then is an additional benefit of performing generator-directed inference.

In the Carter-Kennedy example, the concept NARROW-LEAD was provided with two instances: the instance when Carter narrowed Udall's lead in a primary in 1976, and the time when Hart narrowed Mondale's lead in 1984. (In a fictitious world such as PAULINE's, anachronistic remindings are no stranger than normal ones! The names Hart, Mondale, and Udall were simply chosen because similar instances did in fact occur to them during their bids for the nomination.) When biased, PAULINE uses an appropriate reminding:

(n) KENNEDY DIMINISHED CARTER'S LEAD BY GETTING ALL OF
21850 VOTES IN THE PRIMARY IN MICHIGAN. IN A SIMILAR CASE,
CARTER DECREASED UDALL'S LEAD IN A PRIMARY IN 1976, AND HE
TROUNCED UDALL TO BE NOMINATED BY 2600 DELEGATES. I AM GLAD
THAT KENNEDY IS NOW CLOSER TO GETTING THE NOMINATION THAN HE
WAS BEFORE.

(o) KENNEDY SLIGHTLY DIMINISHED CARTER'S LEAD IN THE
PRIMARY IN MICHIGAN. IN A SIMILAR CASE, HART DECREASED
MONDALE'S LEAD IN 1984, BUT MONDALE EASILY BEAT HART TO BE
NOMINATED BY 1500 DELEGATES. CARTER STILL HAS MANY MORE
DELEGATES THAN KENNEDY DOES.

A reminding found off an interpretation concept obviously has the same structure as the configuration of the relevant input topics. That is what makes it relevant. The details, of course, are different. That is what makes it interesting. Sometimes a reminding may contain parts that do not correspond to any input topic, requiring the generator to decide whether these parts should be included. (There is, for example, no equivalent to Carter's beating Udall for the nomination, since the Carter-Kennedy nomination has not yet, in the hypothetical example, taken place.) Sometimes a concept may furnish more than one reminding, and the generator has to pick the one relevant to its goals. Just as when selecting an interpretation, the generator must choose a reminding whose details serve its goals.

In order to select a reminding, a mapping must be set up between the input topics and/or interpretation and the reminding, so that the corresponding actors, objects, times, places, etc., can be determined. Aspects of the reminding must be replaced with aspects of the input to create the hypothetical case, which can then be used to determine affective suitability. Thus, in the examples, PAULINE "translates" the Carter-Kennedy case into both the Carter-Udall and the Hart-Mondale scenarios and finds that in the former, Kennedy would win the nomination (since in 1972 front-runner Udall lost), and in the latter, Carter would win (since in 1984 front-runner Mondale won). Depending on its sympathies, it selects a suitable reminding. At this point, the generator can either spawn the goal to say the reminding immediately, or it can start doing further topic collection from the aspects of the reminding. (In PAULINE, the decision is based on the the rhetorical goal **RG:haste**: the less hasty, the more time to do further topic collection.) If said immediately, the reminding is woven into the text just after the concept that gave rise to it, using phrases such as "that reminds me" or "in a similar case".

3.8   Conclusion

As generators become larger and more complex, and as they are increasingly used together with other programs, they should use the capabilities of those programs to further their own ends, and, especially, to produce better text. Therefore, we should study the kinds of tasks that generators share with other processes and the purposes generators require them to fulfill. This chapter describes some of the kinds of demands a generator can be expected to place on a general-purpose inference engine. And even with the limited inferential capability described here, PAULINE can greatly enhance the quality of its text and the efficiency of its communication of non-literal pragmatic information.

Chapter 4

Affect in Text

This chapter discusses the communication of opinion. Natural languages contain a large number of linguistic techniques for slanting text — techniques that control both what to say and how to say it. Generator programs require such techniques, explicit opinions, and the ability to derive opinions for related topics. All decisions controlled by these techniques are based upon one general rule, which is derived from the goals speakers must have in order to ensure their hearers' attention.

4.1 Introduction

Any speaker who is sensitive to the pragmatic aspects of conversation must be able to include his or her opinions in the text. People do this all the time; our biases sneak into what we say so easily and so often that producing genuinely unslanted text can be quite a problem! And when we do manage it, the resulting text is often boring:

```
(a) YALE UNIVERSITY PUNISHED A NUMBER OF STUDENTS FOR
BUILDING A SHANTYTOWN, WINNIE MANDELA CITY, ON BEINECKE
PLAZA BY ARRESTING 76 STUDENTS AND TEARING IT DOWN ONE
MORNING IN APRIL. THE STUDENTS WANTED YALE TO DIVEST FROM
COMPANIES DOING BUSINESS IN SOUTH AFRICA. FINALLY, THE
UNIVERSITY COMPROMISED AND ALLOWED THE STUDENTS TO REBUILD
IT.
```

In any real account of the episode, the protesters' version is going to differ appreciably from the university's. The differences will be not be haphazard; each speaker will make the decisions that slant the text in his or her favor:

(b) I AM ANGRY ABOUT YALE'S ACTIONS. THE UNIVERSITY HAD
OFFICIALS DESTROY A SHANTYTOWN CALLED WINNIE MANDELA CITY ON
BEINECKE PLAZA AT 5:30 AM ON APRIL 14. A LOT OF CONCERNED
STUDENTS BUILT IT IN EARLY APRIL. NOT ONLY DID YALE HAVE
OFFICIALS DESTROY IT, BUT THE POLICE ARRESTED 76 STUDENTS.
AFTER THE LOCAL COMMUNITY'S HUGE OUTCRY, THE UNIVERSITY
ALLOWED THE STUDENTS TO PUT THE SHANTYTOWN UP THERE AGAIN.

(c) IT PISSES ME OFF THAT A FEW SHIFTLESS STUDENTS WERE OUT
TO MAKE TROUBLE ON BEINECKE PLAZA ONE DAY --- THEY BUILT A
SHANTYTOWN, WINNIE MANDELA CITY, BECAUSE THEY WANTED YALE
UNIVERSITY TO PULL THEIR MONEY OUT OF COMPANIES WITH
BUSINESS IN SOUTH AFRICA. OFFICIALS HAD TO CLEAR IT FROM
THERE. FINALLY, YALE GAVE IN AND LET THE SHITHEADS PUT IT UP
AGAIN, AND YALE SAID THAT A COMMISSION WOULD GO TO SOUTH
AFRICA TO CHECK OUT THE SYSTEM OF APARTHEID.

The previous chapter describes how one of the possible effects of interpreting
input topics is the slanting of text. But, as these examples show, that is by no
means the only technique to use. Note the adjectives "concerned" and "shiftless
(students)" and "huge (outcry)"; the statements of explicit opinion, such as "I am
angry" and "it pisses me off"; and the suppression of topics that are inappropriate
to each point of view, such as the investigation commission in (b) and the local
community's outcry in (c). Biases can be stated explicitly, using statements such as
"I think X is good", or can be injected into the text at various points during the
realization process. The latter is often more effective, since it incorporates opinion
implicitly into both the content and the form of sentences.

PAULINE uses such strategies to produce the following two versions of the representation of a fight (built by the JUDGE program, a case-based expert system that
models the sentencing behavior of a judge, described in chapter 1 and Bain (1985,
1986)). If PAULINE's sympathies are for Mike, the program says:

(d) FIRST, JIM BUMPED MIKE HARD AND HURT HIM.

MIKE JUST TAPPED JIM ONCE.

AFTER THAT, JIM DID NOT EXPECT THAT MIKE WAS GOING TO
HURT JIM ANY LONGER; ALSO, JIM COULD FORESEE THAT HE WOULD
INJURE MIKE IF HE PURPOSELY STRUCK HIM. HE REALLY SMASHED
HIM. THE RESULT WAS THAT HE INJURED HIM. THE ACTION WAS A
SIMPLE RETALIATION.

NEXT, MIKE HIT JIM, KNOCKING HIM DOWN.

NOT ONLY DID JIM EXPECT NO THREAT FROM MIKE ANY LONGER,
BUT HE COULD FORESEE THAT HE WOULD HURT HIM IF HE REALLY
SLAPPED HIM. HE SLAPPED HIM REPEATEDLY AND HURT HIM.

MIKE REALIZED THAT JIM REALLY HURT MIKE; ALSO, MIKE
EXPECTED THAT JIM'S GOAL WAS TO HURT HIM. JIM WAS STABBED.

AS A RESULT, JIM ONLY DIED.

(...not caring too much about Jim there...). Using the *same input,* if PAULINE is defending Jim, it stresses Mike's actions and culpability and minimizes Jim's:

(e) JIM COULD NOT EXPECT THAT MIKE WOULD BE HURT IF JIM
ACCIDENTALLY BUMPED HIM; ALSO, A REASONABLE PERSON COULD NOT
FORESEE THAT IF HE BUMPED HIM JIM WOULD HURT HIM. HE HAD NO
INTENTION TO BOTHER MIKE. MIKE ONLY WAS BUMPED BY JIM ONCE.
THE ACTION WAS AN ACCIDENT.

THEN MIKE REALIZED THAT JIM HURT HIM. IN ADDITION, MIKE
DID NOT EXPECT THAT JIM WAS GOING TO HURT HIM ANY LONGER.
MIKE'S GOAL WAS TO INJURE JIM. MIKE COULD FORESEE THAT HE
WOULD INJURE HIM IF HE PURPOSELY HIT HIM ONCE. HE HIT HIM.
THE RESULT WAS THAT HE INJURED HIM. HE REQUIRED
JUSTIFICATION FOR CAUSING HIM TO BE INJURED. THE ACTION WAS
AN ESCALATED RETALIATION.

NEXT, JIM REALIZED THAT MIKE INJURED JIM. JIM JUST TAPPED
MIKE ONCE. THE ACTION WAS A SIMPLE RETALIATION.

MIKE DID NOT FORESEE THAT JIM WAS GOING TO HURT HIM ANY
LONGER. MIKE WANTED JIM TO FALL. MIKE COULD EXPECT THAT JIM
WOULD BE KNOCKED TO THE GROUND BY MIKE IF MIKE HIT JIM HARD
ONCE. HE SMASHED HIM, KNOCKING HIM DOWN. HE WAS NOT
JUSTIFIED FOR KNOCKING HIM TO THE GROUND.

JIM REALIZED THAT HE FELL. NEXT, HE ONLY SLAPPED MIKE.

AFTER THAT, MIKE FORESAW THAT JIM WANTED TO HURT HIM.
MIKE WANTED TO KILL JIM TO PREVENT HIM FROM SLAPPING MIKE.
HE COULD EXPECT THAT IF HE STABBED JIM SEVERAL TIMES HE
WOULD KILL HIM. HE STABBED HIM. THE RESULT WAS THAT HE
WOUNDED HIM. MIKE'S CAUSING JIM TO BE KILLED WAS NOT
JUSTIFIED.

AS A RESULT, JIM DIED.

In this chapter, two sets of techniques for slanting text are described: *content-related* slanting techniques, involving judicious topic selection, and *form-related* techniques, involving the use of enhancers and mitigators, the appropriate juxtaposition of topics in phrases, the ordering of sentence parts, and choices of subject, clause content, and words. First, however, we must discuss how to give a program opinions.

4.2   Computing Affect

What does it mean to "slant the text in Jim's favor"? Clearly, to present someone favorably is to try to get the hearer to view him or her sympathetically. In order to do this, the speaker must be able to distinguish between what the hearer is likely to find sympathetic, what he or she is likely to dislike, and what he or she is likely not to care about much. Therefore, at least three values of affect are required to make this decision: GOOD, BAD, and NEUTRAL. (Of course, human affect is not a simple value on a linear range. But *affect* is not used here to mean all human feelings. With the limited denotation used here, three values are sufficient to give the program a great deal of interesting behavior. In this regard it is similar to the work on narrative summarization done by Lehnert, which also uses a simple three-valued affect with very interesting results; see Lehnert (1982).)

In general, affect derives from two sources: from the speaker's own opinions about some contentious topic, and from the intrinsic default affects associated with concepts. For a generator program, these sources are respectively the user and the default affects defined for representation elements. In PAULINE, the first source is simply implemented by having sympathy and antipathy lists which contain user-specified sympathetic and antipathetic representation elements. In the JUDGE examples, when PAULINE defends Mike, the sympathy list contains the concept "Mike" and the antipathy list the concept "Jim"; in the Carter-Kennedy examples, PAULINE is made a Carter supporter by making the element representing Carter's goal to win the nomination a sympathy and making Kennedy's goal an antipathy. In the shantytown examples, PAULINE is given one protagonist and his goals as sympathies and the other and his goals as antipathies. Elements on these lists will be characterized as GOOD and BAD respectively.

The second source of affect is associated with the generic representation elements. Each representation type that carries some intrinsic affect in the example domain has this affect defined. For example, in a neutral context in the JUDGE domain, the concepts "hit" and "die" are BAD, the concept "unintentionally" is GOOD, and all other concepts, such as "Jim" and "Mike", are NEUTRAL. (Similar information is used by the JUDGE program to determine its interpretation of each action.)

In order to determine its opinion about any arbitrary piece of input representation, the given affects must be combined with the concepts' intrinsic affects and must be propagated along the relations between concepts. The rules of affect propagation are:

1. affect is preserved when combined with NEUTRAL

2. like affects combine to GOOD

3. unlike affects combine to BAD

4. affect inverts when propagated along certain relations (for example, the *patient* of a BAD act is GOOD). A special rule of affect propagation must be defined for each such relation.

although their exact form obviously depends on the design of the representation. This rule is similar to the "balance principle" discussed by Abelson and Rosenberg (1958). This works as follows: assume the current topic is the action

```
#{ACTION-UNIT  =  ACT-6
     [ACT :  HIT]
     [ACTOR :  MIKE]
     [OBJECT :  BODY-PART]
     [TO :  JIM]
     [FORESEEABILITY :
            #{STATE  =  STATE-10
               [TYPE :  PHYSICAL-INTEGRITY-VIOLATION]
               [ACTOR :  JIM]
               [DEGREE :  SERIOUS-TEMPORARY]}]
     [NUMBER :  SINGLE]
     [DEGREE :  HARD]
     [INTENTIONALITY :  PRESENT]
     [RESULT :  #{STATE  =  STATE-11
                  [TYPE :  PHYSICAL-INTEGRITY-VIOLATION]
                  [ACTOR :  JIM]
                  [DEGREE :  KNOCK-DOWN]}]}
```

(this is a slightly modified and pruned version of the actual JUDGE representation). Stated neutrally, ACT-6 reads

```
MIKE INTENTIONALLY HIT JIM HARD ONCE AND KNOCKED HIM DOWN
```

In order to slant this, PAULINE has to determine the affect for Mike's role in ACT-6 from its sympathies. If it likes Mike, the program has to combine the intrinsic affect for the type of ACT-6, HIT, (BAD) with its affect for Mike (GOOD) (noting that, since Mike is the ACTOR, the affect doesn't invert), to get the affect BAD. That is to say, in ACT-6, Mike looks bad and by the affect rule (discussed immediately below) the action should be omitted (not possible in this example, since there is only one action) or should be mitigated. One of the ways PAULINE can say this is:

```
MIKE JUST TAPPED JIM ONCE
```

If, on the other hand, PAULINE's sympathies are for Jim, then it combines the affect for HIT (BAD) with its affect for Jim (GOOD), giving BAD. Since Jim fills the role TO (the conceptual role *patient*), this result must be inverted, and so the final affect is GOOD. That is to say, in ACT-6, Jim looks good (ACT-6 is GOOD for the case against Mike). In this case the affect rule suggests that PAULINE enhance the topic. Furthermore, the RESULTant state, STATE-11, carries the same affect, because Jim (GOOD) suffers a PHYSICAL-INTEGRITY-VIOLATION (intrinsically BAD). This result was intentionally (INTENTIONALITY PRESENT) caused by Mike (BAD). The three affects GOOD, BAD, and BAD combine to produce GOOD for Jim in STATE-11, causing it to be enhanced too. Thus, when defending Jim, PAULINE produces the sentence

```
MIKE PURPOSELY SMASHED JIM AND KNOCKED HIM DOWN
```

Which affect the hearer is likely to have for a representation element is computed in exactly the same way, except that the initial sympathies and antipathies are taken from the hearer's sympathies and antipathies.

4.3   The Affect Rule and its Application

Knowing what affect the interlocutors have for each representation element is only part of the story. Next the speaker requires strategies that indicate what to do with GOOD topics and what with BAD ones. With regard to affect, the strategies used in most conversations are all based upon one very general rule. This rule is called here the *affect rule*.

All speakers have the low-level goal to ensure that the hearer will be receptive to the implications of the generated text. That is, the speaker must not say things that will offend the hearer and cause him or her to terminate the conversation. Differences of opinion — i.e., conflicting affective values for topics — is a common cause of offense. Since his or her sympathies and antipathies reflect so accurately the speaker's disposition toward the world, any opinion with which the hearer disagrees signals distance between them, and perhaps even censure on the part of the speaker. The speaker should avoid such opinions to make sure the hearer will continue listening! Therefore, this goal requires that, whenever there is a conflict, or even a potential conflict, between the affective implications of the text and the hearer's opinion, the speaker has to skirt sensitive issues and achieve effects indirectly. On the other hand, when the speaker and the hearer agree on the affect of a topic, this agreement can be stressed to emphasize their kinship.

Fortunately, most languages have a large body of techniques for skirting and emphasizing issues. The application of these techniques (where *enhancers* are words or phrases that strengthen the affect of a concept, and *mitigators* are words or phrases with the opposite effect) is controlled by the

Affect Rule:
In order to convince the hearer that some topic is GOOD or BAD, combine it with other GOOD or BAD topics using enhancers and mitigators:

- for a GOOD effect, say GOOD topics with ENHANCERS and BAD topics with MITIGATORS

- for a BAD effect, say GOOD topics with MITIGATORS and BAD topics with ENHANCERS

This rule is the basis for all affect-related generation decisions. It can, however, be disregarded in certain circumstances. In an argument, the speaker may violate the affect rule and still have the hearer listen. In this case, the hearer is receiving alternative forms of "payment" — even if the only reason he or she continues the argument is the reluctance to walk away and so appear the loser. Another common violation is a comedy act in which the comedian insults the audience. Here the alternative payment is entertainment; a comedian who isn't funny loses. In all such exceptional cases the decision strategies are simply inversions of the normal strategies based on this rule.

The next two sections describe PAULINE's techniques to slant text by enhancing and mitigating affect. The first section deals with decisions of *content* — the "what shall I say?" question — and the the second with decisions of *form* — "how shall I say it?".

4.4 Content: Topic Collection Techniques

Part of a generator's task is to determine what to say. As discussed in chapter 3, it is possible to claim that the generator should say only what it is given, in other words that the task of finding and filtering topics belongs to some other process. However, this constraint can hamper the production of pragmatically sensitive text, of affect-laden text in particular: assume the "other process" decides it is important to say that that Jim was stabbed by Mike. Then if the generator has the goal to support Mike, it should legitimately be able to decide not to say that at all, or at least to mitigate the bald statement "Mike stabbed Jim" by, for example, "...but Jim bumped Mike first". Otherwise, it really cannot do much to help Mike.

By the affect rule, there is no problem when the speaker and hearer agree on the affect of the topic. Such topics can simply be said directly. But when they disagree, the speaker has to be more careful.

4.4.1 Evasion

One strategy the speaker can try is *evasion*: dealing with the topic indirectly, by hinting, implying, or referring to something that is in some way related, and trusting that the hearer will perform the final inferences alone. Various evasive techniques exist. The simplest one is:

- Wishful Suppression and Mitigation:
  - say GOOD topics
  - juxtapose NEUTRAL topics with GOOD ones in enhancer phrases
  - leave out BAD topics altogether, unless they can be mitigated using mitigator phrases and words, or unless they are central to the story

PAULINE uses this strategy in the JUDGE examples. The input from the JUDGE program consists of a list of representation elements, where each element describes an action, its justifiability, and the actor's motivations and culpability, in the JUDGE's opinion. To illustrate, a literal rendering (generated by the JUDGE program) of its representation for the first action of the fight is

```
Jim knew that Mike had not yet hurt him.  He could perceive
no threat against him from Mike.  A reasonable person in
similar circumstances would have perceived no threat against
him from Mike.  Jim could not foresee that Mike would be
hurt if Jim accidentally bumped Mike.  A reasonable person
could not foresee that if he bumped him Jim would hurt him.
He had no intention to bother Mike.  Jim bumped Mike.  The
result of this action was that Mike fell.  Jim's intention
to bump Mike was not justified.  It is simply unclear from
the input as to why Jim acted as he did.
```

Bain (1985)

Instead, when PAULINE is defending Jim, it computes its affect for each part of the representation and, using the wishful suppression and mitigation strategy, decides whether or not to include it. From Jim's point of view, almost all the parts are GOOD: the first three sentence topics are NEUTRAL and are ignored; the fourth is GOOD; it is paired with the NEUTRAL fifth using the *also* enhancer. The sixth is GOOD, and the seventh must be included, since, in this domain, actions are defined to be the central elements of the story. The last sentence is also GOOD. Thus in defense of Jim, PAULINE says (applying, of course, its form-related strategies described in the next section):

(f) JIM, A NICE FELLOW, COULD NOT EXPECT THAT THAT UNPLEASANT MIKE WOULD BE HURT IF JIM ACCIDENTALLY BUMPED HIM; ALSO, A REASONABLE PERSON COULD NOT FORESEE THAT IF HE BUMPED HIM JIM WOULD HURT HIM. HE HAD NO INTENTION TO BOTHER MIKE. MIKE ONLY WAS BUMPED BY JIM ONCE. THE ACTION WAS AN ACCIDENT.

On the other hand, when PAULINE is defending Mike, there is much less to say. From Mike's point of view, the only GOOD part of the input is Jim's action and its result, and PAULINE must make the most of it. Therefore the wishful suppression and mitigation strategy directs PAULINE to say only:

    (g) THAT NASTY JIM BUMPED MY FRIEND MIKE HARD AND HURT HIM.

For the full effect of this strategy, compare the contents of texts (d) and (e) above.

Two other evasive techniques (neither of which PAULINE can do, but which are mentioned here for completeness) are: **if the topic has been forbidden because of some aspect that is sensitive to the hearer, then**

- **Analogy:**
  search for an analogue for the topic that contains an analogue of the sensitive part, and make the analogy. Thus "there's a lid for every pot, for him too" is less harsh than "he's as ugly as sin, but he'll get married", though it can mean roughly the same. The analogue, its parts, and its presentation, are, of course, also subject to the affect rule: there is no point in blindly substituting one sensitive topic for another.

- **Evidence:**
  search for evidence for the new value of the sensitive aspect and, if applicable, evidence against the hearer's particular value of it, and say that. In this rule, *evidence for a value* means any fact, belief, or concept from which the hearer can infer the value. Thus, rather than "your brother is now dead", this strategy suggests saying "your brother was involved in an accident..." and lets the ellipsis signal that further inference is expected. As before, the evidence itself and its presentation are subject to the affect rule.

4.4.2   Selectivity

Rather than simply evading sensitive issues altogether, a generator can choose to say only parts of it. The strategy of *selectivity* enables the speaker to broach unpleasant topics without violating the goal not to offend the hearer. This involves saying aspects of topics that imply that the unpleasantness need not be considered important, or that the difference between what the hearer believes and what the speaker is saying is not too large. Most persuasive discussion is of this type.

This approach requires much more of the generator. In particular, it requires that the generator be able to search not only what it has been given to say, but also through the rest of its concept definition network, in order to find aspects of the topic that help achieve its pragmatic goals. How should the generator know where to search for such useful aspects?

Much work on topic collection for generation was done by McKeown (see, for example, McKeown (1982, 1983), Paris and McKeown (1987)). In her system, the program has goals to answer four different types of descriptive queries to a database. Each goal has a set of strategies, called a schema, that contain instructions indicating which parts of the relevant database entry the generator should pick as answer. These strategies are, in fact, ossified plans or scripts, since they contain a fixed set of instructions in a fixed order. For example, one schema serves the goal to *identify* (i.e., give a definition for) an object. This goal is activated in response to, for example, the request "what is a submarine?". When asked about a whisky-submarine, the *identify* schema directs the generator to say (produced by McKeown's generator TEXT):

```
A whisky is an underwater submarine with a PROPULSION_TYPE
of DIESEL and a FLAG of RDOR. A submarine is classified as a
whisky if its CLASS is WHISKY. All whiskies in the ONR
database have REMARKS of 0, FUEL_CAPACITY of 200, FUEL_TYPE
of DIESEL, IRCS of 0, MAXIMUM_OPERATING_DEPTH of 700,
NORMAL_OPERATING_DEPTH of 100 and MAXIMUM_SUBMERGED_SPEED of
15.
```

McKeown (1982, p. 251)

In similar vein, PAULINE has three plans that indicate where in relation to the current topic it should search for additional sentence topics: the DESCRIBE, RELATE, and CONVINCE plans. The DESCRIBE plan is used to describe objects (subsuming McKeown's four schemas); the RELATE plan to relate events and state-changes; and the CONVINCE plan to help win the hearer over to the speaker's opinion of the topic when they disagree. The CONVINCE plan is described here, since it deals with the affective values of candidate topics.

In contrast to McKeown's schemas, the strategies contained in PAULINE's plans need not be applied in a fixed order. That is why they are called plans and not schemas. When running a plan, PAULINE applies as many strategies as it has time for (depending on its rhetorical goal **RG:haste**), collects their results, and to them, in turn, applies one of the three plans, until it runs out of time or until no new candidates are found. Following that, the program is free to rearrange the candidate topics in order to achieve maximum effect, under guidance of other strategies based on the affect rule and described in the next section. The advantage of using a free-order plan instead of a schema is the additional flexibility it provides. A more detailed overall description appears in chapter 7.

Work in understanding and representing the structure of arguments, from which topic collection strategies can be derived, has been done by Birnbaum, Flowers, and McGuire (1980), Birnbaum (1985), and by Sycara-Kyranski (1985, 1987). Birnbaum (1985) presents a scheme for representing arguments and for reasoning about the status (*established, in jeopardy*) of each of the argument propositions. He describes three rules by which propositions can support (or attack) other propositions in an argument: *appeal to authority, responsibility attribution,* and *justification*. Clearly, when the proposition the generator wants to establish is already represented in an argument graph of this type, with all the support and attack links made explicit, finding supporting topics is no problem. But since different hearers may find different lines of argument compelling, the generator must be able to assemble an argument supporting its opinion from scratch, taking into account the hearer's affects. What's more, it must be able to do so without relying on a hearer to make counterarguments that suggest new aspects as further topics. Thus PAULINE is conceived along the lines of a speechwriter, not a party in an argument.

When saying the argument, the generator should make clear what type of support or attack it is making; this is most easily achieved by beginning the sentence with an appropriate phrase — such as "Well, Einstein said...", "Well, Pete's to blame for...", and "Well, don't you agree it's good that..." respectively for appeal to authority, responsibility attribution, and justification. The type of support or attack a proposition forms is determined by the relation its topic bears with the central topic of the argument: thus, for example, to find topics for responsibility attribution propositions, the generator must inspect the actors of concepts.

Based on these considerations, as well as on analysis of various written arguments (taken from communist newspapers, pro- and anti-labor strike leaflets, etc.) the CONVINCE plan contains the following strategies or suggestions for finding topics that support the speaker's opinion:

The CONVINCE plan:

- Consider **worse examples** of the topic with the sensitive aspect — from the concept(s) immediately superior to the topic in the hierarchically organized memory network, compute the affects of other, similar instances, and collect those with affect equally BAD or worse

- Consider **good results** of the topic with the sensitive aspect — examine all the direct results of the topic, and if it is (part of) a goal, a plan, or a MOP (a stereotypical sequence of scenes; see Schank (1982)), examine the final outcomes too; collect those with GOOD affect

- Consider concepts with **good goal-directed relations** to the topic — compute the affects for the intergoal relations of which the topic is part (e.g., those goals the topic supports, opposes, etc.); collect GOOD ones

- Consider **good side-effects** of the topic — examine all the side-effects of the topic (if it is a plan or an action) and collect the GOOD ones

- **Appeal to authority** — if any of the immediate aspects of the topic refer to people or organizations who share in, have, or support the sensitive aspect, and if the hearer's affect for these authorities is GOOD, collect them

- Simply **enhance or mitigate the topic** with the sensitive aspect — collect the topic so that subsequent realization decisions can slant it appropriately

4.5   Form: Generating with Affect

In answer to the "how should I say it?" question, this section describes strategies to slant the form of text.

After it has collected a number of candidate topics, and before it says any of them, the generator must perform a number of *rhetorical planning* tasks to make its text elegant. Not only should it test the candidate topics for suitability as sentence topics, but it should examine the possibility of interpreting them, reordering them for maximum effect, and casting them into conjunctive phrases to make clear their individual roles in the text and their mutual relationships. Other generators use a number of criteria to make these decisions; for example, *focus* in McKeown (1982); *hearer knowledge* in Cohen (1978) and Appelt (1981); *choosers* in Mann (1983a); *hearer's opinion of speaker* in Jameson (1987). But affect plays an important role as a decision criterion as well, because the other strategies leave much leeway.

4.5.1   Topic Organization: Affect-Bearing Phrases

After reading the following paragraph, complete Martha's and Max's responses:

> Martha and Max are little Pete's parents. Max and Pete are baseball fanatics, but Martha hates baseball. One day, Pete falls off his bicycle and is slightly hurt. Martha forbids him to play his baseball game that afternoon or to go to the movies. Max, who wants his son to be tough, disagrees. Secretly, Pete sneaks out of the house and plays a splendid game, hitting five home runs, and then goes to see a movie. When he gets home, there is a fight between angry Martha and proud Max. The next day, Pete's grandmother calls, and asks both Martha and Max the same question: "So what has Pete done lately?". Max proudly says "He's been great; not only did he play baseball, but...". and Martha angrily says "He's been bad; not only did he play baseball, but..."

Two appropriate responses are:

(a) "Not only did he play baseball, but *he hit five home runs!*"
(b) "Not only did he play baseball, but *he went to the movies afterwards!*"

Max's retort (a) implies that Pete's playing baseball was good, courageous, and tough. Martha's retort (b), in contrast, implies that it was bad and disobedient. Each parent imputes an affect to Pete's playing by juxtaposing the sentence *"he played baseball"* with another sentence of suitable affect.

Clearly, the "not only X but Y" sentence form is used to imply that X and Y carry the same affective value, and in fact that the value is to be strengthened due to their juxtaposition. In contrast, the sentences

> "Pete played the game and he hit five home runs"
> "When Pete played the game he hit five home runs"
> "Pete played the game. He hit five home runs"

carry no such cumulative affective import. The "not only X but Y" form can be called an *enhancer*. More enhancing phrases are:

> "Pete played the game; *also*, he hit five home runs"
> "Pete played the game; *in addition*, he hit five home runs"
> "Pete played the game; *what's more*, he hit five home runs"

When an enhancing phrase juxtaposes two affect-laden sentences, the affect is strengthened; when it juxtaposes an affect-laden sentence with a neutral one, the affect is imputed to the latter. Thus, in addition to stressing affective concepts, a speaker can strengthen his or her case by imputing affect to neutral concepts too! This is, for example, what PAULINE does to produce

(g) NOT ONLY DID JIM EXPECT NO THREAT FROM MIKE ANY LONGER,
BUT HE COULD FORESEE THAT HE WOULD HURT HIM IF HE REALLY
SLAPPED HIM.

when defending Mike. Here Jim's not perceiving a threat from Mike is simply NEU-TRAL, but his ability to foresee the BAD result of his action, coupled with the fact that he did it anyway, is BAD for him. However, when juxtaposed in this way, *both* sentences seem BAD for Jim — exactly what PAULINE wants.

Similarly, phrases with weakening effect are *mitigators*. When a mitigating phrase juxtaposes two sentences carrying opposite affect, the resulting affect is that of the first sentence, weakened; when it juxtaposes an affect-laden sentence with a neu-tral one, the opposite affect is imputed to the latter. In the following sentences, if "John whipped the dog" carries BAD affect, then, if we know nothing more, "he remembered the cat" becomes GOOD:

> "*Although* John remembered the cat, he whipped the dog"
> "John remembered the cat. *However*, he whipped the dog"
> "John remembered the cat. *But still*, he whipped the dog"

Note that the first part, taken by itself, is neutral; it could just as well have been made BAD:

> "*Not only* did John remember the cat, he whipped the dog"

In a two-predicate mitigator, the sentence with the desired affect usually appears last. Two one-predicate mitigators are:

> "*Well*, John whipped the dog, *but...*" (implying that other, as yet unknown, mitigating circumstances may exist)
> "*Oh well, so* John whipped the dog" (implying that the action is not important)

A number of constraints must be met before two topics can be juxtaposed in an enhancer or mitigator phrase. Consider the following examples:

> (c) "Not only did John feed the dog, but he saved the child's life"
> (d) "Not only did John whip the dog, but he saved the child's life"
> (e) "Not only did Pete play the game, but Sam hit five home runs"

Sentence (c) is fine: John's actions are GOOD in both parts. Sentence (d), however, is bizarre, because it is not clear which affect is to be strengthened. Therefore,

> **Constraint 1:**
> Two-predicate enhancer and mitigator phrases can only be used when the parts carry consistent affects; that is,
>
> • in enhancer phrases the two predicates must carry like affect
>
> • in mitigator phrases the two predicates must carry unlike affect
>
> • or else one predicate must be NEUTRAL

In sentence (e), we work hard to infer some relationship between Pete and Sam; we only accept the sentence if there is indeed some team-like conjunction of the two (and perhaps others) to carry the affect. Therefore,

> **Constraint 2:**
> Two-predicate enhancer and mitigator phrases can only be used when the topics in both parts have the same focus concept

Additional criteria for pairing topics in phrases are *topic similarity* and *derivation*. Using topic similarity, a BAD candidate is compared to the GOOD candidates and paired with the one with which it shares the most features, under a simple match that compares the representation types of corresponding aspects of the candidates. Thus, for example, (g) is a better match than (f):

(f) "Although John whipped the dog, he helped the old lady cross the road. He also fed the cat"

(g) "Although John whipped the dog, he fed the cat. He also helped the old lady cross the road"

because "dog" and "cat" are both animals. Alternatively, using the strategy of derivation, the planner may only cast two candidates into a phrase if they are members of the same subtree of topic collection; that is, if they were both collected when the convince plan was applied to their common parent topic. This corresponds to "sticking to the train of thought". In the shantytown example, PAULINE as a protester finds two topics it can use to enhance the destruction of the shantytown: the police arrest and the community's critical response. Since the former is closer to the destruction than the latter (its actor is also officials, its action is also a negation (albeit of someone's freedom rather than of something's construction), its object also directly involves students), the program casts it into the enhancer phrase, getting (h) rather than (i):

(h) NOT ONLY DID YALE HAVE OFFICIALS DESTROY THE SHANTYTOWN, BUT THE POLICE ARRESTED 76 STUDENTS. THE COMMUNITY CRITICIZED YALE'S ACTION.

(i) NOT ONLY DID YALE HAVE OFFICIALS DESTROY THE SHANTYTOWN, BUT THE COMMUNITY CRITICIZED YALE'S ACTION. THE POLICE ARRESTED 76 STUDENTS.

Although PAULINE can use either strategy, the former tends to produce better text. This can be stated as a further constraint:

> **Constraint 3:**
> The predicates in two-predicate enhancer and mitigator phrases should match in as many aspects as possible, under a simple match of representation filler types

4.5.2 Sentence Inclusion: Adverbs and Verbs

Affect-Bearing Adverbs

A number of adverbial stress words (such as "really", "just", and "only" for actions; "very", "extremely", "slightly", and "moderately" for states and adverbs) specifically function as enhancers or mitigators:

"Max *really* smashed Sam" — "Max *just* tapped Sam"
"John was *extremely* happy" — "John was *only* happy"

When these words are used to modify concepts that do not already carry affect, they seem strange, forcing the hearer to postulate affect; consider

"Mary merely looked at the book"

To remedy this, the constraint can be stated as

> **Constraint 4:**
> Adverbial stress words can only be used to enhance or mitigate expressions that carry some affect already

Thus affectively neutral words must not be modified by stress words ("really", "just"), but only by affect-laden adverbs ("hard", "narrowly"):

> "Max hit Sam *hard*" — "Max *really* hit Sam"
> "Sue *narrowly* won the race" — "Sue *just* won the race"

In addition, sentences such as

> "Mike only killed Jim"
> "Sue was merely ecstatic"

give rise to

> **Constraint 5:**
> Irreversible, extreme states and actions should not be mitigated

Affect-Bearing Verbs

Verbs play a very important role in the affective manipulation of text. Often, the verb used determines the content of the predicate, so that the selection of the verb is an important part of the sentence inclusion decision. For example, compare the affective difference between (a) and (b) for a Carter supporter:

> (a) KENNEDY WON THE PRIMARY IN MICHIGAN
> (b) KENNEDY BEAT CARTER IN THE PRIMARY IN MICHIGAN

Just as the mitigator phrase "X; however, Y" imputes to Y the opposite affect of X, the predicate forms of verbs have similar effects. This can be implemented by viewing verbs as having fields with characteristic affective import, for example,

> "A beat B [in C]"

A, B, and C will be called *field fillers*. In the form for "beat", before anything is known about the field fillers, A carries the affect GOOD, B BAD, and C GOOD. These field affects can be used to impute affect, since the relative polarity of the fields remains unchanged: B must carry opposite affect to A and C. Seen from the perspective of verb choice, if the speaker likes Pete, he or she should not use "beat"

(unless Bill and/or the race have previously been established as BAD):
    "[That blighter] Bill beat [my hero] Pete in the [crooked] race"
Similarly, he should not use "lose" either, since in
    "A lost [to B] [in C]"
field A carries BAD to fields B's and C's GOOD affects. However, the speaker could use "win", which doesn't require a direct object, or "get", which avoids the losing altogether:
    "Bill won the race"
    "Carter got 20515 votes"
and hence avoid placing the sympathetic aspect in a BAD field. This is what PAULINE does to produce (a) rather than (b) when it supports Carter in the example above. The effect of this strategy (still supporting Carter) is even more incisive when the sentence is embedded in a phrase:

(c) ALTHOUGH KENNEDY WON THE PRIMARY, CARTER IS AHEAD
(d) ALTHOUGH KENNEDY BEAT CARTER IN THE PRIMARY, CARTER IS
AHEAD

Of course, field affects derive their existence from the semantics underlying the words such as "beat", "lose", and "win". Field affects are not *real* affects. Field affects are simply a concise way of representing the results of standard inferences the hearer is likely to make about the speaker's affects for the field fillers and of using them in generation. Winning is only GOOD, in neutral context, because of an assumed pre-existing set of goals; these are based on the concept WIN and not on the lexical item "win". Before using the field affects, the generator should check for the existence of such goals.

4.5.3   Sentence Organization: Clause Order

Affect has an effect on the organization of the parts of a sentence; specifically, on the choice of the subject and on the order of clauses.

In a typical sentence, almost any aspect of the sentence topic can be selected to be the sentence subject. Since it is a prominent position in the sentence, the subject must be chosen with care; random selection produces incoherent text:

(a) Jane and Susan went to see the new Spielberg movie last night.
The movie grossed $10 million in its first two weeks.
They liked the movie a lot.   — (a1)
The movie really enchanted them.   — (a2)
It had been filmed in Morocco and California.

(b) Jane and Susan went to see the new Spielberg movie last night.
They were really looking forward to it.
The movie really enchanted them.   — (b1)

They liked the movie a lot. — (b2)
Both Jane and Susan considered their money well spent.

In (a), the movie is established as the important topic; in (b), Jane and Susan are. Thus (a2) and (b2), with the movie and Jane and Susan respectively as sentence subjects, follow more naturally than (a1) and (b1). When selecting an aspect of the input topic as sentence subject, the generator must be aware of these constraints.

Grosz (1977), Sidner (1979), Hobbs (1978, 1979), and McKeown (1982), among others, have addressed this problem; the first two from the point of view of language analysis. Sidner and McKeown describe rules for choosing subjects in order to produce flowing, natural text. These rules are based on the notions *current focus* (the focus, usually, the subject, of the current sentence); *potential focus list* (the elements of a sentence that are candidates for the next sentence focus; in practice, most of its aspects); and *focus stack* (a most-recent-first list of the past sentence foci). McKeown's subject choice rules are, in order of preference,

1. select the new focus from the previous sentence's potential focus list

2. maintain the same focus as previous sentence

3. return to a topic of previous discussion from the focus stack

4. select the sentence topic with the most implicit links to the previous sentence's potential focus list

These rules are, of course, underspecific; McKeown's algorithm simply picks the "default" (a predefined entry for each predicate) when a number of focus candidates exist with the same number of implicit links to the potential focus list.

Using affect as an additional criterion for subject choice — either at a low level, simply to help winnow out candidates, or at a high level, to help slant the text very strongly — is another way of injecting affect into text. When the generator has the goal to convince the hearer or to make known its affects, it must use, in addition, the following rule to choose a sentence subject:

5. select the new focus from GOOD candidates for sentences with GOOD affect and from BAD candidates for sentences with BAD affect

4.5.4   Clause Content and Organization

Adverbs play a large role in communicating affect. Stress words were discussed above; in addition, other types of enhancer and mitigator adverbs (from the JUDGE domain) are:

intentionality: "intentionally", "purposely" — "accidentally"
degree: "hard" — "lightly" (hit)
number: "repeatedly" — "once" (stabbed)

During the realization of a sentence, the speaker must find legitimate adverbs (one cannot, for example, misrepresent the contents of the topic to say "lightly" when the aspect DEGREE is HARD), and choose some, usually at most two (when affective adverbs are overused the effect is unnatural; PAULINE has been limited, arbitrarily, to two per sentence):

(a) MIKE JUST HIT JIM ONCE.
(b) JIM COULD FORESEE THAT HE WOULD HURT MIKE IF HE REALLY SLAPPED HIM. HE SLAPPED HIM REPEATEDLY AND HURT HIM.

Within a clause, the speaker has to decide which aspects of the topic to say and how to order them. For example, when making a noun group, the speaker must select the head noun and then decide whether to describe it in full, only give unsaid information, or give an abbreviated version. He or she then has to select and order the modifiers, both pre- and post-nominal (and some modifiers can appear in both positions), before constructing a form from which the eventual noun group will be built. These decisions are determined by the speaker's rhetorical goals of style and of opinion. For example, the speaker's opinion may be expressed by the head noun (a), by an adjective (b), or by a post-nominal modifier (c):

(a) THAT RAT, MIKE
(b) THAT SLIMY MIKE
(c) MIKE, THE JERK

4.5.5   Word Choice: Verbs, Adjectives, and Nouns

Verbs

In addition to determining the form of the predicate, as discussed above, verbs themselves often carry some affect. Often an action can be described by a number of verbs; for example, some enhancing/mitigating verbs are:

"Jane *slammed/tapped* me on the head with a crowbar"
"Mike *wolfed down/nibbled* his supper"

A nice result of constraint 4 is that it helps to organize related words such as "hit", "smash", and "tap" in the lexicon. The sensible way to use these three words is to access "hit" from the representation HIT and then perform a (series of) affective discrimination(s) until the appropriate word "smash" or "tap" is found. (This idea was discussed by Goldman (1975), though his discriminations depend on features of the input concept rather than on the generator's affective goals: INGEST with a liquid OBJECT gives "drink", with solid OBJECT "eat", and with gaseous OBJECT "breathe".) But which words are affectively neutral and therefore good starting points for the discrimination? While this may be immediately clear for "hit" and its variants, it is less so for "punch" or "slap". Chris Owens (personal communication, 1985) suggests that the adverbial stress words can test speakers' intuitions about the affective neutrality of a given word. Of the following sentences, said without stressed intonation,

(a) "Pete really hit Joe"
(b) "Pete really hit Joe hard"
(c) "Pete hit Joe really hard"
(d) "Pete really punched Joe"
(e) "Pete just slapped Joe"

(a) feels awkward and therefore fails the test, so "hit" is neutral. Both (b) and (c) pass it ((c) better than (b), which indicates just where the affect lies). To me, (d) also feels awkward, but (e) seems fine; thus to me "punch" is affectively neutral but "slap" is not. PAULINE's lexicon is organized on these lines; for example, from the action HIT it accesses "hit" and then discriminates to "tap" as a mitigator and "smash" as an enhancer:

(a) JIM JUST TAPPED THAT JERK MIKE ONCE
(b) JIM PURPOSELY SMASHED MIKE AND KNOCKED HIM DOWN

Of course, there is more to sentence affect than this. Sometimes a sentence as a whole carries affect, though each individual word is neutral. In such cases, stress words can be used too. For example,

"The big man hit his aged mother in the mouth"

is certainly not neutral. The sentence creates a sense of incredulity. Applying the Owens stress-word test again, the sentence

"The big man really hit his aged mother in the mouth"

accents exactly this feeling, rather than the action "hit". Much work remains to be done in this regard.

In the shantytown examples, PAULINE uses "tear down" and "destroy" as enhancers and "remove" as a mitigator for the action of disassembling the shanties. For communication of a request, the lexicon contains "order" and "command" as enhancers and "request" and "ask" as mitigators; the neutral word is "tell'. Compare the following extracts:

(c) YALE ORDERED THE STUDENTS TO BUILD THE SHANTYTOWN
ELSEWHERE. LATER, AT 5:30 AM ON APRIL 14, OFFICIALS

DESTROYED THE SHANTYTOWN.

(d) YALE REQUESTED THAT THE STUDENTS BUILD THE SHANTYTOWN
ELSEWHERE, BUT THEY REFUSED TO LEAVE. THE SHANTYTOWN WAS
REMOVED FROM BEINECKE PLAZA BY OFFICIALS ONE MORNING.

In the Carter-Kennedy example, PAULINE uses the enhancers "cream", "trounce", and "triumph" as versions of "beat" (further selection depends on the desired level of formality and floridity, discussed in chapter 5). Variants for the concept "narrow lead" are "narrow", "reduce", "decrease", or "diminish" the lead, as well as "suffer setback" and "lose ground":

(e) KENNEDY [DIMINISHED] CARTER'S LEAD BY GETTING [ALL OF]
21850 VOTES IN THE PRIMARY IN MICHIGAN. IN A SIMILAR CASE,
CARTER DECREASED UDALL'S LEAD IN A PRIMARY IN 1976, AND HE
[EASILY] [TROUNCED] UDALL TO BE NOMINATED BY 2600 DELEGATES.
[I AM [REAL] GLAD] THAT PRESENTLY KENNEDY IS CLOSER TO
GETTING THE NOMINATION THAN BEFORE.

Adjectives

Of course, adjectives can carry affect:

enhancer: "The *wimpy* boy rode home" (compared to "the small boy")
mitigator: "The actress was convincing; she is *adequate*"
(compared to "she is fine")

Depending on the desired level of partiality, formality, and floridity (as described below and in chapter 5), PAULINE can express its opinion by including appropriate adjectives, such as "concerned", "wonderful", "nice", and "nasty".

Nouns

Nouns can also express the speaker's opinions. For example, saying "terrorist" to an IRA soldier may get you shot; saying "freedom fighter" certainly will not! The speaker can express an opinion of an actor when building a noun group by selecting a mitigator or enhancer noun; for example, depending on affect and on the desired level of partiality and formality, PAULINE says:

(a) THAT JERK, JIM, ...
(b) THAT GENTLEMAN, JIM, ...

4.6   When and Where to be Partial

When the speaker's sympathies differ from the hearer's over the topic, the speaker faces a potential problem. By saying the topic he or she may alienate the hearer. He or she can decide not to say the topic at all; otherwise, however, the speaker must decide how explicit to be: merely refer to sensitive aspects obliquely, mitigate them somehow, or say them straight out.

4.6.1   Timidity: The Inclusion of Sensitive Topics

There are at least three points in the generation process when the speaker can decide to ignore sensitive topics:

- **collection of new candidate sentence topics:** Whatever its origin — a topic collection plan, input, a reminding — a sensitive topic or aspect of a topic can simply be excluded from further topic collection. As a result, none of its results, side-effects, or any other aspects will appear in the subsequent text

- **interpretation of candidate topics:** a sensitive topic can be subsumed by an interpretation of it, if one can be found, as described in chapter 3

- **construction of phrases that contain topics:** a sensitive topic can be juxtaposed with others in a phrase that mitigates its affect, if one can be found

The speaker's willingness to include affectively sensitive topics depends not only on the interlocutors' sympathies, but also on aspects of the conversation setting, such as the amount of time available. The less time and the less stylistic flexibility, the less opportunity the speaker has to present the topics in a way that will achieve his goals. Under appropriate circumstances, the speaker may simply decide not to include sensitive topics at all.

These considerations give rise to the following general rule: the speaker should only include sensitive topics if he or she is not overly concerned with the hearer's reaction — that is, if he or she is socially dominant, if the hearer is a stranger, or if the hearer is emotionally distant anyway. PAULINE uses the following version of this rule to activate its rhetorical goal **RG:timidity** that controls the inclusion of sensitive topics. The goal takes a value from the set *timid, normal, reckless* as follows:

1. set **RG:timidity** to *timid* if speaker's and hearer's affects for the topic do not agree, and if the **desired effect on hearer's emotion toward speaker** is marked *like*; or if the **speaker-hearer relative social status** is marked *subordinate*

2. set **RG:timidity** to *reckless* if the **speaker's interest level** is marked *high*, and the **desired effect on interpersonal distance** is marked *distant*; or if

the **speaker-hearer relative social status** is marked *dominant* (since usually a dominant speakers express opinions more freely than a subordinate ones); or if the **desire to involve hearer** is marked *involve* (since the hearer may be goaded into an argument or discussion)

3. otherwise, set **RG:timidity** to *normal*

When activated with the value *timid*, this goal causes PAULINE not to incorporate sensitive aspects encountered during topic collection, interpretation, and phrase construction. With the value *reckless*, the opposite occurs; with the intermediate value, PAULINE includes sensitive topics only if certain other rhetorical goals (such as **RG:haste**) permit.

4.6.2   The Degree of Partiality

How partial should one be? Clearly, this depends on the hearer's own opinions; For example, if the hearer is a protester, he or she will react very differently to the following two sentences:

(j) AS A REMINDER TO YALE UNIVERSITY TO DIVEST FROM COMPANIES
WITH BUSINESS IN SOUTH AFRICA, A LARGE NUMBER OF CONCERNED
STUDENTS BUILT A SHANTYTOWN, WINNIE MANDELA CITY, ON
BEINECKE PLAZA ONE DAY.

(k) A FEW SHIFTLESS STUDENTS TOOK OVER BEINECKE PLAZA ONE
DAY AND BUILT A SHANTYTOWN, WINNIE MANDELA CITY, BECAUSE
THEY WANTED TO FORCE YALE UNIVERSITY TO DIVEST FROM
COMPANIES WITH BUSINESS IN SOUTH AFRICA.

Obviously the latter is more contentious: statements like (b) cause fights. In order to know how explicitly partial to be, the speaker must know a lot about the hearer, the topic, and the conversational circumstances. In general, to remain friendly with the hearer, the speaker's conduct must be governed by the affect rule stated above. These considerations can be stated concisely as the rules PAULINE uses to assign its rhetorical goal **RG:partiality** a value from the set *explicit, implicit, impartial*:

1. set **RG:partiality** to *explicit* if the speaker's and hearer's **affects for the topic agree** and the **desired effect on hearer's emotion toward speaker** is marked *like*; or if the **desired effect on interpersonal distance** is marked *close*; or if the **desired effect on hearer's emotional state** is marked *calm*; or if the **speaker-hearer relative social status** is marked *equal* or *subordinate* (that is, if the speaker does not want to imply social domination over the hearer); or if **atmosphere (tone)** is marked *informal*

2. set **RG:partiality** to *implicit* if the speaker's and hearer's **affects for the topic agree** and the **desired effect on interpersonal distance** is marked *distant* (since being lukewarm about their agreement with the hearer separates them); or if the **speaker-hearer relative social status** is marked *dominant*; or if the **desire to involve hearer** is marked *leave*; or if the **speaker's desire to emphasize** is marked *mention* (in contrast to *emphasize*)

3. otherwise, set **RG:partiality** to *impartial* if their **affects agree**, or if their **affects disagree** and the **hearer's knowledge level** is marked *expert* and the **speaker's knowledge level** is marked *student* or *novice*, and the **desired effect on hearer's emotion toward speaker** is marked *respect* or *like*

4. set **RG:partiality** to *explicit* if the speaker's and hearer's **affects for the topic disagree** and the **desired effect on hearer's emotional state** is marked *anger*; or if the **desired effect on hearer's emotion toward speaker** is marked *dislike*

5. otherwise, set **RG:partiality** to *implicit* if their **affects disagree** and the **desire to involve hearer** is marked *involve*; or if the **speaker-hearer relative social status** is marked *subordinate*

4.7   Conclusion

This chapter describes some techniques a speaker can use to incorporate opinions in the text. To do so, the speaker must be able to determine his or her opinion about any piece of the topic; this can be achieved by combining and propagating affects along the relationships among representation elements. The speaker can emphasize or evade topics he or she likes or dislikes by being selective in the choice of topic, by juxtaposing topics of appropriate affect within affect-imputing phrases, by selecting verbs with appropriate predicate forms, by including appropriate stress words, adverbs, and adjectives, and by choosing verbs and nouns with appropriate affect. All these decisions are based upon the affect rule.

In summary, consider the derivation of a paragraph from the JUDGE example, when PAULINE defends Mike:

AFTER THAT, JIM DID NOT EXPECT THAT [THAT JERK] MIKE WAS GOING TO HURT HIM ANY LONGER;	topic: NEUTRAL enhancer: BAD noun
[ALSO], JIM COULD FORESEE THAT HE WOULD INJURE MIKE IF HE [PURPOSELY] STRUCK HIM.	enhancer: phrase topic: GOOD for Mike enhancer: intent
HE [REALLY] [SMASHED] HIM.	enhancer: stress, verb
THE RESULT WAS THAT HE INJURED HIM.	topic: GOOD for Mike

And one from the Carter-Kennedy example, when PAULINE supports Kennedy:

IN THE PRIMARY IN MICHIGAN,	topic: GOOD for Kennedy
KENNEDY [DIMINISHED] CARTER'S LEAD	enhancer: verb
BY GETTING [ALL OF] 21850 VOTES.	enhancer: stress
IN A SIMILAR CASE, CARTER DECREASED UDALL'S LEAD IN	topic: GOOD reminding
A PRIMARY IN 1976, AND HE [EASILY]	enhancer: stress word
[TROUNCED] UDALL TO BE NOMINATED BY 2600 DELEGATES.	enhancer: verb
[I AM REAL GLAD THAT] PRESENTLY	explicit opinion
KENNEDY IS CLOSER TO GETTING THE NOMINATION THAN BEFORE.	topic: GOOD for Kennedy

Finally, compare two versions of the shantytown episode (both formal):

FOR PROTESTERS	FOR UNIVERSITY	
IN EARLY APRIL, [AS A REMINDER TO] YALE UNIVERSITY TO DIVEST FROM COMPANIES DOING BUSINESS IN SOUTH AFRICA,	IN EARLY APRIL,	mitigator
A [LARGE NUMBER OF] [CONCERNED] STUDENTS	[A SMALL NUMBER OF] STUDENTS [TOOK OVER] BEINECKE PLAZA AND	enhancer/mitigator enhancer opinion interpretation

CONSTRUCTED A SHANTYTOWN, WINNIE MANDELA CITY, ON BEINECKE PLAZA.	CONSTRUCTED A SHANTYTOWN, WINNIE MANDELA CITY,	
	[IN ORDER TO FORCE] YALE TO DIVEST FROM COMPANIES DOING BUSINESS IN SOUTH AFRICA.	interpretation
THE LOCAL COMMUNITY EXPRESSED SUPPORT FOR THE STUDENTS' ACTION.		topic: support
	YALE REQUESTED THAT THE STUDENTS MOVE THE SHANTYTOWN, BUT THEY REFUSED TO LEAVE. [THE UNIVERSITY INTENDED TO BE REASONABLE]. YALE GAVE IT PERMISSION TO EXIST UNTIL THE MEETING OF THE YALE CORPORATION, BUT [EVEN] AFTER THAT THE STUDENTS REFUSED TO MOVE.	topic: request explicit opinion topic: permission enhancer topic: refusal
LATER, AT 5:30 AM ON APRIL 14, THE SHANTYTOWN WAS DISASSEMBLED BY OFFICIALS; [ALSO], AT THAT TIME, THE POLICE ARRESTED 76 STUDENTS. THE STUDENTS REQUESTED THAT YALE GIVE THEM PERMISSION TO REASSEMBLE IT ON BEINECKE PLAZA AND AT THE SAME TIME SEVERAL LOCAL POLITICIANS AND FACULTY MEMBERS EXPRESSED CRITICISM OF YALE'S ACTIONS.	AT 5:30 AM ON APRIL 14, OFFICIALS [HAD TO] DISASSEMBLE THE SHANTYTOWN.	interpretation enhancer topic: arrest topic: request topic: support
FINALLY, YALE PERMITTED THEM TO RECONSTRUCT THE SHANTYTOWN.	FINALLY, YALE [BEING CONCILIATORY TOWARD THE STUDENTS], [NOT ONLY] PERMITTED THEM TO RECONSTRUCT THE SHANTYTOWN, [BUT ALSO] ANNOUNCED THAT A COMMISSION WOULD GO TO SOUTH AFRICA IN JULY TO EXAMINE THE SYSTEM OF APARTHEID.	interpretation enhancer enhancer topic: commission

Chapter 5

Creating Style

This chapter addresses the question "how do we say the same thing in different ways in order to communicate non-literal, pragmatic information?". Since the style of the text — formal, hasty, forceful — can convey much information, any generator worth its salt must use style to help achieve its communicative goals. But what is "style"? Taking an algorithmic approach to the creation of style in language, this chapter shows how rules that prescribe which options to select at decision points in the generation process help to achieve a generator's pragmatic goals.

5.1 The Nature of Style

Text style contains much pragmatic information — in fact, it is so important that hearers tend to remember the precise text form used. This statement is borne out by psycholinguistic research: while testing people's retention of the surface forms of sentences, Keenan, MacWhinney, and Mayhew describe an experiment that shows that subjects were significantly better at remembering the actual form of sentences that had what they called "high interactional content" (that is, much non-literal, pragmatic information, such as "I wish you guys would shut up!") than remembering sentences with low interactional content (such as "Please be quiet!"). Their conclusion (Keenan, MacWhinney, & Mayhew, 1982, p. 323) is that

> ... findings indicate that the parameters which control the retention of surface form information... have yet to be worked out. The present experiment demonstrates the importance of a parameter... [that] involves the degree to which a statement conveys information about the speaker's intentions, beliefs, and attitudes toward the listener. Our results indicate that the impact of this parameter on memory is more dramatic than that of any of the other parameters which have been examined to date.

In order to produce effective, pragmatic-based, goal-directed language, generators have to be able to manipulate style. Therefore, they require an understanding of what it is, what effects various styles have on the hearer, and what information various styles convey. Since, as discussed in chapter 2, classifying all possible styles of text is an impossible task, a number of basic styles can be identified from which more sophisticated and idiosyncratic styles can be built.

So what is style? Typically, handbooks of good writing describe styles in terms of the characteristics of complete paragraphs of text, which is not very useful for a practical, generator-oriented approach. Instead, during the construction of PAULINE, the following fact was found empirically: when you vary the decisions you make during generation, certain types of decisions group together and form stylistically coherent text, and other types, when grouped, produce text that is incoherent or odd. The coherent groupings conform to traditional stylistic concepts. Thus a functional approach is to describe styles in terms of the decisions a generator has to make: decisions such as sentence content, clause order and content, and word selection.

This chapter illustrates a few such coherent groupings, and in doing so develops functional definitions for the text styles **formality, haste,** and **force.**

5.2   Formality

The level of formality of text is one of the most obvious stylistic aspects. It plays a role along the whole range of generator decisions — from the initial topic selections and organization down to the final word selection. All language users have rules for making their text more or less formal; politicians especially have a large number of such rules and hence produce good examples of formal language. But what exactly does it mean for language to "be formal"? No single item in the language can be pinpointed as defining the level of formality; rather, text seems to contain a number of little clues that cumulatively create a certain impression. What are these little clues? Where do they appear and how do we decide to use them? The best way to illustrate is to dissect a piece of text:

> *Yesterday, December 7, 1941 — a date which will live in infamy —*
> *the United States of America was suddenly and deliberately attacked by*
> *naval and air forces of the Empire of Japan.*

> *The United States was at peace with that nation and, at the solic-*
> *itation of Japan, was still in conversation with its Government and its*
> *Emperor looking forward to the maintenance of peace in the Pacific.*

> *Indeed, one hour after Japanese air squadrons had commenced bomb-*
> *ing Oahu, the Japanese Ambassador to the United States and his col-*
> *league delivered to the Secretary of State a formal reply to a recent*
> *American message. While this reply stated that it seemed useless to con-*

tinue the existing diplomatic negotiations, it contained no threat or hint
of war or armed attack.

It will be recorded that the distance of Hawaii from Japan makes
it obvious that the attack was deliberately planned many days or even
weeks ago. During the intervening time, the Japanese Government has
deliberately sought to deceive the United States by false statements and
expressions of hope for continued peace.

["We Will Gain the Inevitable Triumph — So Help Us God", war address
by U.S. President F.D. Roosevelt to joint session of Congress of the United
States, December 8, 1941.]

What characteristics make this address formal? Certainly, one factor is the use of
formal verbs and nouns instead of more common ones, such as "solicitation" instead
of "request". Another factor is the use of full names and titles instead of their
common abbreviations. Accordingly, we replace words and phrases in the address
by less formal equivalents ((a) below), and using the common names for entities (b).
The result, however, is definitely not informal. The sentences still seem long and
involved. In order to simplify them, we (c) remove conjunctions and multi-predicate
phrases, and (d) remove adverbial clauses, or place them toward the ends of sentences
(note the difference this change makes to the very first sentence):

The US (b) was suddenly and deliberately attacked by naval and air
forces of Japan (b) yesterday, December 7, 1941 (d). This date will live in
infamy (c,d).

The US (b) was at peace with that nation. [and, (c)] At the request (a)
of Japan, the US was still talking to (a) its Government and its Emperor
looking forward to the maintenance of peace in the Pacific.

Indeed, one hour after Japanese air squadrons had started (a) bomb-
ing Oahu, the Japanese Ambassador here (a) and his colleague gave (a) the
Secretary of State a formal reply to a recent American message. [While] (c)
This reply said (a) that it seemed useless to continue the existing diplomatic negotiations. [, it contained (a)] (c) There was (a,c) no threat or hint
of war or armed attack.

It will be recorded that the distance of Hawaii from Japan makes it
obvious that the attack was deliberately planned many days or even weeks
ago. The Japanese Government has deliberately tried (a) to cheat (a) the
United States by false statements and expressions of hope for continued
peace in (a) the intervening time (d).

Though not a formal address any longer, the text is not yet informal; in fact, it
seems odd. Phrases such as "looking forward to the maintenance of peace" and "it
will be recorded" do not blend with phrases such as "deliberately tried to cheat". To

improve this, we (e) eliminate the use of passive voice, and (f) refer to the involved parties — speaker, hearer, and others — directly. Also, some phrases sound flowery and out of place. To simplify, some nominalized verbs are converted back to verbs (g); noun groups are simplified by dropping redundant adjectives and nouns (h); and pronominalization is increased (i):

> <u>We were</u> (f) *suddenly and deliberately attacked by naval and air forces of Japan yesterday, December 7, 1941. This date will live in infamy.*

> <u>We were</u> (f) *at peace with* <u>them</u> (i). *At* <u>Japan's request</u> (h), <u>we</u> (f) *were still talking to* <u>their</u> (e) *Government and* <u>[its]</u> (h) *Emperor.* <u>We were</u> (f) *looking forward to* <u>maintaining</u> (g) *peace in the Pacific.*

> *Indeed, one hour after Japanese air squadrons had started bombing Oahu,* <u>their</u> (f) *Ambassador and his colleague gave* <u>our</u> (f) *Secretary of State a formal reply to a recent message. This reply said that* <u>they</u> (f,i) <u>thought it was</u> (e) *useless to continue* <u>negotiating</u> (g). <u>[There was]</u> (g) *But* <u>they</u> (f,i) <u>made</u> (e) *no* <u>[threat or]</u> (h) *hint of* <u>[war or]</u> (h) *armed attack.*

> <u>Note</u> (e,f) *that the distance of Hawaii from Japan makes it obvious that* <u>they</u> (f) <u>deliberately planned</u> (e) *the attack many days or even weeks ago. The Japanese Government has deliberately tried to cheat* <u>us</u> (f) *by false* <u>[statements and]</u> (h) *expressions of hope for continued peace in the intervening time.*

Finally, a few finishing touches: simplified tenses (j); colloquial phrases (k); elision of redundant words where grammatical (l):

> *We were suddenly and deliberately attacked by naval and air forces of Japan yesterday, December 7, 1941.* <u>We'll never forget this date</u> (k).

> *We were at peace with them. At Japan's request, we were still talking to their Government and Emperor. We were looking forward to* <u>having</u> (k) *peace in the Pacific.*

> <u>[Indeed,]</u> (l) *one hour after Japanese air squadrons* <u>had</u> (j) *started bombing Oahu, their Ambassador* <u>[and his colleague]</u> (l) *gave our Secretary of State a formal reply to a recent message.* <u>[This reply said that]</u> (l) *they thought it was useless to continue negotiating. But they* <u>didn't</u> (k) *hint at armed attack.*

> <u>[Note that]</u> (l) *The distance of Hawaii from Japan makes it obvious that they deliberately planned the attack* <u>a while</u> (k) <u>[or even weeks]</u> (l) *ago. The Japanese Government* <u>has</u> (j) *deliberately tried to cheat us by* <u>false expressions of</u> (k) *hope for* <u>[continued]</u> (l) *peace in the* <u>intervening</u> (k) *time.*

Though not colloquial yet, the changes have produced informal text, something Roosevelt might have said to his family but not to Congress:

> *We were suddenly and deliberately attacked by naval and air forces of Japan yesterday, December 7, 1941. We'll never forget this date.*

> *We were at peace with them. At Japan's request, we were still talking to their Government and Emperor. We were looking forward to having peace in the Pacific.*

> *One hour after Japanese air squadrons started bombing Oahu, their Ambassador gave our Secretary of State a formal reply to a recent message. They thought it was useless to continue negotiating. But they didn't hint at armed attack.*

> *The distance of Hawaii from Japan makes it obvious that they deliberately planned the attack a while ago. The Japanese Government deliberately tried to cheat us by pretending to hope for peace in the mean time.*

The oddness of the intermediate texts makes it clear that the transformation rules operate together, as a unit, to manipulate the level of formality. Only then is stylistically coherent text created.

5.2.1 How and When to Make Formal Text

The rules underlying the transformations were gathered from the analysis of a number of texts, ranging from politicians' speeches and writings to discussions with friends. They can be summarized as follows: In order to make text more formal, the speaker or generator must examine the options at each of the following decision points and apply the following strategies:

- **topic inclusion:** to make long sentences, select options that contain causal, temporal, or other relations to other sentence topics

- **topic organization:** to make complex sentences, select options that are subordinated in relative clauses; that conjoin two or more sentence topics; that are juxtaposed into relations and multi-predicate enhancer and mitigator phrases

- **sentence organization:** to make sentences seem weighty, include many adverbial clauses; place these clauses toward the beginnings of sentences rather than at the ends; build parallel clauses within sentences; use the passive voice; use more complex tenses such as the perfect tenses; avoid ellipsis, even though it may be grammatical, in such sentences as "Joe got more than Pete [did]", "When [I was] 31 years old, I got married"

- **clause organization:** to make weighty, formal clauses, include many adjectives and adjectival clauses in noun groups; double nouns in noun groups ("Government and Emperor", "statements and expressions"); include many adverbs and stress words in predicates; use long, formal phrases; nominalize verbs and adverbs as in "their flight circled the tree" instead of "they flew round the tree"; pronominalize where possible; do not refer directly to the interlocutors or the setting

- **phrase/word choice:** select formal phrases and words; avoid doubtful grammar, popular idioms, slang, and contractions (for example, say "man" rather than "guy" and "cannot" rather than "can't")

In contrast, the generator can make text less formal by

- **topic organization:** make simple sentences by not conjoining two or more sentence topics; by not juxtaposing them into relations or affect-imputing phrases; and by not subordinating them in relative clauses

- **sentence organization:** make short simple sentences by including at most one adverbial clause per sentence (placed toward the end of the predicate); by using active voice; by avoiding the perfect and other complex tenses; by eliding words and clauses where this may grammatically be done

- **clause organization:** make simple clauses by selecting at most one adjective in noun groups; by using short, simple phrases; by pronominalizing where possible; by using verbs and adverbs instead of their nominal forms; by referring to the interlocutors and the setting directly

- **word choice:** use informal phrases and words by selecting only simple, common words; by using popular idioms, slang, and contractions wherever possible

Knowing how to be formal is not enough. The generator must also know when formal language is appropriate. Usually, interlocutors establish some level of formality at the outset of their interaction, which, once established, doesn't normally change very quickly. Since formality is not precisely measurable, it is most apparent when the level is suddenly changed or is inappropriate. In order to see the pragmatic effects of using formal language, then, the important question is: *what does the speaker achieve by altering the level of formality?*

First, if you become less formal, you signal a perceived or desired decrease in the interpersonal distance between yourself and the hearer. In any relationship, the participants maintain a certain distance (say, on a range from intimate to aloof) which is mirrored, in conversations, by a corresponding level of textual formality. (Which interpersonal distance corresponds to which level of formality depends, of course, on social conventions, on the interlocutors, and on their relationship; for example, colloquial or informal language is normally used to discuss relatively intimate topics.

The odd feeling produced by exceptions — say, formal language on private topics between psychiatrists and patients — confirms this rule.) Usually, a lower degree of formality permits the selection of more intimate topics and the use of more personal phrases and words (and, of course, more slang, more flexible interruption behavior; for example see Sacks, Schegloff, and Jefferson (1974)). Conversely, greater formality indicates that you feel, or wish to feel, more distant than the conversation had been implying, perhaps after the hearer had offended you, or when you had become uncomfortable with the topic. See Brown and Levinson (1978) on the use of language in formal situations, and Kuno (1973), Harada (1976), and Gasser and Dyer (1986) on Japanese deictic honorifics.

Second, if you alter the level of textual formality, you may perturb the tone or atmosphere of the conversation. Since the conversational atmosphere is also mirrored by textual formality, a serious conversation (a burial speech or a conference talk) requires more formality than an everyday conversation (a report to the family of the day's events). This remains true when a new topic calls for a change in tone, even if the hearers and the setting do not change. To help signal such a change, speakers often use "important" voices or clear their throats. An inappropriate level of formality can affect the hearer's emotion toward you: if you are too informal, you may seem cheeky or irreverent; if you are too distant, you may seem snooty or cold. As mentioned in chapter 2, a large amount of work by sociologists, anthropologists, and psycholinguists describes the characteristics of various settings and the appropriate levels of formality in various cultures (see, for example, Irvine (1979) and Atkinson (1982) on formal events; Goody (1978) and R. Lakoff (1977) on politeness).

Based on these considerations, PAULINE's rules to determine a value (from the set *highfalutin, normal, colloquial*) for its goal **RG:formality** are:

1. set **RG:formality** to

   - *colloquial* when the **depth of acquaintance** is marked *friends*, or when the **relative social status** is marked *equals* in an **atmosphere (tone)** marked *informal*

   - *normal* when the **depth of acquaintance** is marked *acquaintances*

   - *highfalutin* when the **depth of acquaintance** is marked *strangers*

2. then, reset **RG:formality** one step toward *colloquial* if **desired effect on interpersonal distance** is marked *close* or if **tone** is marked *informal*

3. or reset **RG:formality** one step toward *highfalutin* if **desired effect on interpersonal distance** is marked *distant* or if **tone** is marked *formal*

4. and invert the value of **RG:formality** if the **desired effect on hearer's emotion toward speaker** is marked *dislike* (since inappropriate formality is often taken as an insult), or if the **desired effect on hearer's emotional state** is marked *angry*

The effects of these rules are illustrated at the end of this chapter, for the Carter-Kennedy texts, as well as below. PAULINE produces the following two versions of the shantytown story when it is being *highfalutin* (say, when writing about the event for a newspaper) and *colloquial* (say, when describing it to a friend):

HIGHFALUTIN	COLLOQUIAL	Decision Type
[IN EARLY APRIL],	[ ]	clause position
	STUDENTS [PUT]	verb formality
A SHANTYTOWN -- NAMED	A SHANTYTOWN, [ ]	ellipsis
WINNIE MANDELA CITY --	WINNIE MANDELA CITY,	
[WAS [ERECTED] BY]	UP	mode, verb formality
[SEVERAL] STUDENTS		adjective inclusion
ON BEINECKE PLAZA,	ON BEINECKE PLAZA	
	[IN EARLY APRIL].	clause position
[SO THAT]		conjunction
	THE STUDENTS WANTED	
YALE UNIVERSITY WOULD	YALE UNIVERSITY TO	
[DIVEST FROM]	[PULL THEIR MONEY OUT OF]	verb formality
COMPANIES DOING BUSINESS	COMPANIES DOING BUSINESS	
IN SOUTH AFRICA.	IN SOUTH AFRICA.	
[LATER,]	[ ]	conjunction
[AT 5:30 AM ON APRIL 14],	[ ]	clause position
THE SHANTYTOWN	OFFICIALS	
[WAS DESTROYED]	[TORE [IT] DOWN]	mode, verb formality
BY OFFICIALS;	[AT 5:30 AM ON APRIL 14,]	clause position
[ALSO, AT THAT TIME,]	[AND] [ ]	conjunction
THE POLICE	THE POLICE	
ARRESTED 76 STUDENTS.	ARRESTED 76 STUDENTS.	
SEVERAL LOCAL POLITICIANS	SEVERAL LOCAL POLITICIANS	
AND FACULTY MEMBERS	AND FACULTY MEMBERS	
[EXPRESSED CRITICISM]	[CRITICIZED]	verb formality
OF [YALE'S] ACTION.	THE [ ] ACTION.	adjective inclusion
[FINALLY],	[LATER,]	word formality
YALE [GAVE] THE	YALE [ALLOWED] THE	verb formality
STUDENTS [PERMISSION]	STUDENTS	
TO [REASSEMBLE]	TO [PUT [IT] UP]	verb formality
THE SHANTYTOWN THERE	THERE [AGAIN].	
[AND, CONCURRENTLY],	[ ]	conjunction
THE UNIVERSITY [ANNOUNCED]	THE UNIVERSITY [SAID]	verb formality
THAT A COMMISSION WOULD	THAT A COMMISSION WOULD	
GO TO SOUTH AFRICA IN	GO TO SOUTH AFRICA IN	
JULY TO [INVESTIGATE] THE	JULY TO [STUDY] THE	verb formality
SYSTEM OF APARTHEID.	SYSTEM OF APARTHEID.	

5.3 Haste

Haste refers to the amount of time the speaker allows him- or herself to generate language. The less time available, the more pressure, and the less effort the speaker can spend in making the text appropriate and striking. To speed things up, the speaker can minimize processing of non-essential tasks, or even ignore them altogether. Thus the rhetorical goal of haste affects decision points where the speaker can take short-cuts.

Where are these short-cut points? One way to find them is to examine the mistakes people make when they speak under pressure. Typical excuses are:

- *"I ran out of things to say — I said it all immediately, and then all I could do was repeat myself"* — no additional **topic collection** is performed before the main topics are all realized. Thus one decision point controls the use of topic collection plans such as the CONVINCE plan described in chapter 4.

- *"I talked about something I shouldn't have"* — unhappy **topic choice**, alias foot-in-the-mouth disease. Since it is unlikely that the speaker knows beforehand the hearer's opinion on all aspects of the topic, he or she has to determine the likely effects by guessing the hearer's relevant sympathies. For a complex topic, this may take some time. Similarly, the stylistic appropriateness of a sentence topic may also be difficult to determine — weddings and burials, for example, have a number of taboo topics. Thus a second decision point controls the extent of checking the hearer's opinion about and the stylistic appropriateness of topics.

- *"I just said anything as it came into my head"* — inadequate **topic organization** is common. To form coherent paragraphs, sentence topics must be ordered, linked up using introductory and relating phrases, juxtaposed into multi-predicate phrases, and checked for useful interpretations. These tasks are time-intensive, so a set of haste-related decision points control them.

- *"I got all muddled in my sentence and couldn't say what I meant"* — when the sentence topic is complex, badly done or neglected **sentence organization** can cause uncompletable sentences, elucubration, unavoidable repetitions, etc. A haste-related decision controls how much sentence planning is done.

- *"I used the wrong word or phrase"* — inappropriate **word and phrase choice** is a common problem; well-planned text is characterized by apt and imaginative expressions. As with topics, checking affective and stylistic implications of words and phrases depends on the time available.

Errors of these types pervade everyday speech (they are, in fact, far more common than people realize). We illustrate with the following example, a transcript of a conversation between three young women on the question *the current trend towards increased employment of women must ultimately conflict with the child care needs of society.* Undoubtedly the three interlocutors experienced very high pressure to say something — not only were they strangers to each other, but they knew the conversation was being recorded as an experiment, and they had been instructed to arrive at some common conclusion:

> Lisa: *"...I must be the only person who agreed [with the topic]."*
>
> Colleen (interrupting Lisa): *"Wha–why did you agree?"*
>
> Lisa: *"Because I'm a working woman. Because I've seen it. No, I'm not married but I work with — all the women I work with are married and they all have children and n–one in particular is having so many problems right now with trying to care for her children, and so y'know that's what I'm seeing everywhere with with working women is the nnnn is that society just right now — in fact I was discussing this with with one of the men I work with 'cause he's got the same problem with children — society right now is not set up in such a way that um both of the partners in a marriage can work, 'cause all you can do is send the children to school nnnnn babysitters; this guy's a former schoolteacher, so we were talking about the inadequac–inadequacies of the school as far as being a baby sitting system, y'know..."*
>
> Janet: *"Yeah but that's not what they're really there for. It's like like OK there are problems with it, but still, like the men y'know it's like OK for a period of time — why can't the man be home? OK it's like why should it be — in my family my father's the one who's home; he's the one who cooks, does the laundry, and it's just ma–my mother goes out to work and so it's like why can't it be that the man is the one who's home for a few years? Let the wife get her career started off and have her do it while the children are young; the father's there part of the time and then maybe at some point then they switch back, the man is working all the time during the day and the woman either has — then can have her job because the kids are old enough to be in school and have it so that they can come home"*

(Transcript of an experiment made at Cornell University, September 1978; some interruptions and noises of agreement have been omitted.)

Topic organization: The connectedness and flow of sentence topics in Janet's paragraph illustrate how easily this task is sidestepped. A good author would not, as Janet did, begin to state a point of view, suddenly interrupt herself to present an example, and then return to the original topic:

> *"...why can't the man be home OK it's like why should it be — in my family my father's the one who's home; he's the one who cooks...*

> *so it's like why can't it be that the man is the one who's home for a few years..."*

Similarly, Lisa's sentence topics appear in haphazard order:

1. WORKING WOMEN: she is a working woman and has seen it
2. COLLEAGUES: her female colleagues all have children
3. COLLEAGUE: a female colleague has a problem caring for her children
4. WORKING WOMEN: this problem is quite common with working women
5. SOCIETY: at present, society is not properly set up
6. COLLEAGUE: a male colleague has the same problem caring for his children
7. SOCIETY: in current society, school is the only place for some children

Sentence organization: Under pressure, Lisa's performance is poor; consider her tortuous answer to Colleen: from the outset, she is fully aware of the four ideas *children require care, currently, parents provide the only acceptable care, when parents work they can't provide care,* and *many mothers work outside home.* Her difficulty in answering arises from the inability to find phrases capable of expressing the multiple dependencies. So she tackles each part separately, giving specific examples; only after that is she able to state the relation between society, work, and child care:

> *...society right now is not set up in such a way that um both of the partners in a marriage can work, 'cause all you can do is send the children to school*

Given more time, Lisa could have examined the relationships among the four concepts more carefully and used some standard ways of expressing the dependency *if not A then B* (such as "since not A, B" and "A, which causes B") in order to marshal the four topics as follows:

> *Since schools are not babysitters, the only place where children are properly cared for in today's society is at home, which causes a problem if both parents work*

(Of course it is much easier to produce polished text when you are writing at a terminal than when you are speaking into a microphone...) Alternatively, she might have found an interpretation of these topics that would provide her with a ready-made phrase. For example, this configuration of concepts is similar to, but not exactly the same as, the TOP (a high-level goal-plan configuration; see Schank (1982)) characterized by *if you want something done right, do it yourself.* This TOP would have been appropriate if the parents entrusted their children to a school and then at some later time were disappointed in the child care quality; however, Lisa's colleagues knew that schools did not provide good care from the outset. Had she interpreted the four ideas as an instance of this TOP, she may instead have said:

> *If you want your children brought up right, do it yourself; the schools* are
> *not going to look after your children properly. And if you're a working*
> *couple, there's nowhere else you can take your children in current society,*
> *so you have a problem*

In addition, note in Lisa's and Janet's text the many instances of elucubration (a),
false starts (b), rephrased sentences (c), and sentences in which crucial information
is appended to the end (d):

(a) *I'm not married <u>but I work with — all the women I work with</u>*...
(b) *It's <u>like like OK</u> there are problems with it*...
(b) *...but still <u>like the men y'know it's like OK for a period of time</u> —*
(b) *it's just <u>ma–my mother</u> goes out to work*
(c) *that's what I'm seeing everywhere <u>with with working women is the*
    nnnn is that</u> society just right now —
(c) *and the woman <u>either has — then can have</u> her job*...
(d) *we were talking about the inadequac–inadequacies of the school <u>as far*
    as being a baby sitting system</u>, y'know...

Topic selection: Lisa and Janet both include examples. But Lisa's two examples
are essentially identical — why does she mention the male colleague after having
told of the female colleague with the same problem? Obviously she didn't check the
second example well enough to ensure that it contained some new information. Note
that this second example appears directly after her aborted attempt at making the
general statement about society. It seems safe to assume that when she ran into
trouble with that sentence, she needed some other topic to fall back on, and the
extra reminding was the first thing at hand. Had she had more time, Lisa might
have checked, realized that it added nothing new, and decided not to say it.

5.3.1   Controlling the Speed of Generation

When and why does a speaker feel time pressure? In an ideal world, the speaker
would always have time to plan out the text completely, testing each topic, each
phrase, even each word for pragmatic suitability. This would satisfy the default
speaker goal to present topics so that the hearer finds them intelligible and accepts
their implications. However, another default goal calls for the speaker to ensure
that the hearer finds the conditions of the conversation acceptable; specifically, the
speaker should not waste the hearer's time. Thus haste is partially determined by the
amount of time the hearer is willing to wait. (In this regard, hearers have available
a number of signals to speed up the tempo, such as saying "yes, yes" frequently,
completing the speaker's sentences, or repairing the speaker's errors rather than
allowing self-repair; see Schegloff, Jefferson, and Sacks (1977, p. 380). On receiving
such signals, the speaker should strengthen the goal to be quick. The opposite holds
too: If the speaker speaks too quickly or spends too little time on each topic he

or she violates the goal of intelligibility; when the hearer's signals are requests for clarification the speaker should slow down.) A second factor influencing the goal of haste is the amount of time available to complete the conversation (as determined, for example, when making a long-distance telephone call). A third factor is relative social status: when the speaker is subordinate to the hearer the level of haste must increase to help ensure that he or she will be entertaining and/or not waste the hearer's time.

Based on these considerations, PAULINE uses the following rules to activate its rhetorical goal **RG:haste** (taking a value from the set *pressured, unplanned, somewhat planned, highly planned*):

1. set **RG:haste** to *pressured* if the **time** is marked *little*, the **relative social status** is marked *subordinate*, and the **depth of acquaintance** is marked *acquaintances* or *strangers*

2. or set **RG:haste** to *unplanned* if the **time** is marked *little*; or if the **relative social status** is marked *subordinate* and the **depth of acquaintance** is marked *acquaintances* or *strangers*

3. or set **RG:haste** to *highly planned* if the **time** is marked *much* and the **speaker-hearer depth of acquaintance** is marked *friends*

4. otherwise, set **RG:haste** to *somewhat planned*

5. then, reset **RG:haste** one step toward *pressured* if the **hearer's knowledge level** is marked *expert* and the **speaker's knowledge level** is marked *expert* or *student*

The effects of this goal are illustrated later in this chapter. In the program, **RG:haste** is examined to determine whether or not to perform the following tasks:

- **topic search**: run topic collection plans (such as the CONVINCE plan of chapter 4) to find additional topics

- **interpretation**: run interpretation inferences (as described in chapter 3) to find appropriate alternative formulations

- **topic inclusion**: test whether remindings are appropriate (chapter 3)

- **topic inclusion**: check the hearer's opinion on topics before saying them (as described in chapter 4)

- **topic organization**: try to juxtapose topics in enhancer and mitigator phrases (chapter 4) for maximum slanting effect

- **word choice**: check affective and stylistic connotations of phrases and words (chapter 5) for apt formulations

The degree of haste helps make typical spoken text different from typical written text. The prudent generator takes more time to plan when writing than when speaking, because a writer knows that (a) his or her text must be more grammatical than a speaker's, since it cannot contain incomplete sentences, retractions, and other mistakes, and that (b) it is much harder to recover from foot-in-the-mouth and grammatical but uncompletable sentences when they have been written than when they have been spoken or are still being planned.

5.4   Force

Forceful text is straightforward, direct, and has momentum. Consider, for example, the following opus:

> ... *another disgrace. The fact that America's homes are as filthy and messy as pigpens. Until now, I blamed those yappy women's libbers for the sorry conditions of our homes. They're the ones who encourage our gals to get out of the house and find jobs... But now I realize that a lot of the blame for crummy homes belongs to lazy housewives who watch soaps and The Price Is Right. These slobs could take a lesson from my wife Thelma Jean — the best little homemaker in America... I'm proud to say that on the day of the terrible space shuttle disaster, my little honeybun had no idea that anything special had happened. It wasn't until I called her that she knew. Thelma Jean wasn't glued to her TV set like so many of our lazy women.*
>
> (*My America*, weekly column by Ed Anger in **Weekly World News**, March 4, 1986)

In order to determine how people generate forceful text, a number of texts, taken from newspapers, advertisements, style books, speeches, and academic papers, were analyzed and rewritten in the same manner as the formal Roosevelt text in the beginning of this chapter. (This is rather fun to do.) A less forceful version is:

> ... *another disgrace, namely, the fact that America's homes are not clean and neat. Although women's libbers may be given some responsibility for the conditions of homes in this country because they seem to be the ones who encourage housewives to get out of the house and find jobs, perhaps a lot of the blame for messy homes also belongs to less energetic housewives in whose homes TV is a constant distraction. Perhaps these women could learn from Thelma Jean Anger, an exemplary American homemaker, who never watches TV during the day.*

The results of this investigation can be summarized as follows: Aggressive text is calculated to capture and win the hearer's attention and to manipulate him or her by making him or her feel threatened or angry. It shares with incitement the goal to exhort the hearer to behave in a certain way, but inciting text is the carrot where aggressive text is the stick. Direct personal reference is common, both to the hearer and to the speaker; and references to the setting appear as well, together with memories shared by the interlocutors. Hence force is achieved by using a number of independent strategies: incitement, personal reference, aggression, color, warmth. (In the program, in fact, these component strategies are implemented separately as the stylistic rhetorical goals **RG:incitement**, **RG:speaker-reference**, **RG:hearer-reference**, **RG:aggression**, **RG:color**, and **RG:warmth**, for they have characteristic effects that can be combined in other ways to produce different styles.) For the sake of brevity, however, only the amalgam **RG:force** is discussed here.

Based on the analysis, the strategies that a speaker or program must use to make its text forceful when it reaches decision points are:

- **(a) topic inclusion and organization:** enhance the sensitive aspects of topics by using appropriate phrases (such as the enhancer phrases of chapter 4); include direct references to the interlocutors

- **(b) sentence organization:** make declarative and imperative sentences instead of requests or questions (for example, say "He doesn't know what he is talking about" rather than "It seems he doesn't know what he is talking about")

- **(c) sentence organization:** make short, simple sentences, by choosing not to link together sentences; by including at most one adverbial clause; by selecting short phrases; by, during predicate construction, using the active voice

- **(d) sentence inclusion and word choice:** use enhancers — verbs, nouns, stress words — to stress affect-laden aspects of the topic

- **(e) word choice:** rather than flowery or unusual options, select forceful or simple, plain words and phrases

In contrast, in order to make text calm, the speaker must:

- **(a) topic inclusion and organization:** mitigate sensitive topics by using appropriate phrases (such as the affect-imputing phrases) and euphemisms (such as "Uncle John has a bit of a headache after last night's party and will not come and play with you"); also avoid direct references to the interlocutors

- **(b) sentence organization:** make questions, requests, and signal opinions explicitly (using, for example, "I think", "it seems", "don't you agree?")

- **(c) sentence organization:** make longer, more involved sentences, by including many adverbial clauses; by conjoining and subordinating topics; by including words that can be elided; by using the passive voice

- **(d) sentence inclusion and word choice:** select phrases that denote a calm attitude (such as "well, well", "it would seem that", "let's see..."); mitigate sensitive aspects (using mitigators such as "only" and "just")

- **(e) word choice:** select long, flowery, less forceful words and phrases

To illustrate these rules, note their use (numbered a-e, correspondingly) in the following pro-communist newspaper editorial (*Daily World*, November 1, 1984):

Forceful text	Rule	Insipid text
[The time is at hand] to end the presidency of Ronald Reagan.	d	[Now is a good time] to end the presidency of Ronald Reagan
[We must] prevent four more years of policies [dictated] by the [ultra-right].	a c e	[in order to] prevent four more years of [right-wing policies].
If the people turn out to vote in record numbers we will have a new president and a new and better Congress. Every eligible voter [must] [exercise his or her right to] cast their ballot.	e	If the people turn out to vote in record numbers we will have a new president and a new and better Congress. Every eligible voter [should] cast his or her ballot, [because]
That's the [only] way to [assure] a defeat for Reagan and Reaganism.	c d	that's the way to defeat Reagan and Reaganism.
[Everyone] who has been affected by Reaganomics and Reaganism is [needed] to help mobilize the voting population of the United States to produce a record [smashing], [Reaganite smashing] vote on November 6.	e e b e d	[People] who have been affected by Reaganomics and Reaganism are [asked] to help mobilize the voting population of the United States to produce a record vote on November 6.
The [Reagan gang] must cease to govern. They are [union busters] and wage cutters. They have cut Medicare and Social Security.	b e c c e b	[Isn't it time that] [Reagan and his staff] cease to govern, [since] they [oppose unions], cut wages, Medicare, and Social Security?
In the remaining hours of this campaign, and on Election Day, [we] [urge] our readers to...	e a b	In the remaining hours of this campaign, and on Election Day, our readers [are requested] to...
No sector of the electorate should be conceded to the Reaganites. Every vote must be [fought] for and won. It is [critical] that all [victims of Reaganism] not only vote, but also get out the vote. [Start now!]	c e e e c d b c	No sector of the electorate should be conceded to the Reaganites, [therefore] every vote [should] be [worked] for and won. It is [important] that all [who experience Reaganism] not only vote, but also [help to] get out the vote, [so please] start [doing so] now.

To produce a forceful shantytown text, PAULINE used the rules as follows:

FORCEFUL	Decision Type
[IT PISSES [ME] OFF THAT]	opinion, personal reference
[A FEW] [SHIFTLESS] STUDENTS	enhancer, opinion
[WERE OUT TO MAKE TROUBLE]	opinion, informal phrase
ON BEINECKE PLAZA [ONE DAY]:	single clause at end
THEY BUILT A SHANTYTOWN,	
WINNIE MANDELA CITY,	
BECAUSE THEY WANTED YALE UNIVERSITY	
TO [PULL THEIR MONEY OUT]	infomal verb
FROM COMPANIES [WITH]	informal phrase
BUSINESS IN SOUTH AFRICA.	
[I] [AM HAPPY THAT] OFFICIALS	personal reference, opinion
REMOVED THE SHANTYTOWN	
[ONE MORNING].	single clause at end
FINALLY, YALE [GAVE IN AND]	opinion, informal verb
LET THE [SHITHEADS]	opinion, informal verb, adjective
[PUT IT UP] AGAIN,	informal verb, active
AND YALE [SAID]	informal verb
THAT A COMMISSION WOULD	
GO TO SOUTH AFRICA IN JULY	
TO [CHECK OUT] THE SYSTEM	informal phrase
OF APARTHEID.	

The question of activation remains. When should a speaker make the text force-ful? This depends on how forceful text affects the hearer. Since it is short, direct, and has momentum, forceful text is appropriate when the speaker wants to inject energy into the hearer or the conversation — thus, when he or she wants to incite the hearer to action, draw him or her into the conversation, capture his or her attention, sway his or her opinions. In contrast, quiet text is appropriate in more solemn or anguished occasions. PAULINE's rhetorical goal **RG:force** takes a value from the set *forceful, neutral, quiet*, using the following rules:

1. set **RG:force** to *forceful* if the **desired effect on hearer's goals** is marked *activate*, or if the **desire to involve hearer** is marked *involve*, or if the **desired effect on hearer's emotional state** is marked *anger*, or if **atmosphere (tone)** is marked *informal*

2. set **RG:force** to *quiet* if the **desired effect on hearer's goals** is marked *deactivate*, or if the **desired effect on hearer's emotional state** is marked *calm*; or if **atmosphere (tone)** is marked *formal*

3. otherwise, set **RG:force** to *neutral*

5.5 Summary

In summary, this section describes PAULINE's generation of the fictitious primary election between Carter and Kennedy from chapter 1 under five pragmatically different scenarios. The episode consists of a network of about 80 representation elements. After the five texts are listed, a short description follows of how the program acts in each phase of the generation process. Different program behavior results from different activated rhetorical goals; for purposes of illustration, four rhetorical goals will be discussed: **RG:formality**, **RG:partiality**, **RG:detail**, and **RG:haste**.

In **case 1**, PAULINE must inform an acquaintance of the outcome of the primary and of the current status of both delegates. Neither interlocutor has opinions about the topic; both have the usual knowledge of the electoral process. This is achieved by giving PAULINE's characterizations of the speaker and the hearer their default values: normal interest in the topic, no sympathies or antipathies, calm emotional state, informal setting, normal conditions. In addition, PAULINE is given the following interpersonal goals:

- Hearer:

    - affect his knowledge — *inform*

    - affect his opinions of topic — *no effect*

    - involve him in the conversation — *no effect*

    - affect his emotional state — *no effect*

    - affect his goals — *no effect*

- Speaker-Hearer Relationship:

    - affect hearer's emotion toward speaker — *make like*

    - affect relative status — *make equal*

    - affect interpersonal distance — *make distant*

These values activate the following rhetorical goals: **RG:formality** is *colloquial*, **RG:partiality** is *impartial*, **RG:detail** is *details*, and **RG:haste** is *somewhat planned*. In this case, the program says

> **Case 1.**
> ON 20 FEBRUARY, CARTER AND KENNEDY WERE THE CANDIDATES IN A
> PRIMARY IN MICHIGAN. CARTER LOST TO KENNEDY BY 1335 VOTES.
> KENNEDY HAS A BETTER CHANCE OF GETTING THE NOMINATION THAN
> BEFORE AT PRESENT. CARTER IS ALSO CLOSER TO GETTING THE
> NOMINATION THAN BEFORE. BOTH CARTER AND KENNEDY WANT TO GET
> THE NOMINATION.

In **case 2**, PAULINE is sympathetic to Kennedy, while the hearer, the program's knowledgeable sibling, supports Carter. In this case the hearer is defined to have the knowledge state *expert*, with depth of acquaintance *intimate*, relative social status *equal*, and emotion *like*. The program has the goals to *make close* the interpersonal distance and to *inform* the sibling. These values activate the rhetorical goals as follows: **RG:formality** is *colloquial*, **RG:partiality** is *implicit*, **RG:detail** is *details*, and **RG:haste** is *somewhat planned*. In this case, PAULINE says

Case 2.
WELL, SO CARTER LOST THE PRIMARY TO KENNEDY BY 1335 VOTES.

Case 3 is similar to case 2, but the hearer is a *friend* and social *equal* (say, a colleague) who is not as expert as the sibling (i.e., knowledge level is *student*). But now both interlocutors have opinions: PAULINE's sympathy is for Kennedy and the hearer's for Carter. The conversational tone is still *informal*, which gives PAULINE the time to prepare its text well, in order to try to convince Bill that Kennedy is going to win. The rhetorical goal **RG:formality** takes the value *colloquial*, **RG:partiality** is *implicit*, **RG:detail** is *all* (details and interpretations), and **RG:haste** is *planned*. The program says

Case 3.
KENNEDY DIMINISHED CARTER'S LEAD BY GETTING ALL OF 21850
VOTES IN THE PRIMARY IN MICHIGAN. IN A SIMILAR CASE, CARTER
DECREASED UDALL'S LEAD IN A PRIMARY IN 1976, AND HE EASILY
TROUNCED UDALL TO BE NOMINATED BY 2600 DELEGATES. I AM REAL
GLAD THAT KENNEDY IS NOW CLOSER TO GETTING THE NOMINATION
THAN BEFORE.

In **case 4**, PAULINE is a Carter supporter and is speaking formally — say, making a speech at a debate — so that the conversation time is only *some* and the tone is *formal*. The audience is presumed to support Kennedy, while the program supports Carter. Thus PAULINE has the goal to *switch* the hearers' opinions of the topic, to make them *respect* the speaker, and yet feel *distant*. These values activate the rhetorical goals as follows: **RG:formality** is *highfalutin*, **RG:partiality** is *explicit*, **RG:detail** is *details*, and **RG:haste** is *somewhat planned*. PAULINE says

Case 4.
I AM PLEASED TO INFORM YOU THAT CARTER HAS IMPROVED HIS
CHANCES OF WINNING THE NOMINATION. AT THE PRESENT TIME,
CARTER HAS MANY MORE DELEGATES THAN HE HAD IN THE PAST;
ALSO, CARTER HAS MANY MORE THAN KENNEDY DOES.

Finally, in **case 5**, PAULINE is a Carter supporter and is speaking to its boss, an irascible Kennedy man. They are making a long-distance telephone call, which gives the program *little* time and makes conversational conditions *noisy*. Furthermore, the program is *distant* from its boss, does not wish to anger him (desired emotional effect is *calm down*), and still wants to make him feel socially *dominant*. The four rhetorical goals get the following values: **RG:formality** is *colloquial*, **RG:partiality** is *implicit*, **RG:detail** is *interpretations*, and **RG:haste** is *pressured*. To its boss, the program says

> **Case 5.** ...

...nothing!

Note that PAULINE does not generate widely different versions of the central topic. To do so would be easy: the program would simply have to discriminate to one of a number of greatly different sentence forms (however they are represented) and then fill it in. But this would prove nothing beyond the fact that PAULINE uses relevant pragmatic aspects in its discrimination process. In this work, the question is more subtle: how is additional information *implicitly* encoded in text? — in other words, how can the same phrases and words be selected, rearranged, and juxtaposed in order to convey different information? When this question has been answered, generating greatly different sentence forms will be easy to do as well.

5.5.1   Topic Collection

In all five cases, PAULINE is given a single input element that represents the primary election between Carter and Kennedy as the central topic of conversation. (This is done for purposes of comparison; any of the 80 representation elements required for the story could be given as input topic(s), but the resulting texts would, of course, be different, and usually not very interesting.) From the central topic, PAULINE can search for relevant additional sentence topics. As described in chapter 4, the program has three topic collection plans: RELATE, DESCRIBE, and CONVINCE.

Using the selection rules described, the RELATE plan is used in case 1 (speaking to an acquaintance), since the interlocutors do not hold different affects for the topic, and the CONVINCE plan is selected in the other four cases. The plan's steps are applied to the representation in order to suggest candidate topics. In case 5, speaking to the boss under *pressured* **RG:haste**, PAULINE has to say each candidate topic as soon as it is found; in the other cases, it can apply all the plan steps and collect a number of candidate topics before proceeding with further planning. In cases 2 and 3, the candidates are the topics that support a pro-Kennedy argument, namely Kennedy's and Carter's outcomes and Kennedy's current delegate count. In cases 4 and 5, the collected topics are Carter's delegate count, including the facts that it is larger than it was before and still is larger than Kennedy's.

5.5.2 Topic Organization

After it has collected candidate topics and before it says them, PAULINE performs a number of topic organization tasks (described in more detail in chapter 7): it orders the topics; checks whether the topics can be appropriately interpreted; it checks whether sentences of explicit opinion (such as "I am angry about that") should be included; and it tries to juxtapose topics in multi-predicate phrases.

When PAULINE speaks to its boss (case 5), the candidates it collects all oppose his sympathies. Since **RG:partiality** is *implicit*, the program is required to mitigate such sensitive topics (say, by using appropriate multi-predicate phrases or using an interpretation that subsumes them). However, these are time-consuming tasks, and the program's rhetorical goal **RG:haste**, with value *pressured*, does not permit PAULINE to do more than test the candidates for affective suitability; hence, in this case, PAULINE cannot say *anything*! (The first time PAULINE did this, I thought it was a bug in the program.)

In case 3, however, PAULINE has more time to perform the planning tasks. In particular, the collected facts (Carter was and still is ahead though Kennedy won the primary) match the pattern defining the interpretation *narrow lead*. Indexed under the interpretation, as described in chapter 3, the program finds two remindings: Hart narrowing Mondale's lead in 1984 (but still losing the nomination), and Carter narrowing Udall's lead in 1972 (and eventually winning). Since **RG:detail** is not set to *details*, the program is allowed to say the interpretation; also, the value *planned* for **RG:haste** allows time to select the appropriate reminding (by mapping the equivalent role fillers and checking affects) and to cast all this in suitable phrases. (In addition, the newly created interpretation is added to memory; when PAULINE tells the example again the interpretation is immediately found and can be said directly.)

In case 2, PAULINE's goal **RG:detail** calls for low-level details, and thus it doesn't search for interpretations but simply says the two outcomes. Similarly, in case 1, the program organizes its details *impartially* by alternating topics with opposing affects. And in case 4, since it doesn't find interpretations off the collected Carter-supporting topics, the program simply orders them and casts them into multi-predicate phrases.

5.5.3 Sentence Organization and Word Choice

When realizing a sentence, PAULINE must select the subject, select which adverbial clauses to say before the subject, select a verb that doesn't require pragmatically sensitive aspects (such as "win", with no direct object, rather than "beat"), and order the predicate clauses. Furthermore, it must select appropriate aspects to say as adverbs and adjectives, build noun groups, and select appropriate words.

In cases 2, 3, and 4, the strategies for partial text (described in chapter 4) cause PAULINE to include the clauses "I am glad that", "I am pleased to inform you", and the affective adjectives and stress words "many", "all of", and "easily". In case 4, when PAULINE formally addresses the hostile audience, its strategies select the wording "I am pleased to inform you" and "at the present time", place the latter clause before the sentence subject instead of after it, and include the extra verb "does". In order to produce explicit and implicit partial text, the program selects nouns and verbs that carry affect; also, in case 4, formal words and phrases help achieve the goal of **RG:formality**.

5.5.4   Analysis

In summary, the following tables illustrate the effects of the rhetorical goals:

Case 1 (to an acquaintance): *colloquial, impartial, details, somewhat planned*

Topic: central topic	RELATE plan	
[ ] CARTER AND KENNEDY WERE	no clauses before	*colloquial*
THE CANDIDATES IN A PRIMARY		
[IN MICHIGAN] [ON 20 FEBRUARY].	clauses after subject	*colloquial, planned*
Topic: result	RELATE plan	
CARTER [LOST]	neutral verb	*impartial*
TO KENNEDY BY [1335] VOTES.	neutral details	*impartial, details*
Topic: outcome with good affect for Kennedy	RELATE plan	*impartial*
AT PRESENT, KENNEDY		
HAS A BETTER CHANCE		
OF [GETTING] THE NOMINATION	informal word	*colloquial*
THAN [ ] BEFORE.	elide *he had*	*colloquial*
Topic: outcome with good affect for Carter	RELATE plan	*impartial*
CARTER IS ALSO CLOSER	separate sentence	*colloquial*
TO [GETTING] THE	informal word	*colloquial*
NOMINATION THAN [ ] BEFORE.	elide *he was*	*colloquial*
Topic: actors' goals (twice)	RELATE plan	
BOTH CARTER AND KENNEDY [WANT]	informal verb	*colloquial*
TO [GET] THE NOMINATION.	informal verb	*colloquial*

Case 2 (to an expert sibling): *colloquial, implicit, details, somewhat planned*

Topic: results with good affect for Kennedy	CONVINCE plan	*implicit, planned*
[WELL, SO] CARTER LOST THE PRIMARY	informal, to sibling	*colloquial*
TO KENNEDY BY [1335] VOTES.	details	*details*
Topics: outcomes with good affect for Kennedy	CONVINCE plan	*details*
...	suppressed due to hearer knowledge	

Case 3 (to a friend): *colloquial, implicit, all* (details and interpretations), *planned*

Topic: results with good affect for Kennedy	CONVINCE plan	*implicit*
[ ] KENNEDY	no clauses before	*colloquial*
[DIMINISHED] CARTER'S [LEAD]	interpretation	*all, planned*
BY [GETTING]	informal verb	*colloquial*
[ALL OF]	stress word	*implicit*
[21850] VOTES	details	*all*
[IN THE PRIMARY] [IN MICHIGAN].	clauses after subject	*colloquial*
Topic: reminding	indexed off interp	*planned*
IN A SIMILAR CASE, CARTER DECREASED	reminding	*implicit, planned*
UDALL'S LEAD IN A PRIMARY		
IN 1976, AND HE [EASILY]	stress word	*implicit*
[TROUNCED] UDALL TO BE NOMINATED	stress verb	*implicit*
BY [2600] DELEGATES.	details	*all*
Topic: outcome with good affect for Kennedy	CONVINCE plan	*implicit*
[I AM REAL GLAD THAT]	informal opinion	*colloquial, explicit*
KENNEDY IS [NOW] CLOSER TO	clause after, informal	*colloquial*
[GETTING] THE NOMINATION THAN	informal verb	*colloquial*
[ ] BEFORE.	elide *he was*	*colloquial*

Case 4 (making a speech): *highfalutin, explicit, details, somewhat planned*

Topic: results with good affect for Carter	CONVINCE plan	*explicit*
...	none	
Topic: outcome with good affect for Carter	CONVINCE plan	*explicit*
[I AM PLEASED TO INFORM YOU] THAT	formal opinion	*highfalutin, explicit*
CARTER HAS [IMPROVED HIS CHANCES]	formal phrase	*highfalutin*
OF WINNING THE NOMINATION.		
Topic: outcome with good affect for Carter	CONVINCE plan	*explicit*
[AT THE PRESENT TIME], CARTER HAS	clause before, formal	*highfalutin*
[MANY] MORE DELEGATES THAN	stress	*explicit*
[HE HAD] IN THE PAST;	no elision	*highfalutin*
[ALSO], CARTER HAS	long sentence	*highfalutin, planned*
[MANY] MORE THAN	stress	*explicit*
KENNEDY [DOES].	no elision	*highfalutin*

Case 5 (to the boss): *colloquial, implicit, interpretations, pressured*

Topic: results and outcomes for Carter	CONVINCE plan	*implicit*
...	no time for mitigation	*pressured*

5.6   Conclusion

In chapter 1, we asked the question "why and how is it that we say the same thing in different ways to different people, or even to the same person in different circumstances?". This chapter described part of the answer to the "how" question. It suggested an algorithmic approach to the creation of style in language. Though many of the program's rules for achieving rhetorical goals of style may need refining, the underlying claim — that style is the result of following a coherent policy when making decisions during the process of generation — is undeniable.

Chapter 6

Grammar and a Phrasal Lexicon

The question addressed in this chapter is: how should language be represented in a generator? In particular, where should the information required by the generator reside? What is the relation between this information, the concepts the generator must express, and pragmatic and stylistic considerations? The argument presented here is that all the structural aspects of language — rules of grammar, phrases, word patterns — should be represented together in the lexicon in the form of phrases and features of words and that the lexicon should be closely bound to the system's concept representation network, so that the selection of stylistically appropriate forms of expression is facilitated.

6.1   The Three Tasks of a Generator

All generators have to perform three principal functions: inclusion, ordering, and casting. These functions arise from the nature of their task: they start with complex, large, non-linear input and from this produce chunked, linear output.

To explain these terms and to outline the issue, we make a number of assumptions. Assume that the generator's input is a list of structures built using a representation scheme that is not based on the syntax of any language. (An example of such a scheme is Conceptual Dependency Theory, Schank (1972, 1975), extended in Schank and Abelson (1977) and Schank (1982); a similar scheme is developed in Jackendoff (1985).) One consequence of its semantic nature is that the input does not specify a unique realization in language. Next, assume that the representation structures are defined within a property inheritance network such as those in common use (as described, for example, in Stefik and Bobrow (1985), Charniak, Riesbeck, and McDermott (1980), Bobrow and Winograd (1977), or Brachman (1978)). Assume also that these structures have been assembled by some encapsulating system or text planner that plays a further role in the realization process only to guide decisions,

105

as described below. If now an element can be said directly, in one word or frozen phrase, the generator's task is easy; otherwise, the generator has to break up the element into parts and concentrate on each part, recursively. Assume finally that the order in which it examines the parts will be reflected in the order of the words of the text; hence, the generator must use the ordering conventions of the language to guide its traversal of the input.

During its traversal, the generator must consider progressively "smaller" pieces of the input element, or it must consider pieces from a progressively "narrower" point of view, so that it will eventually produce text and not just blindly continue traversing the whole network in which the elements are defined. That is to say, if the generator starts out with the goal of making a sentence about some input X, then its next goal could be to make a sentence subject of some part X1 of X, and its next goal to make a noun phrase of some part X2 of X1, and so forth. This sequence of goals must eventually end in the "narrowest" goal, namely the goal to output one or more words from the lexicon without spawning any further goals. Though this sequence need not monotonically decrease in scope (since, for example, whole sentences can be relativized and subordinated to other sentences), it must always terminate. (Of course, the pieces of the input do not really become "smaller", however size is measured; it is simply convenient to think of them doing so, in the sense that the agent of an event is somehow contained within the event and that the agent's age is in turn contained within the agent, which means that more words of the sentence describe the event than the agent, and in turn more words the agent than the age.)

Therefore, from the piece of the input under consideration, the generator must select the following: which section(s) it is going to work on next, in what order it is going to do so, and what work it is going to do on each section, — in such a fashion that it is guaranteed eventual termination. Thus the generator must perform three tasks:

- **inclusion:** select which of the input elements, and perhaps which portions of them, to consider. Only those selected will eventually appear in the text. Thus not all the input need eventually appear, as discussed chapter 3; the criteria for determining this are pragmatic and are queried by the text planner)

- **ordering:** select the order in which to consider the input elements. They will appear in the text in this order

- **casting:** select, for each element, a syntactic class or type. This class determines the form of the eventual realization — that is, the syntactic category in which the element will appear in the text

Consider the following example, using representation terms based on Conceptual Dependency notation (Schank, 1972, 1975, 1982), where MTRANS means "transfer of information":

```
#{ACTION  =  MTRANS-6
    [ACT :  MTRANS]
    [ACTOR :  JIM]
    [OBJECT :  #{STATE-CHANGE  =  DEATH-10
                    [TYPE :  HEALTH]
                    [ACTOR :  JANET]
                    [FROM :  ALIVE]
                    [TO :  DEAD]
                    [TIME :  PAST]}]
    [FROM :  JIM]
    [TO :  SUE]
    [MANNER :  QUIET]
    [TIME :  PAST]}
```

From this representation, a generator should be able to produce at least the following
sentences:

1. Jim told Sue that Janet died

2. Jim told Sue of Janet's death

3. He told her of Janet's dying

4. He whispered to her that Janet died

5. Jim quietly told Sue

6. Quietly, Jim let Sue know that Janet died

7. Jim whispered

8. Sue was told by Jim that Janet died

9. Sue heard of Janet's death

10. She heard of Janet's dying from him

11. Sue was quietly informed of Janet's death

12. Janet's death was what Jim quietly informed Sue of

13. That was what Sue heard from Jim

These sentences are produced in the following way: Initially, of course, the generator
simply has the goal to make a sentence from MTRANS-6. Its first decision is: which
aspects should be included? JIM and SUE and DEATH-10? Only JIM and SUE?
Only DEATH-10? Then, if more than one are selected, it has to choose a sentence

subject (in sentences (1) through (8), JIM is the subject, and in (9) through (12), SUE is). It also has to decide whether to include the adverb QUIET and how to order it with respect to the rest of the sentence (compare (5), (6), and (7)). When it starts building the subject, the generator must make a casting decision — actions and state-changes must be cast as nominals or pronominalized (DEATH-10 in (13) and (14)); objects can be named, described or pronominalized ((1) and (3)). Later, when it builds the predicate, inclusion decisions pertain to adverbs ((5) and (6)) and to other parts of the topic ((10) and (11)); casting decisions include verb choice ((1), (5), (10)) and predicate form (see (1), (2), and (3)). These decisions are made by the text planner, which we assume has access to the speaker's goals with respect to the hearer and to some characterization of the conversational situation and of the hearer.

The form of each generated sentence is determined by the sequence of inclusion, ordering, and casting decisions made in the realization process. At any point in the process, the generator needs information on which linguistic options exist — which decision tasks it must/may perform on the current input. The question of interest in this chapter is *how and where in the generator should this information reside?*

6.2   Formative Information

Most work on the representation of the structure of language makes a distinction between the *grammar* and the *lexicon*. The former is a body of the rules that govern how words can be put together; the latter is the collection of words and their idiosyncratic features. See, for example, Chomsky (1965) (his italics):

> The grammar will contain no rules... that introduce the formatives belonging to lexical categories. Instead, the base of the grammar will contain a *lexicon*, which is simply an unordered list of all lexical formatives. (p. 84)

In this spirit, the simplest generator programs contain as distinct entities: a set of grammar rules, a lexicon, and a mechanism that produces text (by accepting an input representation, building a syntactic tree structure on applying the rules of grammar to the input, inserting into the tree lexical entries that are accessed from the input representation, and finally saying the words).

6.2.1   Rules of Grammar

In this section, the following argument is presented: Clearly, some rules of grammar have formative properties. Also, some individual words have formative properties. If, now, one organizes a generator on functional principles, then the formative information should not be divided between grammatical rules and lexical entries, but should be represented homogeneously and be accessed in the same way.

The rules of English grammar are concerned with phrasal constituents (such as noun phrase and adjective) which we call here syntactic environments. (Later, a more general type of environment, of which phrasal constituents are one subtype, is introduced.) Based on their function, these rules can be divided into two groups. Rules from one group specify the *order of environments* within encompassing environments — for example, within the environment NOUN GROUP, the order

[ARTICLE   ADJECTIVES   HEAD-NOUN   POST-NOMINAL-MODIFIERS]
or, within a PREDICATE environment, the order of various noun groups:

[NG (subject)   VERB   NG (object)   { NG (location)   NG (direction)   ...}]
Rules from the other group specify *how different environments and their relationships are signalled* — for example, the case information provided by " 's" in "John's book" or by the preposition in "to the store"; or the number agreement between subject and verb.

Some attempts at writing rules of the first kind — the ordering or *formative* rules — don't take any actual words into account at all. Words are simply inserted during the generation process (see, for example, Simmons and Slocum (1972)). But divorcing the formative rules from the lexical entities can cause problems. For example, generators built along these lines run the risk of building a syntax tree into which they cannot grammatically insert words, as in (b):

(a) John beat Pete in the race
(b) * Pete lost John in the race   (*i.e.:* Pete lost the race to John)

To ensure that this doesn't happen, you must either (a) make the formative rules of grammar smart enough to distinguish between such cases as subjects that win and subjects that lose, or you must (b) associate the various sentence structures with the words that control them (such as "beat" and "lose"), and make the rules examine the words in order to build appropriate trees. Obviously, alternative (a) amounts to building rules that depend on words in any case, so most systems opt for (b) by associating with certain words in the lexicon information about how they can combine with other words and syntactic environments. However, this information does not completely specify formation (ordering). For example, in the lexicon in Stockwell, Schachter, and Partee (1972), the word "let" includes the features

"let":
+ V
− ADJ
+ TO-DEL
+ [___ +NEUT   +DAT   −LOC   −INS   +AGT]
+ DAT → OBJ

(that is, "let" is a verb but not an adjective (which some linguists consider a type of verb); "to" is deleted (otherwise, "John let Pete to win the race"); the predicate may not contain the cases INSTRUMENTIVE or LOCATIVE). Still, these constraints are not sufficient to prohibit sentences such as "John let win the race Pete" or "win the race let John Pete"; additional rules are required in the grammar.

Associating this grammatical information with individual words subsumes part of the function of formative grammar rules into the lexicon. The subsumption takes place to varying degrees. In the transformational approach (see, for example, Chomsky (1957, 1965) or Stockwell, Schachter, and Partee (1972, p. 719)), the generator accesses the lexicon twice: once (after applying phrase structure rules that build the basic sentence pattern, but before the transformation rules that reorganize it) for the words, such as verbs, with information used by the formative grammar rules, and once again (at the end, just before realization into speech or writing) for the words without this information, such as prepositions and pronouns.

In the deep case approach (Fillmore, 1968), the syntactic environments of sentences are determined by functional primitives called *cases*. The cases provide lexical entries as well as features that determine appropriate syntactic environments. Fillmore (1971) states that the lexicon of a generative grammar

must make available to its users, for each lexical item, at least

1. the nature of the deep-structure syntactic environments into which the item may be inserted;

2. the properties of the item to which the rules of grammar are sensitive;

3. the presuppositions or 'happiness conditions' for the use of the item, the conditions which must be satisfied in order for the item to be used 'aptly';

4. its meaning; and

5. the phonological or orthographic shapes which the item assumes under given grammatical conditions.

In order to subsume the formative rules of grammar into the lexicon, we should add to these requirements the following:

6. the order of the syntactic environments required by the item

In the tradition of systemic grammar (Halliday, 1961, 1976), the generator traverses the grammar (a discrimination network), setting features throughout the traversal, until it arrives at a fully specified consituent order, by which time it has completed specifications for the appropriate words as well; see Davey (1979), Mann (1982), Mann and Matthiessen (1983), Matthiessen (1984), Cumming (1986a, 1986b). Thus though lexical elements themselves do not contain ordering information, they can only be found by the time the ordering has been specified. Ordering is thus implicit in the structure of the network, which makes extensions and additions extremely difficult to accomodate.

In other approaches, the subsumption is stronger: the definitions of words also include ordering information explicitly. This is the case with functional grammar (Kay, 1979), unification grammar (Kay, 1984), lexical functional grammar (Kaplan & Bresnan, 1983), and the grammar developed by Gross (1984) and Danlos (1984, 1987a). For example, the verb "beat" would contain the formative pattern:

"beat":
[VERB [OBJECT loser (mandatory)] [PREPGROUP instance *in*]
    [DIFFERENCE *by*]]
"She [beat] [him] [in the election] [by 3 votes]"

Here *loser* and *instance* indicate which aspects of the input element to say in the environments. In comparison, the verb "win" would contain:

"win":
[[VERB [OBJECT instance] [DIFFERENCE *by*]]
"She [won] [the election] [by 3 votes]"

and "lose" would contain:

"lose":
[[VERB [OBJECT instance] [PREPGROUP winner *to*] [DIFFERENCE *by*]]
"He [lost] [the election] [to her] [by 3 votes]"

This method works well for cases where words — typically, verbs and nouns — require idiosyncratic combinations of words. Whenever the generator encounters a word with formative information, it uses that information to help build its sentence. But what of the general formative rules that are not tied to specific words? For example, in unification grammar, the functional description for NOUN PHRASE is

$$
\begin{aligned}
\text{CAT} &= \text{NP} \\
\text{PATTERN} &= (\, \ldots \text{N} \ldots \,)
\end{aligned}
$$

either: [ADJ = NONE]
or: [PATTERN = (ADJ ...)]
    [ADJ = [CAT = ADJ]]
    [[LEX = ANY]]

either: [PP = NONE]
or: [PATTERN = (... PP)   ]
    [PP = [PATTERN = (PREP NP)]]
    [[CAT = PP   ]]
    [[PREP = [CAT = PREP]]]
    [[[LEX = ANY]   ]]
    [[NP = [CAT = NP]   ]]

(Reading from the top, this means: a NOUN PHRASE must have a NOUN. It need not have adjectives, but if it does, they are ANY words of CATegory ADJ and precede the noun. The noun phrase need not have any preposition phrases either, but if it does, they are of CATegory PP and follow the noun. Here, PPs consist of a PREP, where the preposition is ANY word of CATegory PREP, and an NP. This grammar is used in the generators of Appelt (1983), McKeown (1982), and Jacobs (1985), and the latter mentions some implementational difficulties and proposes solutions to them.)

Rules such as these have but one function: to provide the types and the order of the constituents of syntactic environments. But this is exactly the function of the formative patterns associated with verbs and nouns, as described above! From a functional perspective, there is no reason why general formative rules of grammar should be viewed as being different from the formative patterns contained in the lexicon. They serve the same purpose. Therefore, they should be defined and used in the same way as the verb patterns are. In other words, *all* formative information should either be contained in rules of the grammar or be associated with words in the lexicon. PAULINE includes a computer implementation of the latter option. Hence, though not associated with specific verbs and nouns, all the standard phrasal constituents (S, VP, etc.) are incorporated into the lexicon and accessed in a unified manner.

6.2.2   Becker's Phrasal Lexicon

There is a lot more to language than grammar and words. Though not discussed as much by linguists, frozen and partially frozen phrases must also appear in the lexicon; a generator should be able to use them to create sentences in the same way it uses grammar rules and words. This view is engagingly described by Becker (1975, from the abstract):

> ... [U]tterances are composed by the recitation, modification, concatenation, and interdigitation of previously-known phrases consisting of more than one word. I suspect that we speak mostly by stitching together swatches of text that we have heard before... A high proportion of utterances are produced in stereotyped social situations, where the phatic and ritualistic functions of language demand not novelty, but rather an appropriate combination of formulas, clichés, allusions, slogans, and so forth.

Becker estimates that we know about as many stock phrases as we know single words (about 25,000), and about as many lexical similes (such as "pleased as punch" or "white as a sheet") as there are strong verbs in English (some 100). Thus any study of language that limits itself only to words and ignores phrases is hopelessly incomplete.

Becker's categorization of the types of phrases (p. 6) ranges from multi-sentence paragraphs (such as the Pledge of Allegiance), through "sentence builders" (such as

X gave Y a song and dance about Z; sell X short), to polywords (such as *for good; two bits; the facts of life*). But not all phrases are so colorful, Becker says,

> ... most of the lexical phrases that we actually use are too humble and un-
> interesting that they would never appear on a list devoted to picturesque
> expressions like *Davey Jones's Locker*. Yet these humble expressions do
> most of the work of language production for us. (p. 32)

Clearly, phrases such as these provide a lot of formative information — the same kind of information provided by formative grammar rules and by certain words. With respect to formative function, no principled difference exists between general patterns such as [SUBJECT   VERB   OBJECT] and specific ones such as [*the facts of life*], since intermediate patterns exist along the whole range of generality — patterns such as [[VERB *bury*] *the hatchet*] (giving "buried the hatchet" and "will bury the hatchet", but not "bury the hatchets" or "bury the red hatchet"). Thus multi-predicate phrases such as the enhancer phrase

[*not only* [SENTENCE (verb relocated, with *"do"*)] , *but* [SENTENCE]]

(described in chapter 4) exist in the lexicon side by side with the verbs "beat", "win", and "lose", discussed earlier. (The use of such phrases in language analysis is described in Wilensky (1981) and Riesbeck and Martin (1985), and some research on how they may be learned is reported in Zernik and Dyer (1986).)

Taking this view seriously, I believe that all formative aspects of language should be treated as phrasal. Multi-predicate phrases, formative rules of grammar, and words with idiosyncratic formative requirements — all entities that deal with the ordering of words and syntactic environments — should be contained in the lexicon as frozen, semi-frozen, and very general phrases. The lexicon should be the sole repository of the patterns that make up language — some very specific, some very general. (Note, however, that this does not advocate "template generation", in which, for example, whole predicates are represented as units and are simply linked to subjects with appropriate features. This scheme works for very limited domains (see Kukich (1983a, 1983b)) but obviously doesn't provide anything like the flexibility real communication requires.)

Just as for verbs and nouns, phrases in the lexicon are associated with the concepts in memory that they describe. If an idiosyncratic phrase exists for the expression of a memory concept, the generator must have the option of using it instead of general all-purpose sentence-formation rules. Though there is no reason to associate the rule [SUBJECT VERB OBJECT], or even the verbs "huff" and "puff", specifically with the story of the three pigs, the fixed phrase "he huffed and he puffed" belongs just there. Similarly, "kick the bucket" is tied to the state change DIE; "the big apple" is tied to New York City. And *nothing prohibits specific phrases from contradicting general rules.* ("You pays your money and you takes your chances" and "I ain't done nothing" are not ungrammatical; they're just rather special.) This fact makes it impossible in principle to capture all the forms of language in a few general rules; thus, the endeavor of trying to create a formal, complete, consistent set of rules to describe all of language tries to describe structure where there is none, and is therefore destined to fail.

Thus, in summary, verbs, nouns, and other words in the lexicon are associated with the representation elements they describe. When idiosyncratic forms of expression exist, the forms are associated with the lexical entries. Similarly, fixed and semi-fixed phrases are associated with representation elements and have similar patterns. Formative patterns consist of other formative patterns and of lexicon entries. Although the general formative rules of grammar are not associated with any specific representational element, their formative patterns are defined similarly. This homogeniety enables the generator builder to add new forms of expression — words, phrases, or rules of grammar — with ease.

6.3   Syntax Specialists

6.3.1   PAULINE

Many generators rely on some central process to examine the input representation, to check its features, and to perform the inclusion, ordering, and casting of its aspects. This approach is most practical when the three decision types are relatively straightforward. This is the case in most functional/systemic generators to date: typically, the inclusion decisions simply are of the form "does aspect X appear in the functional description (the formative pattern)?"; ordering is given by the pattern; and casting is given by the pattern and by the feature constraints of the parts of the input. However, generators that are able to realize the same input in various ways (say, by taking into account pragmatic issues, as PAULINE does) have to make more complex decisions. In addition to syntactic constraints, their inclusion decisions depend on the pragmatic import of the pieces of the input; their ordering decisions, where alternatives exist, may carry pragmatic weight; and pragmatic issues can affect how pieces are cast as well, as described in chapters 4 and 5. And, just as it makes sense to associate information about idiosyncratic syntactic phenomena with the words that control them, it makes sense to associate the pragmatic decisions with words (and other lexicon elements) as well. It is sensible to encode all the relevant decisions in the functional descriptions of the lexicon entries themselves; that is, to spread the functionality of the central process into the lexicon.

In PAULINE, the extended functional descriptions are called *syntax specialists* — each syntactic goal is achieved by a procedure, the specialist, that accepts a piece of input, performs the three tasks, and produces an ordered list of words and/or other syntactic goals, each associating another specialist with a piece of the input. Thus syntax specialists are the repositories of information about the linguistic options. They control the performance of the three types of decision. Sometimes the specialists are very simple — so simple that they contain no procedural information

— and then they are implemented as patterns. Alternatively they may be quite complex — directing much processing and altering the state of the generator — and then they are implemented as procedures.

The specialists correspond to the *clause templates* of Danlos (1985, 1987), or to the *realization classes* of McDonald's generator MUMBLE (for example, McDonald and Pustejovsky (1985)); they can be viewed as implementations of the *systems* in the systemic grammar of Halliday (1976) (for a clear exposition, see Patten and Ritchie (1987)), and so resemble the systems in Nigel, the systemic grammar implemented by Mann and colleagues (1982, 1983a, 1983b). However, PAULINE's specialist functions differ from systems in a number of ways: most importantly, they are not activated whenever their input conditions are fulfilled, but rather are activated in a sequence determined by their predecessors (described at the end of the chapter). This is a simplification of the systemic scheme. PAULINE's specialists differ from Nigel's systems in particular in that they can index phrases as well as words in the lexicon; they can index to more than one word via discrimination nets, as is described below; and their decisions refer to pragmatic criteria as well as to grammatical criteria.

Each syntax specialist must achieve the goal to create its syntactic environment with the input it receives. Thus the generator's NOUN GROUP and RELATIVE CLAUSE specialists make different decisions when given the same input element. Starting with the representation of "John shot Mary with a gun", when the generator's goal is to make a SENTENCE, it can say that sentence; if its goal is to make a noun group, the NOUN GROUP specialist can return "John's shooting of Mary with a gun"; and the RELATIVE CLAUSE specialist may produce "that John used to shoot Mary" or "who shot Mary with a gun". Each specialist must know of the different ways its goal can be achieved, and must be able to select an appropriate alternative. For example, an alternative noun group formulation for the above example is "John's use of a gun to shoot Mary"; and an alternative relative clause is "who was shot with a gun by John". The criteria by which these decisions are made can be grouped into three classes: syntactic, semantic, and pragmatic. *Syntactic criteria* are binding; if they are ignored, ungrammatical sentences result. (For example, when saying a verb, choices concern singular or plural endings, appropriate tenses, and aspect.) *Semantic criteria* depend on the nature of the input and its relations to other concepts and the constraints of use of words. (For example, for the representation elements INGEST, the verb must match features of the OBJECT: a liquid gives "drink", a solid "eat", and a gas "breathe". This idea was first described by Goldman (1975).) Clearly, some input representations may be handled by a number of such syntax specialists. Picking one can be a problem. In this regard, pragmatic criteria can help make the decision[1].

---

[1]McCawley (1978) notes that additional information is conversationally implicated, under the Gricean cooperative principle, when the speaker chooses a less direct way of saying something than the most straightforward one, if such exists. For instance, he uses Householder's example (Householder, 1975, p. 75) that "pale red" is not "pink", whereas "pale blue", "pale yellow", "pale green", etc., all correspond to [color + white] in the color wheel. Similarly, in contrast to "let me in", "let me come in" implies that the speaker doesn't want to partake in the activities inside. This point indicates

Pragmatic criteria relate to the affective values of words and their interactions with the speaker's goals, and are determined by strategies such as those described in chapters 3, 4, and 5. The responsibility for accessing the relevant syntactic, semantic, and pragmatic information resides within each specialist.

6.3.2   Specialists and Phrase Structure Symbols

It is quite natural to identify certain syntax specialists with their equivalent phrase structure entities. This identification can help answer some linguistic questions. For example, at issue for a number of years has been the question whether certain SVO languages are configurational (i.e., whether they have a verb phrase or not). Rather than follow the traditional lines of argument by constructing test sentences for each language, one can go and build a generator and note whether a number of decisions have to be made before the verb can be uttered, once the subject has been said. Certainly, for example, this is the case in English: both the sentences "she seeks the ball" and "she searches for the ball" derive from the same semantic source, yet "search" requires a preposition for the object. If a VP specialist exists, it will do the work of accessing the verb, finding the required preposition, and associating the preposition with the goal to create the object environment; after that, the verb specialist can proceed with conjugation, etc. On the other hand, if no verb phrase specialist exists, then the verb specialist will have to post the object's preposition so that, after its completion, the object specialist can find it.

Now from a linguistic point of view, there is nothing wrong with this transferral of information across specialists; however, programming experience with large systems with many interacting modules has taught that it is to be avoided[2]. This principle of encapsulation of information is very useful to the generator builder, since it helps delimit the extent of syntax specialists. By it, for example, English has a verb phrase. Whether or not other languages should have one is a purely practical matter: this will depend on the types of decisions required to produce predicates. And, with respect to configurationality, the notion that there exists a distinct entity called verb phrase, an entity that is the same in all languages with verb phrases, is certainly false. It is quite conceivable that two languages each have some decisions that must be made across the whole predicate, but that the decisions are not at all similar; in this case, though they would both have "verb phrases", the contents of these specialists would be completely dissimilar.

---

that the generator's casting decisions must take into account the conversational implicature that each specialist would have, if used. This idea of implicature is useful to the phrasal lexicon builder: it provides him or her with a criterion of organization — the pseudo-syntactic class (i.e., the syntax specialist) that expresses the input *without* implicature must be the one most closely associated with it in the network.

[2] "If a variable is not local it is said to be a *free variable* or a *special variable*. It is bad style to use special variables because it is difficult to understand a program if variables appear in it whose values and 'meaning' are given elsewhere." (Charniak & McDermott, 1985, p. 74, their italics)

However, not all rules of grammar deal with information that can be neatly encapsulated in parts of sentences. Some rules operate across specialists. These are the non-formative rules described earlier — the rules that deal with tense, number agreement, declension, etc., anything relating to the scoping and interrelations of syntactic environments. For example, number agreement (in, say, English) is scoped within sentences, and adjectival declension (in, say, German) is scoped within preposition/noun groups. That is, information about head-noun number that is determined by the subject specialist is used for conjugation by the verb specialist in English and German, and, in German, gender information that is determined by the head-noun specialist is used with article information determined by the noun group specialist to determine the appropriate endings for adjectives. This information is scoped over (has to be kept available for the duration of) the governing syntactic environment. These rules do not require separate syntax specialists. Rather, they are implicitly contained within the specialists. Thus they can apply anywhere the general and the specific formative phrases are used.

Thus, where functionally justified, syntax specialists exist, and may correspond to the traditional phrase structure entities, where each specialist creates a specific syntactic environment and, in doing so, may spawn goals to create other environments. But PAULINE's syntax specialists are not limited to the standard phrase structure symbols. As described earlier, some multi-predicate phrases and some words contain formative information just as phrase-structure symbols do. Accordingly, specialists exist to create the requisite phrasal and word-bound environments. This approach to organizing language recognizes many more symbols than standard linguistic systems do: in fact, *any* grouping of the information and decisions that are applicable to more than a single instance may be considered a specialist. For example, English has a number of highly idiomatic ways of referring to money. This knowledge must appear somewhere in a generator's lexicon, and it seems sensible to group the indices to the relevant patterns as well as the criteria for deciding among them together in a specialist. Though not a phrase structure entity, a phrase, or a word, this specialist exists in the lexicon and performs its function similarly. Similarly, PAULINE has, in its phrasal lexicon, a specialist that knows how to say (i.e., that creates an environment appropriate for expressing) the time; another specialist for saying colors; another for measurements, ages, etc. These specialists are described in more detail in appendix B.

6.3.3   Relations among Elements of the Lexicon

What is the relationship between verb-based formative patterns, general formative rules of grammar, special-purpose entities such as the color specialist, and phrases such as Becker describes? If they exist side by side in the lexicon, which ones are accessed by the generator under which circumstances? How do specific patterns differ from more general ones of the same form?

In the main, some generalities hold across the formative patterns. Very general

rules, such as [SUBJECT   VERB   OBJECT], seem to apply at all times, even to
very specific ones that express specific concepts. Sometimes, however, patterns can
be ungrammatical, as were some examples from before: [*you pays your money and
you takes your chance*] or [SUBJECT *ain't done nothing*]. This is consistent with
the general theory of memory organization described in Schank (1982), in which special cases, exceptions, and idiosyncracies remain associated with specific episodes in
memory while less specific cases are generalized to the point of maximum applica-
bility.

Other patterns appear to be instances of general rules without in fact being so.
For example, to announce Pete's demise, you can say "Pete kicked the bucket" or
"Pete died", where the former uses the idiosyncratic phrase accessed directly from
the state change DIE:

    1. [SUBJECT [VERB *kick*] *the bucket*]
and the latter uses the general phrase

    2. [SUBJECT   PREDICATE]
Phrase 1 is, of course, a partially frozen expression with only one meaning. In
a phrasally organized lexicon, this phrase will be indexed only under the concept
DIE and nowhere else; in contrast, phrase 2 is part of the general sentence-building
knowledge, able to produce many more different sentences than phrase 1. But that
does not imply that the two phrases are different *in nature*. Both consist of an
ordered list of elements, where some elements are words and others determine the
syntactic environments into which words will eventually be placed. How, now, are
phrases 1 and 2 related? After replacing PREDICATE in phrase 2 by its definition,

    2a. [SUBJECT   VERB   OBJECT   PREPOSITION-PHRASES]
phrase 1 seems to be a specialization of phrase 2. This is not, however, the case; *the
bucket* in phrase 1 is not part of an OBJECT environment, since this phrase cannot
become "the red bucket" or "the buckets". It is consistent instead to view *the bucket*
as part of the VERB environment, making "kick" an intransitive verb here. This
explains the unacceptability of (b):

> (a)   He tied the noose around his neck, kicked the chair from under
> himself, and kicked the bucket
> (b)   * He tied the noose around his neck, kicked the chair from under
> himself, and the bucket

Therefore, obviously, no explicit relationship exists between phrase pattern 1 and
phrase pattern 2.

In general, when syntactic generalities do exist between phrases and words, these
generalities should be exploited (say, by the creation of a specialist). This idea was
noted by Jacobs (1985):

> ...a system which deals only with "core" grammatical and productive
> constructs will handle but a small portion of the language... On the

other hand, failing to take advantage of linguistic generalizations can introduce redundancy and possibly inefficiency into the knowledge base. Robust and efficient language processing therefore demands a balance between specialized and generalized knowledge. (p. 42)

As mentioned above, this approach results in the creation of a large number of pseudo-syntactic classes to capture the generalities. For example, Jacobs describes a concept called *transfer-event*, of which one *view* (see Wilensky (1984)) uses "take" and another uses "give". This transfer-event is not a semantic concept (that is, it is not part of his concept representation network); in PAULINE, it would be implemented as a syntax specialist. It produces the sentences

- (a) "Frazier gave Ali a punch"
- (b) "Ali took a punch from Frazier"
- (c) "John gave Mary the book"
- (d) "Mary took the book from John"

It should be clear that formative grammar rules, phrasal patterns, and syntax specialists are but slightly different incarnations of the same type of information: inclusion, casting, and ordering requirements. The differences are caused by ease of use in a system; what is a specialist function in one system with one notation may easily be a pattern in a more powerful system.

Why does one care about the relationship between the rules of grammar and the lexicon? One cares because, if all the formative grammar rules can be incorporated into the lexicon, and if the elements of the lexicon are inextricably tied to the system's network of concept representations, then the right way to build a set of representations is to pay a lot of attention to the ways in which the representation elements are expressed in language — not only the words existing for entities, but also the phrases and sentences. If the elements under consideration do not easily support such words and phrases they are suspect. Hence, generating from a representation is an excellent way of discovering its shortcomings (which is a paraphrase of McGuire's maxim: *when the generating gets tough, check that representation*).

6.4   A Phrasal Grammar

PAULINE's grammar consists of a set of phrases. Some phrases prescribe actions the generator must perform, and are implemented as syntax specialist functions; other phrases simply provide inclusion, ordering, and casting information and are implemented as patterns.

The phrases can be arranged in a rough hierarchy depending on how much effect they have on the final text. At the level of largest effect, the phrases control the formation of multi-predicate sentences, such as enhancer and mitigator phrases and relations between topics. At the next level, the phrases determine sentence content and organization to form various types of sentences (questions, imperatives). At lower levels, constraints on the content and organization of predicates, adverbial clauses, and noun groups are represented. And since the lexicon is part of the grammar, the individual words appear as well. This hierarchy does not reflect the order in which phrases actually do their work during the generation of sentences: halfway though the generation of a sentence, words will already have been chosen for some pieces of the input while other pieces are still completely uninterpreted. Furthermore, the hierarchy is not strict: for example, the choice of verb has an effect on the sentence wider than simply one word, for it often determines the presence and order of preposition groups and other words. This is one reason for combining lexical and grammatical information.

The phrases that constitute PAULINE's grammar are listed in Appendix B. They can be categorized as follows:

- **Multi-predicate phrase patterns:** When appropriate, depending on the relationships between the sentence topics and on the desired slant, these patterns are used for the juxtaposition of more than one sentence topic. Multi-predicate patterns express the following:

  - **Slanting phrases:** "Not only X, but Y" and "X, however, Y"
  - **Reminding phrases:** "X, which reminds me of Y"
  - **Goal-relationship phrases:** " X in order to Y" and "X so that Y"
  - **Result-relationship phrases:** "X. As a result, Y" and "Y because X"
  - **Other relationship phrases:** "X is larger than Y" and "After X, Y"

- **Standard phrase structure entities** such as predicate, noun group, pronoun, etc.: Most of these require the generator to perform inclusion, ordering, and casting decisions, and are thus implemented as syntax specialist functions; a few (such as noun group form) are patterns

- **Other standard patterns and idiomatic phrases:** Additional patterns of language, such as the frozen ways of referring to money, age, titles, places of residence, greetings, expressing likes and dislikes, etc.

6.5   A Small Example of Realization

The rest of this chapter briefly describes how PAULINE's syntax specialists realize a sentence in order to make clear the interaction of grammatical and lexical information.

The realizer starts with a semantic-based input representation. The application of a high-level specialist produces a seminal sentence which, after a series of expansions, becomes the actual English.

The central generator data structure is a *stream* (see Charniak, Riesbeck, and McDermott (1980)) — a list of units. Of it, only the first unit (the stream head) is always evaluated. Each unit is one of three things: a *word*, a *topic goal*, or a *syntax goal*. If it is a word, the unit is output and removed from the stream; otherwise, if it is a topic goal, the text planner (including topic collector, as described in chapters 4 and 7) are activated on the topic, and its results — a list of syntax goals — are replaced at the front of the stream. In this section, we are only interested in the expansion of syntax goals. A syntax goal represents the generator's instruction to create a syntactic environment (say, a sentence, or a noun group) from the input representation element. Initial syntax goals are spawned by the planner; after that, each syntax goal gives rise to a list of other syntax goals and/or words (this process was described as a "cascade" in McDonald (1981)), until all the words have been said. The principal components of a syntax goal are its specialist function (henceforth called the *say-function*; it produces the required syntactic environment) and its topic (the subpart of the representation upon which the specialist is to operate). Of course, the type of specialist determines what type of goal it is. Depending on the type of goal, additional information may be relevant to the creation of the environment (either pragmatic information such as desired slant, or syntactic information such as gender, case, head noun). Thus inclusion decisions are reflected in the choice of topic, casting decisions in the choice of specialist, and ordering decisions in the order of syntax goals.

Generation proceeds by applying the say-function to the topic and replacing whatever the say-function produces on the front of the stream. This is a straightforward way to implement the left-to-right generation of language. The generator can thus be viewed as performing a depth-first traversal of the syntax tree of each sentence, where each node in the tree corresponds to a specialist function (though the tree need never be built explicitly; in PAULINE it isn't). The central expansion function simply loops until the stream is empty.

During expansion, the generator must maintain certain information for certain periods of time. This information helps satisfy the non-formative requirements of the grammar. For example, for the duration of a noun group, the generator must have available information about case (and in languages with more explicit declension such as German and French, about number and gender); for the duration of a sentence (a "verb group"), it requires information on number and mode (for subject-verb agreement), tense (for verb-time clause agreement), etc. The requisite information for noun groups and "verb groups" (sentences) is maintained on two stacks in *context records*; for example, when a noun group is started, a new context is created on the noun group context stack and given values (case, etc.) by the relevant specialist functions; when the noun group is finished, the dummy say-function POP-NOUN-GROUP pops the context. Records on the verb group stack maintain pertinent information for the scope of the verb group; this enables the generation of embedded clauses, reported events, reports of mental actions, etc. For pronominalization, the generator also creates a list of the topics it has already said, together with appropriate syntactic information such as gender, case, and part of speech.

6.5.1 Input Topic

We begin with one syntax goal on the stream:

```
#{SYNTAX-GOAL
    [SAY-FUNCTION : SAY-SENT-TOP]
    [TOPIC : MTRANS-6]}
```

where MTRANS-6 represents "Jim told Sue that Janet died" and JIM, JANET, QUIET, HEALTH, etc., are all either atomic symbols or defined in the system's representation network:

```
#{ACTION  =  MTRANS-6
    [ACT : MTRANS]
    [ACTOR : JIM]
    [OBJECT :  #{STATE-CHANGE  =  DEATH-10
                  [TYPE : HEALTH]
                  [ACTOR : JANET]
                  [FROM : ALIVE]
                  [TO : DEAD]
                  [TIME : PAST]}]
    [FROM : JIM]
    [TO :  #{PERSON  =  SUE
              [AGE :  #{MEASURE  =  AGE-23
                         [UNIT : YEAR]
                         [NUMBER : 23]}]
              [NAME : SUE]
              [RESIDENCE : NEW HAVEN]
              [SEX : FEMALE]
              [SIZE : SMALL]}]
    [MANNER : QUIET]
    [TIME : PAST]}
```

6.5.2 Sentence Content and Organization

The stream contains only one syntax goal; the generator applies SAY-SENT-TOP to MTRANS-6. This specialist determines what type of sentence to make: since MTRANS is an event, it returns the following syntax goal, which is placed on the stream:

```
#{SYNTAX-GOAL
    [SAY-FUNCTION : SAY-EVENT-SENT]
    [TOPIC : MTRANS-6]}
```

This goal is now the head of the stream. Its specialist SAY-EVENT-SENT is applied to MTRANS-6. First, it checks whether the rhetorical strategies call for nominalization of the input topic; if so, it would return

```
#{SYNTAX-GOAL
    [SAY-FUNCTION : SAY-PRONOUN]
    [TOPIC : MTRANS-6]}
```

which would eventually expand to "that", as in "That was what happened". Otherwise, the specialist performs the following tasks: it selects a subject, selects pre-subject adverbial aspects, and sets the sentence context information for tense (from the TIME aspect, if any) and mode (PASSIVE when the subject is the OBJECT (or, in an MTRANS, the TO) aspect; ACTIVE otherwise). The criteria for subject selection are both syntactic (using rules of topic coherence such as those discussed in chapter 4) and pragmatic (such as the rules described under **RG:formality** in chapter 5). The criteria for including pre-subject clauses and selecting from the available candidates are also pragmatic. In the example, only one adverb, MANNER, has been given; other possibilities are TIME, LOCATION, and INSTRUMENT. If the pragmatic criteria call for its inclusion, and decide to make JIM the subject, this specialist returns:

```
#{SYNTAX-GOAL
    [SAY-FUNCTION : SAY-PRE-SENT]
    [TOPIC : MTRANS-6]
    [ASPECTS : (MANNER)]}
#{SYNTAX-GOAL
    [SAY-FUNCTION : SAY-SUBJECT]
    [TOPIC : JIM]}
#{SYNTAX-GOAL
    [SAY-FUNCTION : SAY-PREDICATE]
    [TOPIC : MTRANS-6]}
```

This sequence of syntax goals will eventually expand into sentences such as "Quietly, Jim told Sue...". Alternatively, under appropriate pragmatic circumstances, the rhetorical criteria could prescribe the selection of DEATH-10 as the sentence subject, which would eventually produce "Janet's death was what Jim told Sue of". Or, if the criteria suppress all pre-subject adverbials and select SUE as the subject (to give "Sue was told..."), the result would be:

```
#{SYNTAX-GOAL
    [SAY-FUNCTION : SAY-SUBJECT]
    [TOPIC : SUE]}
#{SYNTAX-GOAL
    [SAY-FUNCTION : SAY-PREDICATE]
    [TOPIC : MTRANS-6]}
```

6.5.3   Clause Organization

The specialist SAY-SUBJECT creates a new noun group context in the nominative case and pushes it on the noun group context stack. It checks whether the topic is a single entity or whether it should build a list of entities (as in "Thomas, Richard, and Harold went..."), and returns one or more goals:

```
#{SYNTAX-GOAL
    [SAY-FUNCTION : SAY-NOUN-GROUP]
    [TOPIC : SUE]
#{SYNTAX-GOAL
    [SAY-FUNCTION : POP-NOUN-GROUP]}
```

SAY-NOUN-GROUP then queries the rhetorical strategies to select a head noun from the aspects PAULINE's grammar can handle (namely, TYPE, OCCUPATION, TITLE, NATION, RESIDENCE, AGE, NUMBER, GENDER, LOCATION, and SIZE, in that order, all other things being equal), as well as from the generator's own opinions (if any), using syntactic and pragmatic criteria, as described in chapters 4 and 5. This specialist also determines pre- and post-nominal modifiers. In this regard, some possibilities are ruled out by syntactic text flow rules (one doesn't say "the New Haven female 23-year-old Sue Brown, a comptroller"); other decisions are made by strategies that query the activated rhetorical goals and the affective values of the aspects. These strategies determine the affective and knowledge-related suitability for each of the candidate modifiers, as described in the preceding chapters, and return the permissible candidates in order of preference. Then SAY-NOUN-GROUP selects some number of these candidates, depending on its syntactic adjective combination rules and the value of the rhetorical goals **RG:detail** and **RG:haste** (for example, when the latter goal is *pressured*, no aspects are included, as described in chapter 5). Finally, the specialist associates each selected candidate with an appropriate say-function specialist (maintaining the preferred order), syntactic ordering constraints are checked, and the resulting list of syntax goals is returned.

Different types of topic require different noun group forms: locations ("X was where..."); states ("Peter's feeling ill..."); possessives ("the man's large car..."). This specialist also has pragmatic strategies select and order pre- and post-nominal modifiers. For example, SAY-NOUN-GROUP produces and places on the stream the following (the last element, SAY-PREDICATE, was on the stream already):

```
#{SYNTAX-GOAL
    [SAY-FUNCTION : SAY-ARTICLE]
    [TOPIC : SUE]}
#{SYNTAX-GOAL
    [SAY-FUNCTION : SAY-PRE-NOUN-MODS]
    [TOPIC : SUE]
    [ASPECTS : (SIZE)]}
```

```
#{SYNTAX-GOAL
    [SAY-FUNCTION : SAY-HEAD-NOUN]
    [TOPIC : SUE]
    [ASPECT : AGE]}
#{SYNTAX-GOAL
    [SAY-FUNCTION : SAY-POST-NOUN-MODS]
    [TOPIC : SUE]
    [ASPECTS : (RESIDENCE NAME)]}
#{SYNTAX-GOAL
    [SAY-FUNCTION : POP-NOUN-GROUP]}
#{SYNTAX-GOAL
    [SAY-FUNCTION : SAY-PREDICATE]
    [TOPIC : MTRANS-6]}
```

6.5.4 Word Choice

The stream head is now the article:

```
#{SYNTAX-GOAL
    [SAY-FUNCTION : SAY-ARTICLE]
    [TOPIC : SUE]}
```

The definite article is used for nouns such as "police", for topics that already have been said, for topics that have enough specifying information (such as specific time or place), or for phrases such as "the most". The article is suppressed when the topic is commonly known or is a proper noun (such as "Mexico"). "That" is used with an explicitly opinionated noun ("that jerk"). Otherwise, as in the example, the specialist SAY-ARTICLE returns the word

====> THE

which is placed on the stream, and then popped off the stream and said. The next specialist, SAY-PRE-NOUN-MODS, casts the aspect into an appropriate say-function:

```
#{SYNTAX-GOAL
    [SAY-FUNCTION : SAY-SIZE]
    [TOPIC : SMALL]
    [NG-POSITION : PRE]}
```

which produces

====> SMALL

The SAY-HEAD-NOUN specialist finds an appropriate word or phrase from the representation element (perhaps using pragmatic factors in its discrimination), and then pluralizes if necessary. Sometimes, as in this example, it requires a specialist with specific phrasal knowledge:

#{SYNTAX-GOAL
    [SAY-FUNCTION : SAY-AGE]
    [TOPIC : AGE-23]
    [NG-POSITION : HEAD]}

which given the right pragmatic and stylistic criteria could return words such as "youngster" and "kid"; though now it produces the prosaic

    ====> 23-YEAR-OLD

SAY-POST-NOUN-MODS casts adjectival aspects using appropriate specialists:

#{SYNTAX-GOAL
    [SAY-FUNCTION : SAY-RESIDENCE]
    [TOPIC : NEW HAVEN]
    [NG-POSITION : POST]}
#{SYNTAX-GOAL
    [SAY-FUNCTION : SAY-NAME]
    [TOPIC : SUE]
    [NG-POSITION : POST]}

which produce

    ====> FROM NEW HAVEN
    ====> *CMA* SUE *CMA*

Now the dummy specialist POP-NOUN-GROUP is encountered and the noun group context stack is cleared.

    The next task is to build the predicate. The most important task here is to select a verb; as described before, all the formative information can then be found — either from it, or from the representation element, or by using the default form. To find verbs in the lexicon, PAULINE uses discrimination nets attached to its representation primitives. It searches the concept definition network 'near' the topic, starting with the type of the topic and proceeding up the property inheritance hierarchy until a filled WORD aspect is found; this will point to a verb or to a (discrimination) procedure that will eventually point to a word. Near the top of the hierarchy all elements are organized under some Conceptual Dependency primitive.

    PAULINE's lexicon contains more than 20 words to express MTRANS; amongst others, "tell", "inform", "whisper", "shout", and "broadcast". Since the mode in this example is passive, some verbs (such as "say") are not available and others (such as "hear"), normally unavailable, are. The discrimination criteria are semantic and pragmatic, as described earlier. If the verb "hear" is selected, the generator must use the sentence form

[SAY-VERB [SAY-PREPGROUP (aspect OBJECT) *of*]
[SAY-PREPGROUP (aspect ACTOR) *from*] SAY-POST-SENT]

whereas the verb "tell" specifies the form

[SAY-VERB [SAY-OBJECT (aspect TO)] SAY-ADVERB SAY-POST-SENT
that [SAY-COMPL (aspect OBJECT)]]

Choosing the latter, and inverting for the passive mode, this specialist returns

```
#{SYNTAX-GOAL
    [SAY-FUNCTION : SAY-VERB]
    [TOPIC : MTRANS-6]
    [WORD : tell]
    [MODE : PASSIVE]}
#{SYNTAX-GOAL
    [SAY-FUNCTION : SAY-PREPGROUP]
    [TOPIC : JIM]
    [PREPOSITION : by]}
that
#{SYNTAX-GOAL
    [SAY-FUNCTION : SAY-COMPL]
    [TOPIC : DEATH-10]}}
```

The specialist SAY-VERB conjugates the verb, producing

====> WAS TOLD

and SAY-PREPGROUP expands via SAY-NOUN-GROUP directly into SAY-HEAD-NOUN:

====> BY JIM

The next element on the stream is the literal "that", which is just said:

====> THAT

6.5.5   The Process Repeats

Only one syntax goal remains: the clause expressing DEATH-10. Its syntax special-ist, SAY-COMPL, creates a sentence without initial adverbial clauses, linking words, and opinions, by activating SAY-SENT-TOP with appropriate switches (which are simply listed here as part of the syntax goal):

```
#{SYNTAX-GOAL
      [SAY-FUNCTION : SAY-SENT-TOP]
      [TOPIC : DEATH-10]
      [SUPPRESS : (PRE-ADVERBIALS LINK-WORDS OPINIONS)]}
```

As before, SAY-SENT-TOP must determine what kind of sentence to make. A state-change is made by using SAY-EVENT-SENT, which expands into

```
#{SYNTAX-GOAL
      [SAY-FUNCTION : SAY-SUBJECT]
      [TOPIC : JANET]}
#{SYNTAX-GOAL
      [SAY-FUNCTION : SAY-PREDICATE]
      [TOPIC : DEATH-10]}
```

Proceeding as before, SAY-SUBJECT and SAY-PREDICATE expand into

```
====>  JANET
====>  DIED
```

Since the stream is empty, a period can be added. Otherwise, the subsequent sentence will expand first to SAY-PRE-SENT, which could produce a run-on sentence, given appropriate stylistic settings, or could just start a separate sentence.

Instead of saying "died", PAULINE could be more frivolous. Since the frozen phrase

[[SAY-VERB *kick*] *the bucket*]

is associated with the state-change DEATH, SAY-PREDICATE could select this option (under appropriate pragmatic conditions such as, say, *colloquial* **RG:formality**):

```
#{SYNTAX-GOAL
      [SAY-FUNCTION : SAY-VERB]
      [TOPIC : DEATH-10]
      [WORD : kick]
      [MODE : ACTIVE]
   the
   bucket
```

thereby expressing its irreverence.

6.6 Conclusion

In this chapter, we ask: How should language be represented in a generator program? In particular, how do the concepts the generator must express, the grammar it is to use, and the words and phrases with which it must express them, relate? The answer presented here is that all linguistic knowledge — all language — should be contained in the lexicon. The argument is the following: In order to produce language from representations, a generator must perform a series of actions that involve decisions of three types: inclusion, ordering, and casting. The decisions determine the form and content of the text. Which decisions are available at any point in the process — that is, which linguistic options exist — is information provided by three sources: by the grammar of the language, by the fixed and semi-fixed phrases of the language, and by idiosyncratic constraints associated with certain words in the language. Since, to a generator, no sharp line of demarcation exists, there is no compelling reason why some of this information should be contained in a body of rules called the grammar and the rest of it in a collection of words (and even of phrases) called the lexicon. It makes sense to collect in the lexicon all the information pertaining to the decisions. Groupings of information can be thought of, and implemented, as specialist functions (when certain types of generator action are required) or as phrasal templates (otherwise). In a phrasal lexicon, groupings exist for all regularities in human language: multi-predicate phrases, the standard grammatical phrase structure entities, predicate patterns associated with verbs, the patterns used to express notions such as age, measure, money, etc.

Chapter 7

Planning and Realization

Traditional (blocks-world) hierarchical expansion planning is not suitable for all text planning tasks. A more appropriate method, which can be called limited-commitment planning, interleaves planning and realization. This method consists of both prescriptive (blocks-world) planning and of restrictive planning (monitoring realization and, at unprovided-for decision points, selecting among options with reference to the status of active goals). All existing text planners perform prescriptive planning at present. However, a large number of planner tasks, especially those concerned with the pragmatic content of text such as style and slant, are most easily performed restrictively. PAULINE's architecture, the kinds of tasks suited to each planning style, and the way PAULINE performs limited-commitment planning, are described.

7.1 Introduction

As our understanding of language generation has increased, a number of tasks have been separated from realization and put together under the heading "text planning". So far, however, the meaning of this term has never been defined, in the sense that nobody has enumerated all the various kinds of tasks that a full text planner is required to do. (This vagueness is due, in part, to the fuzziness of the boundary between generators and encapsulating processes, as discussed in chapter 3, and also due to the fact that a number of aspects of text planning, such as the scoping and control of hypotheticals and assumptions, or the use of slant and affect, have never been attempted.)

In the planning that has been done, two principal approaches were taken. With the *integrated* approach, planning and generation is one continuous process: the planner-realizer handles syntactic constraints the same way it treats all other constraints (such as focus or lack of requisite hearer knowledge), the only difference being that syntactic constraints tend to appear late in the planning-realization process. With the *separated* approach, planning takes place in its entirety before realization starts; once planning is over, the planner is of no further use to the realizer.

As explained below, neither approach is satisfactory. Though conceptually more attractive, the integrated approach makes the grammar unwieldy and is extremely slow and impractical — after all, the realization process proper is not a planning task — and furthermore, it is not clear whether one could formulate all text planning subtasks in a sufficiently homogeneous set of terms to be handled by a single planner. On the other hand, the separated approach typically suffers from the stricture of a one-way narrow-bandwidth interface; such a planner could never take into account fortuitous syntactic opportunities — or even be aware of any syntactic notion!

A better idea is the *interleaved* approach, in which distinct planning and realization processes exist and can pass information and queries for guidance to and fro. This approach requires a fundamentally different kind of planning, in which information and queries from the realizer drive the planning process although they are not necessarily part of any current plan and do not necessarily work together toward achieving any goal. Thus, taking the interleaved approach is not just a matter of interrupting the planner occasionally to let the realizer catch up; rather, the planner has to perform a dual planning function, acting both as a standard goal-plan expander and as a process monitor. This is the approach taken in PAULINE.

7.2   The Trouble with Traditional Planning

In the traditional planning paradigm, one or more initial goals are transformed, after a hierarchical goal-plan expansion cycle, into a series of steps that are executed by some agent (see, say, Sacerdoti (1977)). Accordingly, in the integrated text planning approach, the initial goals (to communicate information to the hearer) are hierarchically expanded, producing progressively more detailed realization instructions until, eventually, specific enough instructions have been assembled to realize each part of the input directly as one or more words. This approach is exemplified by KAMP, Appelt's planner-generator (Appelt, 1981, 1982, 1983, 1985).

Of course, planning all the way down to the actual details of word choice requires that the planner have access to as much syntactic knowledge as the realization component itself. This obviates the need for a realization component. For example, suppose the generator wants to create in the hearer sympathy for a 65-year old beggar in the sentence "the [SAY-AGE #AGE-1] woman is homeless". In this case the specialist SAY-AGE should return "old" or even "ancient" rather than "65-year old". For the planner to precompute this lexical choice, it will have to compute all the decisions (via SAY-SENTENCE and SAY-SUBJECT, etc.), such as selecting a subject, a head noun, and adjectives, before it will be in a position first to realize that #AGE-1 is to be said as an adjective, and second to determine what the options are in this case. In order to do this computation, the planner will have to have access to information which one would like to claim is properly the exclusive concern of realization, such as syntactic and lexical knowledge. (For this reason, Appelt's planner contains grammatical knowledge spread throughout. Appelt alludes to the problems that this causes in Appelt (1981, p. 113).) Clearly, if the planner is going to do all this work, down to the level of individual words, it subsumes the role of the realizer. Therefore, the syntactic information must be represented in the same terms as other planning constraints (such as prerequisites on the hearer's knowledge). This is unwieldy, because the nature of syntactic information (as discussed in chapter 6) is very different from the nature of information relevant to other planning tasks (such as interpretation inferencing). What's more, in such a top-down approach, the planner-realizer cannot begin to say anything before it has planned the whole utterance — which may be many sentences — because only on completion of the plan is it guaranteed success. And finally, this approach is restrictive in that it requires every new planning task to be formulated in the same set of terms the planner can handle. It is not clear that this is possible for all text planning tasks; it certainly cannot be done easily.

The separated approach is more commonly encountered. The text planner continues planning until enough instructions have been assembled to enable the realizer to produce the text. The realizer – usually, little more than a grammar — accepts the planner's output as its input. Though the separation permits the use of different representations for the planning and realization tasks, this solution is hardly better: once the planning stage is over, the realizer has no more recourse to it; if the realizer is able to fulfill more than one planner instruction at once, or if it is unable to fulfill an instruction, it has no way to bring about any replanning! Therefore, in practice, separated generators perform only planning that has little or no syntactic import — usually, the tasks of topic choice and sentence order. This is the case in the generation systems of McKeown (1982), McCoy (1985), Rösner (1986, 1987), Novak (1987), Paris (1987), and the ideas described in McDonald and Pustejovsky (1985). These planners do not address such intrasentential questions as slanted text, interpretation, extensive lexical choice, and sentence and clause construction.

Both these models, therefore, are unsuitable for real text planning. Furthermore, they both run counter to human behavior: When we speak, we do not try to satisfy one or two goals, and we operate (often, and with success) under conflicting goals for which no resolution exists. We usually begin to speak before we have planned out the full utterance, and then proceed while performing certain planning tasks in bottom-up fashion. That is, when we start speaking, we have usually made some decisions and have postponed others — we have some vague notion about what topics we want to cover, and maybe even of the desired slant and a particular phrase we want to use; we leave the details — even some non-syntactic details — for later consideration.

7.3   A Solution: Interleaved Planning

Taking this into account, a better solution is to perform planning only when necessitated by the realization process. This approach interleaves planning and realization and is characterized by a two-way communication at the realizer's decision points. In other words, the planner assembles only a partial set of generator instructions — enough for the realization component to start working on — and then continues planning when the realization component requires further guidance. This approach has advantages the others lacked. First, it allows the separation of planning and realization tasks, enabling them to be handled in appropriate terms. (In fact, it even allows the separation of different planning tasks, so that special-purpose tasks with idiosyncratic representational requirements can be accomodated in special-purpose planners.) Second, it allows planning to take into account unexpected syntactic opportunities and inadequacies. Third, in addition to such computational advantages, this approach accords well with psycholinguistic research that suggests that the model of strictly sequential separate planning and realization components is incorrect (see, say, Bock (1987), Rosenberg (1977), Danks (1977)), as well as with the research on incremetal generation described in De Smedt and Kempen (1987), Kempen and Hoenkamp (1978), Kempen (1977, 1976), and Levelt and Schriefers (1987).

However, interleaving planning and realization comes at a cost. It requires that the planner be altered to perform both standard hierarchical expansion planning as well as a kind of execution monitoring. The reason is that hierarchical expansion planning is usually prescriptive: it determines a series of actions over an extended range of time (i.e., text). However, when the planner cannot expand its plan to the final level of detail — remember, it doesn't have access to syntactic information — then it has to complete its task by planning in-line, during realization. And in-line planning is very different from prescriptive planning, because it usually requires only a single decision, a selection from the syntactically relevant options. Subsequent processing continues as realization — at least until the next set of unprovided-for options. Unfortunately, unlike hierarchical plan steps, subsequent planning options need not work toward the same goal (or indeed have any relation with each other); the planner has no way to guess even remotely what the next set of options and satisfiable goals might be. It's a hierarchical planner's nightmare: any request for further planning could appeal to any of the extant goals; the planner can do nothing to further a specific goal unless the current state of the realizer gives it the opportunity to select an option that does so. It has lost its absolute control; it plays only a guiding role. Hierarchical plan expansion is not possible with in-line "planning"; what is required is something quite different: strategies that guide selection decisions, based on the state of satisfaction of active goals.

A second reason for augmenting traditional hierarchical expansion planning is the following: it is impossible to formulate workable plans for certain types of goals that speakers frequently have. This is true especially for pragmatic goals. A speaker may, for example, have the goals to impress the hearer, to make the hearer feel socially subordinate, and yet to be relatively informal. These goals play as large a role in generation as the speaker's goal to inform the hearer about the topic. However, they cannot be achieved by constructing and following a plan — what would the plan's steps prescribe? Certainly not the sentence "I want to impress you, but still make you feel subordinate"! Pragmatic effects are best achieved by making appropriate subtle decisions during the generation process: an extra adjective here, a slanted verb there. Typically, this is a matter of in-line planning.

A third shortcoming of traditional planning is the following: Some goals can be achieved, flushed from the goal list, and forgotten. Such goals (for example, the goal to communicate a certain set of topics) usually activate prescriptive plans. In contrast, other goals cannot ever be fully achieved. If you are formal, you are formal throughout the text; if you are friendly, arrogant, or opinionated, you remain so — you cannot suddenly be "friendly enough" and then flush that goal. These goals, which are pragmatic and stylistic in nature, must be handled differently.

Generation, then, requires two types of planning. Certain tasks are most easily performed in top-down fashion (that is, under guidance of a hierarchical planner, or of a fixed-plan (schema or script) applier), and other tasks are most naturally performed in a bottom-up, selective, fashion. That is, some tasks are *prescriptive* — they act over and give shape to long ranges of text — and some are *restrictive* — they act over short ranges of text, usually as a selection from some number of alternatives. Prescriptive plan steps are purposefully directed toward achieving some goal; restrictive strategies are not contained in any plan but are brought up by the realization process; their steps work in disjoint fashion toward achieving any of a set of goals. A restrictive planner cannot simply plan *for*, it is constrained to plan *with*: the options it has to select from are presented to it by some other component (in generation, the realizer). It cannot even use current options to control future decisions for two reasons: first, the options only have relatively local effect, and second, the information that controls the sequence of decision types and hence of the options (namely grammar) is not available for planner inspection.

The difference between prescriptive and restrictive planning is captured neatly in the location, organization, and use of the information required to guide the generation process from its initial goal (to say the topic) to a final state (the said utterance). When the information is contained in a set of plan steps (ordered or unordered) and when this information directs which specific actions are to be performed, then the plan is prescriptive. On the other hand, when the information is contained elsewhere (say, it is information in the lexicon on affect), and the planner uses this information to query its goals for guidance, then this information, together with the strategies used for the query, for resolving any goal conflicts, etc., constitutes a restrictive 'plan'. Prescriptive strategies are formative: they control the construction and placement of parts in the paragraph and the sentence. Under guidance of its prescriptive plans, the generator makes some commitment to the final form of the text (such as, for example, the inclusion and order of specific sentence topics). Restrictive strategies are selective: they decide among alternatives that were left open (such as, for example, the possibility of including additional topics under certain conditions, or the specific content of each sentence).

This interleaved planning paradigm is a natural way to implement *limited-commitment planning*. Limited-commitment planning is ubiquitous in daily life; it does not apply to generation only. We very seldom do pure hierarchical expansion planning. For example, Birnbaum (1986) describes the limitations of pure top-down planning in argumentation:

> An exclusively top-down approach to planning can work in situations which are more or less under the control of the planner... But conversations do not, in general, meet those requirements... Thus, unless a speaker can predict, rather specifically, how his adversary will respond, his utterances cannot be completely planned in advance. (p. 176)

McDermott describes a general problem solver/planner that uses a theorem prover to retrieve plan schemata for attacking problems. When it finds more than one schema, it retrieves choice rules to help select one. Here "task reductions" correspond to prescriptive plans and "choice rules" to restrictive plans (McDermott, 1978):

> ... sometimes the user will want to be able to express rules for synthesizing a brand new alternative task reduction 'on the fly' when two task reductions have been suggested... The solution is to face up to the necessity for treating 'choice between alternatives' as a basic situation for problem solving. (p. 76)

7.4   Performing Restrictive Planning: Monitoring

Due to its bottom-up, run-time nature, restrictive planning differs from traditional planning in the type of information it requires and in the way it uses that information. For example, limited-commitment planners have to face up to and compromise on goal conflicts, rather than employ procedures called critics (in the planner NOAH, Sacerdoti (1977)) to notice when conflicts occur and to plan around them. In generation, conflicts arise all the time: if you are instructing someone, you have stylistic permission to change the topic whenever you think it appropriate; but if the hearer is socially dominant, he or she should control topic change. For traditional planners such as NOAH this conflict poses a serious problem. However, this is what gives generation its spice! People can speak while holding conflicting goals; generators must be able to merge conflicting plans into sensible generator instructions.

Thus, an important difference between the two types of planning is that a restrictive planner is unable to guarantee that all its goals will necessarily be achieved; it can, by making appropriate decisions, merely ensure that no goal gets too seriously thwarted. The satisfaction statuses of its goals are constantly changing in ways it cannot predict.

What information, then, does it require?

Obviously, after each decision, the statuses of the affected goals must be altered. This task is called execution monitoring in a real-time planning system with an agent (see Fikes, Hart, and Nilsson (1972), Sacerdoti (1977), Miller (1985), Doyle, Atkinson, and Doshi (1986), Broverman and Croft (1987), Firby (1987)); we will use the term *monitoring* here, appropriate for a system that does not take into account the world's actual reaction (in generation, the hearer's actual response), but that trusts, perhaps naively, that the world will react in the way it expects. Monitoring can be performed by the restrictive planner, since it deals with the effects its options have on the goals. This task requires checking, updating, and recording the following:

- 1. the current satisfaction status of each goal

Furthermore, to perform both planning and monitoring, the restrictive planner must know (or be able to compute), for each option,

- 2. which goal(s) it will help satisfy, to what extent, and in what ways
- 3. which goal(s) it will thwart, to what extent, and in what ways

— that is, it must be able to judge the effect of each option as far as permitted by restrictive planning. In practice, of course, this cannot be too far, because as soon as the planner tries to increase the extent by replacing the information it is given with more detailed information, from whatever source, it is performing top-down (i.e., prescriptive) planning. (Thus, in generation, the principal line of demarcation is the way additional information is used; other than this, there is no natural division in the generation process before which a prescriptive planner should run and after which a realizer (and with that, a restrictive planner) should take over.) Hence the restrictive planner must be provided not only with options, but also with some indication of which goal(s) each option will affect and in what way it will do so. Obviously, this information should reside in the subsystems or specialist functions that present the options to the planner.

One problem remains: conflict resolution. To decide, for example, whether during instruction to change the topic or to wait for the socially dominant hearer to change it, a restrictive planner must know

- 4. the relative priority of each goal

When the planner is uncertain about which long-term goals to pursue and which sequence of actions to select, the following strategies are useful:

- prefer *common intermediate* goals (subgoals shared by various goals; Durfee & Lesser, 1986))

- prefer *cheaper* goals (more easilty achieved goals; (Durfee & Lesser, 1986))

- prefer *discriminative intermediate* goals (goals that most effectively indicate the long-term promise of the avenue being explored) (Durfee & Lesser, 1986))

- prefer *least-satisfied* goals (goals furthest from achievement)

- prefer *least-recently satisfied* goals (goals least recently advanced)

- use a *combination of the latter two* strategies (a goal receives higher priority the longer it waits and the fewer times it has been advanced)

The introduction of explicit priorities permits the formulation of additional high-level prescriptive plans to control the planner's overall approach. (In generation, this is expressed as the *tenor* of longer texts; for example, in a speech, the speaker may start off distant and forceful, and then gradually become more friendly and relaxed. Appropriate plans, when worked out, may be implemented in the style of the meta-plans described by Woolf and McDonald (1984).)

Restrictive planning is implemented in PAULINE in the following way: None of the program's pragmatic goals are ever fully achieved and flushed; they require decisions to be made in their favor throughout the text. (That is to say, you cannot at some point simply flush the goal to be appropriately formal, but you can give it a lower priority for a while.) An option can affect a goal in one way only — by adding one "point" to its satisfaction status — so that the satisfaction level of each goal is simply the number of times some option that helps achieve it has been selected. Of course, a single item may help satisfy a number of goals concurrently. For conflict resolution, PAULINE uses the *least-satisfied* strategy: When making decisions, the program computes the combined effects of each option — the total of all increased satisfaction statuses — and chooses the option corresponding to the goals with the lowest total. In order to do this, it must know which goals each option will help satisfy. Responsibility for providing this information lies with whatever produces the option: either the lexicon or the language specialist functions in the realizer (such as a clause constructor). This implementation rests on the assumptions that all the program's rhetorical goals are equally important and that every option helps satisfy its goals by the same fixed amount. These simplifications produce a quite reasonable approximation of the stylistic behavior of speakers; that is, analysis of spoken texts indicates that people often alternate their rhetorical strategies when pursuing conflicting goals.

At the end of a text, PAULINE displays the number of times each rhetorical goal was satisfied. See, for example, the end of appendix A.

By its bottom-up nature, restrictive planning provides the generator with a kind of opportunism (a very limited version of the kind described as slips of the tongue by Freud (1935) and discussed in Birnbaum (1986)). Whenever the restrictive planner selects options that help satisfy a number of goals and that, in addition, uncover new possibilities (such as for additional topic inclusion), it can be said to be acting opportunistically. For true opportunism, a system has to check incoming possibilities and their effects against *all* its goals; as Birnbaum points out, a potentially expensive operation. However, when each option is explicitly marked with the goals it can help satisfy, the resulting limited form of opportunism becomes tractable.

7.5 Program Architecture

The program consists of over 12,000 lines of T, a Scheme-like LISP developed at Yale. As input, before each run, PAULINE is given descriptions of the situation and of the hearer, as well as appropriate pragmatic goals. It is also given the principal topics of conversation. The program's structure is:

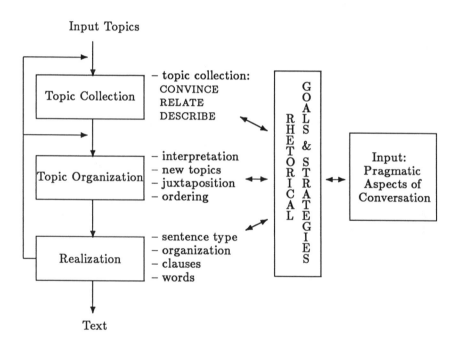

PAULINE's Architecture

Prescriptive planning is mostly performed in the topic collection and topic organization phases and restrictive planning is mostly performed during the realization phase. All stylistic and pragmatic queries are directed to the activated rhetorical goals and their associated strategies, which, to make their decisions, inspect the options given to them and any relevant pragmatic aspects of the conversation.

7.6   Planning in PAULINE

The rest of this chapter describes the implementation of PAULINE's text planning
processes. In PAULINE, the following tasks comprise text planning: topic collection
(prescriptive); topic interpretation (prescriptive and restrictive); additional topic
inclusion (restrictive); topic juxtaposition (restrictive); topic ordering (prescriptive);
intrasentential slant and style (restrictive). An annotated trace of a session with
PAULINE appears in appendix A.

7.6.1   The Program's Input and Opinions

PAULINE's input is represented in a standard case-frame-type language based on
Conceptual Dependency (Schank, 1972, 1975; Schank and Abelson, 1977) and is embedded in a property-inheritance network (see Stefik and Bobrow (1986), Charniak,
Riesbeck, and McDermott (1980), Bobrow and Winograd (1977)). In the shantytown
example, for instance, the shantytown disassembly is represented as follows (where
the entities with numbers are individualized instances of general entities):

```
#{CONSTRUCT  =  CONSTRUCT-2
   [ACTOR :  OFFICIALS]
   [OBJECT :  SHANTYTOWN-1]
   [MODE :  DISASSEMBLE]
   [LOC :  BEINECKE-PLAZA-1]
   [TIME :  TIME-5]
   [RELATIONS :
     (REL-SUBGOAL-TO :
         #{HAVE-GOAL  =  GOAL-2
            [ACTOR :  YALE]
            [DESIRED-STATE :  ORDERLINESS]
            [TIME :  PAST]
            [RELATIONS :  ... ]}
      REL-WHILE :
         #{M-ALTER-FREEDOM  =  ARREST-1
            [ACTOR :  POLICE]
            [OBJECT :  STUDENTS-2]
            [MODE :  ARREST]
            [TIME :  TIME-5]
            [RELATIONS :  ... ]}
      REL-RESULT :
         #{SUPPORT-2 ... }
      REL-RESULT :
         #{MTRANS-7 ... })]}
```

The whole example contains about 120 entities, from which PAULINE generates all the different versions. No intermediate representation (say, one that is more syntactic or that varies depending on the desired slant and style) is created.

PAULINE's opinions are based on the three affect values GOOD, NEUTRAL, and BAD, as described in chapter 4. Its rules for affect combination and propagation enable the program to compute an opinion for any representation entity. For the representation above, when PAULINE speaks as a protester, its sympathy list contains STUDENTS-1 (the protesters) and GOAL-1 (the protesters' goal that Yale divest), and its antipathy list contains YALE and GOAL-2 (Yale's goal that the university remain in an orderly state). To work out its affect for CONSTRUCT-2, the program first negates the intrinsic affect of a CONSTRUCT (which is GOOD) because the action is a disassembly, and then combines this BAD affect with its affect for the actor, which is NEUTRAL. Finally, it combines the result, BAD, with the affect of the goal that the action serves, which is BAD, to get the result GOOD — that is to say, CONSTRUCT-2 should be included, and even stressed, in the text. In contrast, when PAULINE speaks as a Yale official, the resulting affect for CONSTRUCT-2 is BAD. So is ARREST-1, the arrest of the 76 students, after similar derivation.

In order to know when to slant the text, PAULINE uses strategies controlled by its rhetorical goals of opinion, listed in chapter 2. These goals are defined as patterns or configurations of representation elements (see chapter 3). For example, one goal to present the opponents as unreasonable is:

- *Coercion:* they force their will on others (corresponding to the university speaker's "wanted to force"; stated here in English rather than in the pattern language used in the program):

  ```
  IF the current topic is an ACTION,
     AND it is an antipathy,
     AND the action serves one of the opponents' goals
     AND the goal is to have some other party do some act
     AND the other party is a sympathy
  THEN imply that the opponents force their will on them
       (using verbs such as ''force'', ''make them do'')
  ```

These goals affect the generation process in a variety of ways. Correspondingly, they are best implemented in various ways. Some goals are more naturally implemented top-down: for example, the goals that prescribe the inclusion of sentence topics that are not necessarily part of the input topics at all, such as the sentences "we deplore the whole affair" and "they started it". These sentences are added purely for slanting effect; it is doubtful that any non-generator process (other than an argument builder) would routinely include such topics in its output. Other goals function best in bottom-up fashion: They respond to syntactic opportunities to include and use appropriately slanted aspects such as stress words and adjectives, nouns, and verbs (as described in chapter 4); this causes the production of such phrases as "a few shiftless students".

7.6.2   Topic Collection (Prescriptive)

This task — collecting appropriate additional sentence topics — is pre-eminently prescriptive. Good examples of topic collection plans (also called schemas) can be found in McKeown (1982), Paris and McKeown (1987), and Rösner (1986); they instruct the planner where in the representation network (in relation to a given topic) to search for suitable additional sentence topics. In this spirit (as described in chapters 2 and 4), PAULINE has three plans — the DESCRIBE plan to find descriptive aspects of objects, the RELATE plan to relate events and state-changes, and the CONVINCE plan to help slant the text in order to convince the hearer of some opinion. Whenever it performs topic collection, PAULINE applies the prescriptive steps of the appropriate collection plan to each candidate topic, and then in turn to the newly-found candidate topics, for as long as its pragmatic criteria (amongst others, the values of **RG:haste** and **RG:openmindedness**) allow.

Clearly, the details of these plans depend very much on the representation scheme used. For example, following the **good results** strategy, one of the steps of the CONVINCE plan (also stated in the English equivalent of the code) is:

```
COLLECT, from the topic,
     - all its direct RESULTS
     - if it is a script, its FINAL RESULTS
     - if it is part of a plan or otherwise serves a goal,
       the DESIRED STATE of the goal
FOR each of these results,
     IF it carries the affect GOOD for the speaker
     THEN retain it as a candidate topic
```

PAULINE uses the CONVINCE plan in generating the shantytown texts as follows: When speaking as a protester, the instances of support by the local community and faculty members are obviously GOOD and are included, whereas the fact that Yale was at first lenient and allowed the shantytown to remain in place until the meeting of the Yale Corporation is BAD and is ignored. Also, the arrest of 76 students is GOOD for this point of view and is included, but the commission of investigation is not. The contrary is true when PAULINE is a Yale official.

7.6.3   Topic Interpretation (Prescriptive and Restrictive)

As described in chapter 3, PAULINE has the ability to perform limited inference in order to interpret its input topics in ways that help achieve its pragmatic goals. Some inference strategies are defined as prescriptive plans and others as restrictive ones. Activated rhetorical goals of opinion (such as the abovementioned goal to interpret the opponent's actions as coercive) are prescriptive: they cause interpretation inferences to be applied to the collected candidate topics during topic organization. In contrast, restrictive (bottom-up) inferences reside in the memory network as part of the definitions of concept types and fire when the configuration of input topics matches their structure.

7.6.4 Additional Topic Inclusion (Restrictive)

During the course of topic organization, the generator may find additional candidate topics. Whether or not to include these instances can only be decided when such topics are found; the relevant strategies are therefore restrictive. For example, as described in chapter 3, after interpreting input topics as an instance of some new concept, the new concept may furnish other instances, which could be included using phrases such as "that reminds me...". In PAULINE, the rhetorical goal **RG:color** controls the inclusion of remindings. In addition, under certain circumstances, explicit statements of opinion can be included in the text. Rather than give the generator the prescriptive goal to create such circumstances, which may be very difficult, restrictive plans enable their inclusion to be considered whenever the circumstances arise. These restrictive plans also serve rhetorical goals of opinion, as described above and in chapter 2. For example, under appropriate circumstances, PAULINE has the (restrictive) option to include explicit statements of opinion before sentences, such as "it pisses me off", "I am happy", and "X wanted to be reasonable".

7.6.5 Topic Juxtaposition (Restrictive)

As described in chapter 4, whenever two topics are being generated, the generator can search for suitable multi-predicate phrases (such as "not only X, but Y") in which to frame them in order to achieve desired opinion-related and stylistic effects. The task of topic juxtaposition is best implemented restrictively by presenting the candidate topics as options to strategies that check the restrictions on the use of phrases and select suitable ones. (The equivalent prescriptive implementation amounts to giving the program goals such as [FIND IN MEMORY TWO TOPICS THAT FIT INTO A *not only but* PHRASE], a much less tractable task.)

When PAULINE has the goal to convince the hearer of its affect, and when the rhetorical goals **RG:formality** and **RG:simplicity** do not prohibit long and complex sentences, the program plans phrasal juxtaposition in the following way: First, it determines the hearer's affect for each of the current candidate concepts. By the affect rule, GOOD topics can be said; NEUTRAL ones should be enhanced to look GOOD; and BAD ones should be avoided or mitigated. When there are too few GOOD topics to phrasally mitigate all the BAD ones, some of the latter must be mitigated by other means or not said at all. This decision depends on the rhetorical goal **RG:timidity**: a *reckless* approach permits unmatched BAD topics to be said, hoping that other generator decisions can mitigate them, as described below. A *timid* approach suppresses unmatched BAD topics.

7.6.6   Topic Ordering (Prescriptive)

The ordering of topics in the paragraph is best achieved prescriptively. Different circumstances call for different orderings; newspaper articles, for instance, often contain an introductory summarizing sentence, as in example 1, chapter 1. In contrast to the abovementioned schemas (McKeown-style, etc.), steps in PAULINE's topic collection plans are not ordered; additional plans must be run to ensure coherent text flow. PAULINE uses one of two topic-ordering plans that determine the position in the paragraph of an introductory sentence, descriptive and supporting sentences, etc. These plans are simplified scriptifications of the topic coherence strategies discussed in Hobbs (1978, 1979) and Mann and Thompson (1983, 1987).

7.6.7   Intrasentential Slant and Style (Restrictive)

The goal to produce grammatical text underlies the design of all generators (except perhaps ERMA (Clippinger, 1974)), and causes the (prescriptive) use of grammatical rules and phrases. The syntax-level realization decisions are described in chapter 6. Since, however, syntax and semantics are underspecific — one can express the same semantic information in many ways — pragmatic considerations provide additional criteria for making selections. As argued in chapter 2, pragmatic information is communicated through appropriate slant and style (both restrictive).

In addition to the slanting techniques mentioned above (appropriate interpretation, opinion inclusion, and topic juxtaposition), a number of other techniques exist to help slant text. As described in chapter 4, these techniques include the use of stress words, adjectives, adverbs, verbs that require idiosyncratic predicate contents, nouns, etc. As with style, due to the local (i.e., non-formative) nature of most of these techniques and to the fact that options are only found rather late in the realization process, they are best implemented restrictively.

PAULINE uses two rules to choose a sentence subject in order to produce flowing, natural text. The first involves affect; the second is the equivalent of McKeown's (1982) default rule:

1. select the subject from candidates with GOOD affect for sentences with GOOD affect and from candidates with BAD affect for sentences with BAD affect

2. otherwise, select as subject the sentence topic's AGENT, if it exists

Verb selection must be done with care, since, as described in chapters 4 and 6, verbs can carry some affective import. Just as the mitigator phrase "X; however, Y" imputes to Y the opposite affect of X, the predicate forms of verbs can be viewed as having fields with characteristic affects. For example, in the form for "beat",

"A beat B [in C]"

before anything is known about the field fillers, A carries the default affect GOOD, B BAD, and C GOOD. At the verb selection decision, PAULINE matches the fields of the candidate verbs with the desired affects of the candidate fillers and selects a verb by using the affect rule of chapter 4.

In addition to being slanted, text can be hasty, formal, forceful, etc., as described in chapter 5. Control of style is pre-eminently a restrictive task, since syntactic alternatives typically have relatively local effect: some examples are deciding on conjunction and relativization (i.e., length of sentences); determining the presence and position of adverbial clauses, adverbs, and adjectives; selecting specific words (especially verbs and nouns). When the realizer reaches a decision point between options that are equivalent with respect to semantics and opinion, the restrictive strategies that achieve stylistic effects are queried.

7.6.8   Text Planning, Step by Step

First, the user gives PAULINE one or more topics, all part of the representation of the episode and embedded in the concept representation network. For example, in the shantytown examples, PAULINE is given three representation elements: the construction of the shantytown, its removal, and the subsequent permission to have it rebuilt. Next, the user inputs the characteristics of the speaker, the hearer, and the conversational setting. This includes the interlocutors' sympathies and antipathies, and values chosen from the options listed under PAULINE's characterization of the pragmatic aspects of the conversation, chapter 2.3. Finally, PAULINE is given interpersonal goals with respect to the hearer's opinions, knowledge, relationship to the speaker, etc. These values are also chosen from the options listed in chapter 2.3.

In summary, text planning in PAULINE proceeds as follows:

1. PAULINE activates the rhetorical goals with appropriate values, using the activation rules given in chapters 3.4, 3.7.1, 4.6.1, 4.6.2, 5.2.1, 5.3.1, and 5.4

2. if permitted by **RG:haste** and **RG:openmindedness**, a topic collection plan is activated and its steps applied to the next topic (initially, one of the input topics), as described in chapter 4.4

3. when enough collection has occurred, the program starts topic organization

4. when **RG:simplicity** and **RG:haste** permit, a topic ordering plan is run and the topics appropriate for the next stage of the paragraph are gathered as the current candidate topics, as described in chapter 4.4.2

5. if **RG:detail** and **RG:haste** permit, top-down interpretation occurs: from the interpretation inferences associated with the activated rhetorical goals of opinion, the planner collects all the configurations that match candidate topics, as

described in chapter 3.5.2. Also, if those goals permit, bottom-up interpretation occurs: using each candidate (and sometimes related ones) as a pivot, the planner searches for back-pointers to configurations and collects those that match the candidates (chapter 3.5.1). Then a suitable configuration is selected (chapter 3.6)

6. if not found in memory, the planner builds a new interpretation of the matched candidates and indexes in memory it off the interpretation concept

7. if the newly-found interpretations contain specific instances, these are the remindings. Each reminding probably matches the candidates only in some aspects — the aspects that match the configuration — and probably has other aspects — say, information about events whose equivalents have not yet occurred — which may be of interest to further generation. The planner constructs hypothetical equivalents of the remindings from the input and determines which reminding, if any, to say, subject to **RG:color** (chapter 3.7)

8. the matched candidates and the reminding are packaged into a syntax goal (chapter 6.5)

9. the interpretation process (step 5) is repeated, subject to **RG:haste** and **RG:detail**, until no more interpretations are found

10. next, steps 4-9 of the topic organization repeat, again subject to **RG:haste** and **RG:simplicity**

11. depending on **RG:timidity** and **RG:partiality**, the planner tries to embed one or more of its topics (each in a syntax goal) into multi-predicate enhancer or mitigator phrases (chapter 4.5.1)

12. depending on **RG:simplicity**, **RG:formality**, and **RG:haste**, the planner tries to embed one or more of its topics (each in a syntax goal) into phrases that express intergoal, spatial, temporal, etc., relations (chapter 6.4)

13. steps 11 and 12 are repeated, depending on **RG:haste**

14. finally, topic organization is finished, and realization can begin. An appropriate syntax specialist (chapter 6.3.2, 6.5) is chosen for the topic of each syntax goal

15. the syntax goal is applied to the topic and determines: how, if at all, to link it to the previous sentence (chapter 4.5.1); which verb to use, since this interacts with the mode and constrains the form of the predicate; which aspect to generate as the subject (chapter 6.5.2). All the decisions are made by querying the planner, which inspects relevant rhetorical goals such as **RG:formality** and **RG:simplicity**

16. the sentence subject (always a noun group in PAULINE's limited grammar) is constructed by determining a head noun or pronoun, adjectives, article, etc. (chapter 6.5.3); again most of these decisions are made by the planner

17. when the subject is said, the predicate is expanded. Here the planner must make decisions about adverbial clauses, adverbs, stress words, etc., as described in chapter 6.5.3, 6.5.4, 4.5. The goals **RG:partiality** and **RG:formality** are particularly important here

18. finally, when the whole sentence has been said, the next syntax goal is realized; if no syntax goal remains, the whole process (from step 2) is repeated until no new topics are suggested by the topic collection plans

An annotated trace of a PAULINE session appears in appendix A.

7.7 Two Shortcomings of This Approach

One of the strong points of PAULINE is the use of a phrasal lexicon, in which, as described in chapter 6, words, phrases, and formative syntactic information associated with phrase structure symbols are contained in homogeneous form. In order to facilitate two-way information flow, however, the lexicon's information should be more explicit. As they are implemented, PAULINE's syntax specialists use discrimination nets to find appropriate constructs, phrases, and words — that is, the pragmatic information is procedurally encoded. This is a serious handicap to the planner, and makes the addition of new grammatical classes and lexical elements difficult. Rather, lexical elements should contain explicitly represented rhetorical information: for example, the information that the phrasal pattern "not only X but Y" is *moderately formal, quite complex* (since it contains two predicates and inverts word order), and an *affect-enhancer* in which the first filler, X, must hold some affect for the speaker. When considering this option, then, the planner should be able to inspect these features and compare them to the effects desired by the active rhetorical goals.

Adding all such information to the lexicon explicitly requires, first, the formulation of a set of terms, based on the program's rhetorical goals and strategies, which the planner can manipulate to construct plans, and second, the reformulation of the planner and rhetorical goal value monitor. As it is, the rhetorical planner is too simple: it simply tries to achieve each activated rhetorical goal, preferring, in conflicts, the goals least satisfied so far. It keeps no record of the number of times a rhetorical goal was actually thwarted or blocked, and is thus unable to recognize the need to repair mistakes. Including rhetorical information explicitly in the lexicon — both about goals achieved and about goals thwarted — will enable the planner to know when to perform repairs. Of course, the planner must then also have repair strategies and be able to decide what strategies are required.

7.8   Conclusion

The selections distributed throughout the generation process are not just a set of unrelated ad hoc decisions; they are related in ways that permit the creation of style and slant. Therefore, they require control. Since, however, traditional top-down prescriptive planning is unable to provide this control, a different *kind* of planning that is bottom-up is required. With this approach, we can identify the tasks that require such planning as restrictive and build plans and strategies to control them in a uniform fashion. This enables us to interleave realization with the most appropriate style of planning, either prescriptive or restrictive, and the result, limited-commitment planning, greatly enhances our ability to build generators that produce good, pragmatically appropriate text.

Chapter 8

A Review of Language Generation

Traditionally, language generation has been concerned with the questions *what shall I say?* and *how shall I say it?*. Almost all generators focus primarily on one or the other of these questions, and in doing so avoid a number of hard issues. PAULINE, however, faces both questions, and therefore cannot finesse the hard issues. The solution involves a third question, namely *why should I say it?*, by which pragmatic information is introduced in the generation process. This chapter surveys the development of "generation science" with respect to the three questions.

8.1 The Three Questions of Generation

The study of natural language generation by computer has traditionally focused on two questions: *what shall I say?* and *how shall I say it?*. The former question has been investigated by philosophers of language; the latter has been attacked mostly by linguists. Since linguists tend to produce more easily encodable results than philosophers, early AI language generation work concentrated on the latter question, with the result that at the current time, using available knowledge, one can quite easily build a useful (though limited) sentence generator program, but one cannot so easily build a program that selects topics and performs the planning required to organize them into coherent text.

The early generators, as well as many existing ones, ignore the *what* question — the issues of topic selection and organization — completely. For these generators the task is simply: someone (or some program) feeds them a chunk of representation, and they find a way of saying it — the whole chunk and nothing else. Their answer to the *what* question is simply *say it all!*. On the other hand, the few programs that do attempt topic selection and organization tend to skimp when it comes to the *how* question; in fact, some do not even pretend to make sentences, and most

149

of the others use "canned" language (templates). To make matters worse, a number
of generator tasks, such as interpretation and multi-predicate sentence construction,
lie between the two questions, are not properly addressed by either of them alone,
and consequently have never really been attempted by any program.

Putting the two sets of tasks together is difficult for a number of reasons — the
interaction between them is not understood, and neither is their relative timing.
In addition, combining them intensifies the sheer difficulty of guiding the generator
through the large number of topic-related and syntactic opportunities that exist in
language, because when implemented separately, each task usually assumes that the
other does a lot of the hard work. Specifically, topic collection and organization
programs typically expect that their (assumed) syntactic components will be able to
make good, coherent, flowing text with whatever is handed to them, and language
realizer programs assume that their (assumed) planning components will perform a
large amount of difficult but necessary structuring on the input topics.

When you attempt both tasks together, you have to address all these issues.
Immediately a third question arises: *why should I say it?*. The thesis of this book
is that the answer is largely provided by pragmatics. And since the *why* question is
very complex, more difficult to answer than either the *what* or the *how* questions,
it has to date remained unaddressed in natural language processing. But we cannot
avoid it forever. If we want programs to produce natural, high-quality text, we have
to take pragmatics into account.

This chapter contains a brief overview of AI work in language generation and
describes PAULINE's relation to it.

8.2   How shall I say it?

As used here, this question is one of syntax — following the description in chapter
6, a matter of selection, ordering, and casting. Through the years, a number of
techniques have been developed to encode and use grammatical information in a
program.

8.2.1   Transformational Grammar

When given the task to build a generator, transformational grammars seem at first
glance to be eminently suitable for answering the *how* question. However, they are
not; in fact, as Chomsky said, TG was originally meant to be purely descriptive, not
functional (Chomsky, 1965):

> ...it seems absurd to suppose that the speaker first forms a generalized
> Phrase-marker by base rules and then tests it for well-formedness by
> applying transformational rules to see if it gives, finally, a well-formed
> sentence. But this absurdity is simply a corrollary to the deeper absurdity

of regarding the system of generative rules as a point-by-point model for the actual construction of a sentence by a speaker. (p. 139)

Transformational grammar can be a basis for building a generator only if neither the psychological validity of the generator nor its efficiency are important issues.

8.2.2 Augmented Transition Networks

In the earliest generation work, no text planning phase ever appeared. Typically, an ATN was defined to embody some subpart of the grammar of the target language. It was given representation elements defined in a semantic-type network. Under guidance of the input, the ATN was traversed until some path was found that ended in an end state of the ATN and that exhausted the input; the traversal route then provided the sentence. In this way the linearization of the input was achieved in simple and highly unhumanlike ways (ATNs, for example, cannot make mistakes). But the technology is clean, easy to write and extend, and works. For an excellent description of an ATN generator, see Simmons and Slocum (1972).

ATNs are well suited for storing grammatical information; they are not, however, suited for storing all the other information a generator requires. For example, when more than one word exists for a piece of the input, additional processing is needed. Goldman's ATN generator BABEL (Goldman, 1973, 1975) used discrimination nets with semantic tests in order to find words for its input elements. For example, when confronted with the Conceptual Dependency element INGEST (Schank, 1975, 1977), the program inspected the nature of the OBJECT role filler; if it was a liquid, the word chosen was "drink", if a solid, "eat", and if a gas, "breathe". Another nice aspect of BABEL was its ability to express paraphrases of a sentence to varying levels of precision: "John strangled Mary" could be said as "John put his hands around Mary's neck and choked her" or as "John put his hands around Mary's neck and squeezed her windpipe shut and caused her not to be able to breathe which caused her to die". However, BABEL had no idea when each paraphrase was appropriate! The answer, clearly, is based upon a *why* question.

8.2.3 Syntax in the Lexicon and Templates

A number of people have investigated ways of representing syntactic information in the lexicon. In an extreme form, this approach reduces to template generation, which is probably the easiest and most frequently used solution for small domains in which generality is not required. A template is associated with each representation element type, in such a way that the templates can nest in the way representation elements nest. Generation then becomes a matter of filling in the blanks. Template-based generators can produce very impressive text, but, of course, are hardly flexible. Typical examples are in Swartout (1981) and Bain (1986); more sophisticated template generation is performed by Kukich (1983a, 1983b).

Danlos (1983, 1985, 1987) developed a phrasal grammar similar to but richer than PAULINE's grammar as described in chapter 6 and appendix B. By comparing linguistic classes of French and English, she justifies each syntax specialist and identifies syntactic and semantic conditions under which specialists may be used. A similar generator is part of the translation system of Lytinen (1984). Jacobs (1985a, 1985b) developed a representation language for a phrasal lexicon that captures syntactic and semantic commonalities in language, enabling quasi-metaphorical expressions such as "Frazier gave Ali a punch" and "Ali took a punch from Frazier" to be generated easily.

8.2.4   Systemic Grammar

Based on the ideas of Halliday (see Halliday, 1961, 1976, 1978]), a number of systemic generators have been built. As with ATNs, systemic grammars contain the structure of the grammar encoded in a network. A systemic grammar is a large collection of discrimination nets called systems, where each system (one or more discriminations) computes the value(s) of one or more grammatical features such as number and mood. Processing continues in the network until enough features have been computed to specify the sentence completely. Collections of systems thus perform the functions of the syntax specialists described in chapter 6. Although some systems' activation preconditions depend on specific feature values (which forces a degree of sequentiality upon processing), systems do not have to be activated sequentially — they can become active and perform their tasks as soon as their input conditions are satisfied. This fact makes systemic implementations potentially far more powerful than phrase structure grammars.

One of the primary assumptions of systemics is that all three aspects of communication — interpersonal (i.e., pragmatic), ideational (i.e., semantic), and textual (roughly, syntactic) — can in fact be represented as collections of aspects whose values can be computed via discriminations. Insofar as this is the case, systemic grammar offers a clean and powerful formalism with which to build a generator. Patten and Ritchie (1987) give a formal definition of systemic grammar, upon which Patten's generator (Patten, 1986) is based; the generator of Davey (1979) describes tic-tac-toe games; Penman, the world's largest systemic generator, is described in Mann (1982, 1983a, 1983b), Mann and Matthiessen (1983). All these efforts concentrate on syntax. A systemic treatment of pragmatics appears in Fawcett (1980).

8.2.5   Other Ways of Constructing Syntactic Representations

A number of more recent generators use rules to construct explicit syntactic representations of sentences; in a second pass, they substitute words and produce the text. For example, Tree Adjoining Grammars (see Joshi (1987a, 1987b), Kroch and Joshi (1986)) contain rules for constructing and embedding syntax trees in ways that produce valid sentences. Wong describes a more limited generator in Wong (1975). The Functional Grammar of Dik (1978, 1980) is implemented in [Tjoe-Liong 87].

Functional unification grammars (Kay, 1979, 1984) resemble template grammars in that their entities contain ordered parts, each with idiosyncratic constraints. The input representations are matched against the entities; those aspects whose features match the constraints are unified "into" the templates and generated. For examples, see McKeown (1982, 1985), Paris (1987), Jacobs (1985).

The syntactically most sophisticated generator at present is MUMBLE (McDonald, 1980, 1981, 1986; McDonald & Pustejovsky 1985). Entities called *realization classes* (corresponding roughly to PAULINE's syntax specialists) communicate using an elaborate protocol to construct complex syntax trees that are then uttered after a second pass lexical substitution phase. MUMBLE exemplifies prehaps best of all generators the position of autonomous syntax; this position has the advantage that the boundaries of the generator are well-defined and that, in time, a program can be constructed that embodies most of (or all?) the syntax of English. Unfortunately, this position also has a disadvantage: being autonomous means not relying on outside influences, meaning that once the generator starts working on its input it runs alone. Since pragmatic and semantic issues influence the generation of text, this position requires that these issues' effects be somehow already incorporated in the input to the generator. In practice, this means a large amount of difficult pre-structuring work.

8.3 What shall I say?

The second question of language generation, *what shall I say?*, has received less attention. Intrinsically, it is a much harder question to answer, because it depends on factors about which the speaker can never have complete knowledge, such as the hearer's knowledge and beliefs. It is much easier always to make grammatically correct sentences than always to say appropriate things!

In the simplest text planning systems, the planners make only very high-level decisions and play no further role in the realization process. One example is Cohen's (1978) program that reasoned about the hearer's knowledge state in order to decide on an appropriate speech act. The program had no realization component.

8.3.1 Scriptal Planning

A major planning task in the construction of a paragraph is the collection and ordering of sentence topics. McKeown (1982) made the following breakthrough: she defined four so-called schemas which are, in essence, generation scripts that direct the topic collection process and (together with rules of topic flow) control the ordering of sentence topics. Thus, for example, the IDENTIFICATION schema prescribes first saying the object's name and type, then giving (some of) its attributes, then its uses, specializations or instances, etc. The other schemata are ATTRIBUTIVE, CONSTITUENTS, and COMPARE & CONTRAST. Her generator produced output for a database question-answering system that contained information about war machines.

Being script-like, these schemas are tailored to specific circumstances. For hearers with different levels of knowledge, schemas must prescribe appropriate details of the topic. This problem was investigated by Paris (see Paris, 1985, 1987; Paris and McKeown, 1987). For hearers with different interests, different aspects of the central topic are relevant; McCoy (1985, 1987) uses different schemas to correct different hearer misconceptions in different ways. She describes using a *salience value* for aspects of topics and in schemas to help decide what additional sentence topics the schemas should collect. In her system, the salience values reflect characteristics of the hearer and are determined by the hearer's questions.

A variety of other special-purpose generators use script-like topic collection and ordering strategies; for example, Kukich (1983) describes the generation of stock market reports; Novak (1984, 1987) develops strategies for describing relative motions of objects; Reithinger (1984, 1987) generates referring expressions and answers in interactive systems; Rösner (1986, 1987) translates Japanese reports and descriptions into German. Woolf (1984) and Woolf and McDonald (1984) describe a program that tutors students, by planning which schema to select and when to change it, based on its representation of their knowledge and misconceptions.

8.3.2   Non-Scriptal Planning

In systems with more flexible plans, a lot more work must be done before actual realization can be started. Appelt's planner KAMP (Appelt, 1981, 1982, 1985]) is the most general and powerful text planning program yet developed, being an implementation of part of the general-purpose planner NOAH (Sacerdoti, 1977). KAMP starts with a number of goals to inform the hearer of a number of facts; while reasoning about the hearer's knowledge state, it constructs utterances that contain an appropriate amount of information in an appropriate order. In Appelt (1981) the impression is given that the program introduces grammatical constraints midway in the plan expansion process and finally works exclusively with syntactic constructs to produce the text. This turns out to be difficult to do; on p. 113, Appelt expresses dissatisfaction with this way of integrating grammatical and other planning constraints on the grounds that (a) the grammar cannot easily be evaluated without running the program and (b) the grammar cannot easily be altered. In practice, however, KAMP initially used simple templates for the actual text forms and later used a functional unification grammar back end (Appelt, personal communication, 1986). In subsequent work, Appelt has split off the syntactic component and uses KAMP simply for the "normal" planning activities.

However, KAMP does not address a number of text planning issues. The problem of selecting and ordering sentence topics into coherent multi-sentential paragraphs has been studied by Hobbs (1978, 1979), who postulated a number of intertopic relations, and by Mann (Rhetorical Structure Theory; Mann (1984), Mann and Thompson (1983, 1987), whose relational structures result from the study of some 200 texts. A planner that uses these relational stuctures as plans to determine coherent paragraphs is described in Hovy (1988b).

8.3.3 Other Planning-Related Work

Much work has been done on describing the structure of multi-sentential interactive texts such as conversations. Grosz (1977, 1980) and Sidner (1979) discuss rules of focus shift, topic flow, and anaphora; in later work they collaborate and are currently developing a theory of conversations using notions such as speaker intention and attention (Grosz, 1985; Grosz & Sidner, 1986). Reichman (1981) constructed a grammar for the structure of discourse. Kamp's discourse representation theory (Kamp, 1981) presents a way to represent and nest parts of a discourse so that problems in pronominal reference are easily solved. Related work on conversational interaction can be found in the cognitive science and psycholinguistic literature. For example, on turn-taking in conversations, see Garvey (1975), Garvey and Berninger (1981) and Sacks, Schegloff, and Jefferson (1974); on self-correction see Schegloff, Jefferson, and Sacks (1977); Levin and Moore (1977) discuss dialogue-games.

Sanford and Roach (1987) are working on representing the pragmatic import of typical text forms and using this information when parsing and generating. J. Moore (1987) is working on the planning of text by which expert systems can explain their activities.

8.3.4 General Problems with Planning

In almost all existing text planner-generators (whether implemented or described), information flows one-way, from the planner to the realizer (Appelt, 1981, 1985; McKeown, 1982, 1985; McDonald, personal communication, 1984; McDonald and Pustejovsky 1985). In these systems, two approaches are possible: either all the requisite information is pre-planned before realization starts, or planning and realization are interleaved and the planner continues whenever the realization phase completes a subtask. Appelt follows the former option; McDonald advocates the latter. Pre-planning the requisite information is comparatively easy if the criteria for these decisions are based on relatively uniform grounds (for example, syntactic grounds only, including notions such as sentence focus and stress), since they are then relatively simple and only impinge on expansion at a small number of points, such as subject choice and clause content. (This is one reason why Appelt's program KAMP could operate as it did — it took into account only the hearer's knowledge state, and never had the scope to produce wide variations of text.) When less homogeneous, more complex information is taken into account, however, pre-planning all the likely decisions a generator may require is an overwhelming task — the planner must effectively span the space of possible locutions — which is not a practicable solution to the problem. In later work, (McDonald, Vaughan & Pustejovsky, 1987), McDonald argues together with the psycholinguists Levelt (Levelt & Schriefers, 1987) and Bock (1982, 1987) that the two stages, planning and realization, interface at the so-called *message* level.

However, simply interleaving the processes doesn't solve the problem. As argued in chapter 7, generation requires the two-way flow of information — queries in the form of syntactic options and their pragmatic effects from the realizer to the planner, and the corresponding guidance in the form of selections back. Generators must be able to reason about *why* they say what they say. This is the way PAULINE is implemented.

8.4   Why should I say it?

To date, only a handful of programs, in answer to this question, explicitly represent speaker goals to motivate the decisions they make. Jameson (1987) is building a system that constructs its text by selecting utterances from scripts of templates, based on the desired pragmatic import of the final text. Clippinger (1974, 1975) built a complicated system ERMA that modelled one paragraph of text produced by a person in a psychiatric session. ERMA consisted of five modules: CALVIN (topic collection and censoring), MACHIAVELLI (topic organization, phrasing, etc.), CICERO (realization), FREUD (monitoring the origins of generator tasks), and LEIBNITZ (concept definition network). Different parts of the program had characteristic effects on the text, and the hope was that ERMA's text would produce some of the false starts, hesitations, suppressions, etc., that people make when they speak. Since ERMA was *built* to model the paragraph of text, it did, of course; however, though the program is interesting and four of the five parts believable (perhaps, with more examples, the function of FREUD would be clearer), the overall theoretical contribution of ERMA is not clear. Certainly we are a long way from being able to assess all the claims made about the work.

This brings us to PAULINE. PAULINE was built to illustrate the utility of pragmatic information in making planning and realization decisions that are otherwise not decidable. It was inspired by the work of McGuire (see McGuire (1975)), who first worked on what eventually became the Carter-Kennedy example; it has been called "a parameterization of ERMA" (McDonald, personal communication, 1986).

PAULINE is an attempt to state in programming terms, for the first time, the kinds of interpersonal and stylistic issues we all know play a role in language generation. Unfortunately, the sheer magnitude of this task prevents the construction of a complete and satisfactory solution. The most obvious shortcoming of this work is the lack of sophistication of the pragmatic features used in PAULINE: each feature — hearer knowledge, opinion, interpersonal relation, relative social status — is a field of study in itself. Even so, however, the rhetorical goals posited here (for all *their* unsophistication) provide a useful level of organization of text planning information, midway between the airy world of pragmatics and the concrete requirements of generators. That is to say, any generator that can realize a given input in different ways requires reasons for choosing one way over another, and these reasons will always pertain to the stylistic and opinion-based considerations — the rhetorical goals and strategies — discussed in this work. On the other hand, any system that manipulates information of pragmatic nature and wishes to use this information to guide a generator will always do so using intermediate strategies that correspond to the rhetorical goals. The clumsiness of the rhetorical strategies and of the goals' activation conditions, as described in chapters 3, 4, and 5, is due to the unsophisticated nature of the terms used to characterize pragmatic information and generator decisions; increasing the level of sophistication, and experimenting with combinations of strategies to form different rhetorical goals, should be the focus of continued research.

As "generation science" develops — as our understanding of grammar and of text organization becomes more complete — the *why?* question will become increasingly important. Researchers in this field should bear it in mind always.

Appendix A

A Short Annotated Example

In order to illustrate the interleaving of prescriptive and restrictive planning and text realization, this appendix contains an annotated trace of PAULINE's generation of a shantytown text. In the example, PAULINE is a protester trying to convince its audience at a meeting; though it is somewhat formal, it is not pressed for time:

```
AS A REMINDER TO YALE UNIVERSITY TO DIVEST FROM COMPANIES
DOING BUSINESS IN SOUTH AFRICA, A LARGE NUMBER OF STUDENTS
CONSTRUCTED A SHANTYTOWN --- NAMED WINNIE MANDELA CITY ---
ON BEINECKE PLAZA IN EARLY APRIL. AT 5:30 AM ON APRIL 14,
YALE HAD OFFICIALS DESTROY IT; ALSO, AT THAT TIME, THE
POLICE ARRESTED 76 STUDENTS. A LARGE NUMBER OF LOCAL
POLITICIANS AND FACULTY MEMBERS EXPRESSED CRITICISM OF
YALE'S ACTION. FINALLY, THE UNIVERSITY GAVE THE STUDENTS
PERMISSION TO REASSEMBLE IT.
```

At the outset, the program is given a set of values that characterize the setting and its goals. The input topics are the building of the shantytown (CONSTRUCT-1), its being demolished (CONSTRUCT-2), and Yale's permission for its reconstruction (MTRANS-8). PAULINE is a protester; as sympathies, it is given the protesters' goal to have Yale divest from companies with business in South Africa (GOAL-1). The hearer, a pro-Yale person, has as sympathies Yale's goals to keep the university orderly (GOAL-2) and to be reasonable in the face of argument (GOAL-3):

```
SPEAKER'S INTERPERSONAL GOALS:

Speaker's conversation with UNIV
   about (CONSTRUCT-1 CONSTRUCT-2 MTRANS-8)
```

159

```
CONVERSATION SETTING:
  Setting:
   - Available time: MUCH
   - Tone: FORMAL
   - Conditions (noise, etc.): GOOD
  Speaker:
   - Sympathies: (GOAL-1)
   - Antipathies: (GOAL-2 GOAL-3)
   - Knowledge level: EXPERT
   - Interest level: STRONG
   - Emotional state: NORMAL
  Hearer:
   - Sympathies: (GOAL-2 GOAL-3)
   - Antipathies: (GOAL-1)
   - Knowledge level: STUDENT
   - Interest level: SOME
   - Emotional state: CALM
   - Language ability: NORMAL
  Relationship:
   - Depth of acquaintance: STRANGER
   - Hearer's social status relative to Speaker: EQUAL
   - Emotion between interlocutors: LIKE


SPEAKER'S GOALS:
   - Topic collection plan: *CONVINCE-PLAN*
   - Conversation time: MUCH
  Desired effect on Hearer's Knowledge and Beliefs:
   - Hearer knowledge level: TEACH-TALK
   - Hearer opinions: SWITCH
  Desired effect on Hearer's Goals and Emotions:
   - Alter Hearer's goals: SWITCH
   - Hearer's emotional state: NORMAL
  Desired effect on Hearer's Relationship to Speaker:
   - Distance between interlocutors: NORMAL
   - Hearer emotion toward Speaker: LIKE
   - Relative status between interlocutors: EQUAL
```

Next the rhetorical goals are given values, using the activation rules described in chapters 3, 4, and 5:

```
Setting up rhetorical goals from interpersonal goals...

  SPEAKER:  PROTESTER
  HEARER:   YALIE
  SPEAKER'S RHETORICAL GOALS:
    AFFECT GOAL -- *CONVINCE-GOAL*     KNOWLEDGE GOAL -- ()
    TOPIC SLANT PLAN -- *OPINION-PLAN* TOPIC COLLECTION PLAN -- *CONVINCE-PLAN*
    FORMALITY -- HI                    DETAIL -- MED
    FORCE -- MED                       HASTE -- MED-LO
    TIMIDITY -- LO                     PARTIALITY -- MED
    SPEAKER-REF -- HI                  HEARER-REF -- MED
```

```
COLOR -- HI                    FLORIDITY -- MED
RESPECT -- MED-HI              SIMPLICITY -- MED
WARMTH -- HI                   VERBOSITY -- MED
AGGRESSION -- MED              INCITEMENT -- MED
```

In order to elaborate on the input and produce better text, the program can search for additional topics. Of course, such topics will be related to the input in some way; thus to know where to find likely candidates, PAULINE follows the prescriptive instructions of one of its topic-collection plans. As described in chapter 4, since its sympathies differ from those of the hearer, the program selects the CONVINCE plan. (First, however, it must check whether (a) it has time to do topic collection, and (b) whether the hearer's opinions about some aspect of the topic disagree with its own, otherwise there is nothing to dispute!):

```
-------------------------------------------------------------------------
Topic collector considering new topic:  CONSTRUCT-1
    PRAGS: level of HASTE for extent of topic collection
    -->checking rhet goal: RG:HASTE
  Searching for a topic-expansion plan for goal CONVINCE-GOAL
  Deciding whether to convince about CONSTRUCT-1's affect
    -- checking whether I agree with hearer on all its aspects
  Working out *SELF*'s affect for SHANTYTOWN-1  ...none
  Working out *UNIV*'s affect for SHANTYTOWN-1  ...none
  Working out *SELF*'s affect for STUDENTS-1  ...none
  Working out *UNIV*'s affect for STUDENTS-1  ...none
  Working out *SELF*'s affect for SBG:CONS1-G1  ...GOOD
  Working out *UNIV*'s affect for SBG:CONS1-G1  ...BAD
    ... no: we differ about its RELATIONS (SBG:CONS1-G1)
  Checking amount to be said ... there is enough to say
CONVINCE-PLAN is appropriate
-------------------------------------------------------------------------
```

```
Now applying *CONVINCE-PLAN*'s steps to CONSTRUCT-1
 - trying plan step to find worse example
 - trying plan step to find good (or not bad) result
 - trying plan step to find good goal
   found the following: -> GOAL-1 is the SUBGOAL-TO of CONSTRUCT-1
 - trying plan step to find good (or not bad) relations to concepts
   found the following:
   -> GOAL-1 is a SUBGOAL-TO relation of CONSTRUCT-1
   -> SUPPORT-1 is a RESULT relation of CONSTRUCT-1
 - trying plan step to find good side-effect
 - trying plan step to find appeal to authority
 - trying plan step to find suitably slanted affect
   found the following: -> CONSTRUCT-1 can be said with suitable slant
CONSTRUCT-1 spawned the following topics: (SUPPORT-1 GOAL-1 CONSTRUCT-1)
```

Since the speaker and hearer have different opinions about GOAL-1 (the protesters' goal to have Yale divest), the CONVINCE plan can be applied to the input topic; this directed search produces two additional topics: GOAL-1 and SUPPORT-1 (the support given the protesters by the local community).

At this point, CONSTRUCT-1 has been examined and can be said directly — that is, the realization phase can begin. Indeed, if the rhetorical goal **RG:haste** had the value *pressured*, this is what would happen, although this would mean that the program could not perform further topic organization tasks (such as interpretation and phrasal juxtaposition) since it would have no additional topics. This is the first point at which interleaving between planning and realization could occur. However, since the program is not hasty, it can continue the search for additional topics in order to facilitate such planning. Thus, after checking **RG:haste**, PAULINE examines SUPPORT-1 next; it finds the CONVINCE plan appropriate but collects no new sentence topics. Throughout, the states of satisfaction of certain rhetorical goals are updated, in order to enable appropriate restrictive planning.

```
PRAGS: start topic organization yet? (checking haste and topic derivation)
-->checking rhet goal: RG:HASTE
 ...no
-----------------------------------------------------------------------
Topic collector considering new topic: SUPPORT-1
  Deciding whether to convince about SUPPORT-1's affect
  CONVINCE-PLAN is appropriate
-----------------------------------------------------------------------
Now applying *CONVINCE-PLAN*'s steps to SUPPORT-1
 .....
SUPPORT-1 spawned the following topics: (GOAL-1 SUPPORT-1)
```

Similarly, GOAL-1 provides no new topics either. Now all the topics reachable from CONSTRUCT-1 have been examined, and, rather than continue collecting topics off the other inputs (which occurs under conditions that call for extremely well planned, complex, unpressured text), the program can start the topic organization phase. Three syntax goals are created, one for each candidate sentence topic:

```
Topic collector sending to planner:
<Goal to express CONSTRUCT-1
 Nomination: Goal CONVINCE-GOAL; Derivation: original topic>
<Goal to express SUPPORT-1
 Nomination: Goal CONVINCE-GOAL; Derivation: Parent CONSTRUCT-1; Role: RESULT>
<Goal to express GOAL-1
 Nomination: Goal CONVINCE-GOAL; Derivation: Parent CONSTRUCT-1; Role: SUBGOAL
```

The topic organization phase includes the following tasks (some of which can be ignored under certain conditions): topic reordering, insertion of explicit opinions, interpretation, phrasal juxtaposition, new topic inclusion. The first task, reordering, is achieved under guidance of a (prescriptive) paragraph construction plan (of which PAULINE has two). In order to open a paragraph, this plan prescribes using the initial topic and the goal it serves:

```
Starting to organize topics into phrases...
-----------------------------------------------------------------
Reordering input topics
   PRAGS: is there time to do REORDERING-INPUT?  ...yes
Final order is: (CONSTRUCT-1 SUPPORT-1 GOAL-1)
-----------------------------------------------------------------
Proceeding to next stage of paragraph...
  Grouping together topics suitable for introducing initial topic
  Using topics (CONSTRUCT-1 GOAL-1)
    PRAGS: is there time to do SLANTING with (CONSTRUCT-1 GOAL-1)?  ...yes
    Getting affect of CONSTRUCT-1 (slanting strategy is ENHANCE)
    Getting affect of GOAL-1 (slanting strategy is NONE)
  Starting to build phrases with CONSTRUCT-1
```

Next, the planner checks whether the rhetorical goals of opinion call for the inclusion of a sentence of explicit opinion (such as "I am angry about Yale's actions"), and if so whether conditions allow the insertion of such a sentence. This is a restrictive task. Since, however, conditions are not favorable (amongst others, no text has been produced yet, and the rhetorical goal **RG:timidity** prevails during monitor conflict resolution), no sentence is included...

```
Checking active opinion strategies (COMMENT) on CONSTRUCT-1
  Rhet goal conflict resolution...
   -->checking rhet goal: RG:FORCE  RG:VERBOSITY  RG:TIMIDITY  RG:PARTIALITY
  Chosen to satisfy RG:TIMIDITY
  No applicable strategy found
```

Following this, the program checks whether the rhetorical goals have activated any interpretation inferences. As explained in chapter 3, this task is executed both bottom-up and top-down. Three possible interpretations are found bottom-up, but none of them are affectively suitable (remember, the program is speaking as a protester!):

```
Checking active opinion strategies (INTERPRETATION) on CONSTRUCT-1
  Found possible interpretations:

  [<CONFIG-TAKE-CONTROL> on CONSTRUCT-1  :
     [ACTOR  :  STUDENTS-1 (= ?X)]
     [INSTR  :  INTO-PLAZA-1]
      [TO   :  STUDENTS-1 (= ?X)]]
  Working out *SELF*'s affect for INTERP-TAKE-CONTROL.434: no applicable strat

  [<CONFIG-CONFRONTATION> on CONSTRUCT-1  :
     [ACTOR  :  STUDENTS-1 (= ?X)]
     [RELATIONS   :  SBG:CONS1-G1]
       [CONC2  :  GOAL-1 (= ?Y)]
         [RELATIONS  :  OPPO:G1-G2]
           [CONC2  :  GOAL-2 (= ?Z)]
             [ACTOR  :  YALE (= ?W)]
```

```
        [OPPOSITES:  :  () (= ?W) (= ?X)]
     [RELATIONS  :  OPPO:G1-G2]
        [CONC1  :   GOAL-1 (= ?Y)]]
Working out *SELF*'s affect for STUDENTS-1
Working out *SELF*'s affect for INTERP-CONFRONT-CONCEPT.436: no applicable s


[<CONFIG-PUNISH> on CONSTRUCT-1  :
   [ISA  :   CONSTRUCT (= T) (= ?P)]
   [ACTOR  :   STUDENTS-1 (= ?X)]
   [RELATIONS  :   SBG:CONS1-G1]
     [CONC2  :   GOAL-1 (= ?Y)]
        [RELATIONS  :   OPPO:G1-G2]
          [CONC2  :   GOAL-2 (= ?Z)]
           [ACTOR  :   YALE (= ?W)]
            [OPPOSITES:  :  () (= ?W) (= ?X)]
            [RELATIONS  :   OPPO:G1-G2]
             [CONC1  :   GOAL-1 (= ?Y)]
            [RELATIONS  :   SBG:CONS2-G2]
             [CONC2  :   GOAL-2 (= ?Z)]
             [CONC1  :   CONSTRUCT-2 (= T)]
              [ISA  :   CONSTRUCT (= ?P)]]
Working out *SELF*'s affect for INTERP-PUNISH-CONCEPT.438: no applicable str
```

PAULINE checks whether memory contains another instance of a CONSTRUCT to be used as a reminding, and then tries to use a multi-predicate enhancer or mitigator phrase. Since, however, the hearer doesn't share the program's opinion of GOAL-1, such a phrase may not have the intended effect; thus the program decides not to slant CONSTRUCT-1 in this way.

```
Starting to work on remindings similar to CONSTRUCT-1
    PRAGS: include a reminding?  ...yes
    Checking if CONSTRUCT-1 is very similar to other topics in memory  ... no

Starting to build affect phrase around CONSTRUCT-1
    PRAGS: should use a phrase to ENHANCE the topic?
    -->checking rhet goal: RG:PARTIALITY  RG:SIMPLICITY
    ...yes
    PRAGS: slant topics on own bias only?
    Rhet goal conflict resolution...
    -->checking rhet goal: RG:PARTIALITY RG:SIMPLICITY RG:AGGRESSION RG:TIMID
    Chosen to satisfy  RG:SIMPLICITY
    ...no
Found no suitable other topic
```

Finally, though, a strategy does work: the program finds that the relation between its two topics — SUBGOAL-TO — can be expressed as an enhancer by using the linking phrase "as a reminder to". (Since this phrase requires the use of the desired state, not of the goal itself, PAULINE changes the topic to DIVESTED-1).

```
Starting to cast topic CONSTRUCT-1 into relational phrase
  Searching for another topic from
    - Goals: (GOAL-1)
    PRAGS: is CONSTRUCT-1 simple enough to be conjoined?  ...yes
  Will use GOAL-1 (a SUBGOAL-TO relation of CONSTRUCT-1) to build a phrase

  Checking active opinion strategies (LINK-PHRASE-GOAL) on CONSTRUCT-1
  (slanting strategy on CONSTRUCT-1 is ENHANCE)
  Running strategy to use phrase <PHRASE %AS-A-REMINDER>
  (altering topic from GOAL-1 to DIVESTED-1)
  Strategy successful
```

The program has now assembled the composite syntax goal to build the first sentence, starting with the protesters' goal, and then stating their action:

```
Finished organizing topic CONSTRUCT-1; built up syntax goals:
(<Goal to express DIVESTED-1
  Nomination: Goal CONVINCE-GOAL activated plan; role is SUBGOAL-TO
  Derivation: Parent CONSTRUCT-1 via relations (GOOD-GOALS *CONVINCE-PLAN*)
  Affect: Desired affect is GOOD; Goals call for () strategy
  With preceding words (*DOT* AS A REMINDER TO)
  Followed by
          (<Goal to express CONSTRUCT-1
            Nomination: Goal CONVINCE-GOAL activated plan; role is INITIAL-TOPIC
            Derivation: original topic
            Affect: Desired affect is GOOD; Goals call for ENHANCE strategy
            With preceding words (*CMA*)>)>)
```

The phase of topic organization is now complete: each syntax goal has enough information associated with each sentence topic to enable realization to begin. The other two input topics, CONSTRUCT-2 and MTRANS-8, are still waiting for topic collection and subsequent organization, and consequently have almost no information associated with them yet. At this point, realization interleaves with planning: the program continues planning to satisfy its rhetorical goals while realizing the syntax goal it has assembled.

The program starts by deciding what type of sentence — a description, an event, or a relation — to build. Complex sentences such as relations and sentences containing nominalized actions satisfy goals of low simplicity and high formality; here, their satisfaction state (restrictively) selects a normal event sentence. The linking phrase is first:

```
Generator starting to produce text...

-------------------------------------------------------------------
Sentence top: setting up DIVESTED-1 with modifiers (GOOD-GOALS COMPL INFINIT)
    PRAGS: nominalize DIVESTED-1?  ...no
    PRAGS: include pre-sentence adverbial clauses?
    Rhet goal conflict resolution...
    -->checking rhet goal:  RG:FORMALITY  RG:SIMPLICITY
```

```
      Not satisfying any of these goals
      ... building a normal event sentence
      ------------------------------------------------------------------
      Setting up words or phrases linking new sentence to previous one

      ====>   *DOT*
      ====>   AS
      ====>   A
      ====>   REMINDER
```

Next, the program must select an appropriate sentence subject. Of the two candidates, the one most interesting (central in the story), YALE, is selected. Then the rhetorical goals of opinion are checked to see if opinions should be added, and the noun group is built:

```
      Searching for a subject for sentence about DIVESTED-1
         PRAGS: which slot to select from (ACTOR OBJECT) as SUBJECT?
         Rhet goal conflict resolution...
         -->checking rhet goal: RG:HASTE RG:SIMPLICITY RG:FORMALITY
         Ordering (ACTOR OBJECT) of DIVESTED-1  ...order is (ACTOR OBJECT)
      Found sentence subject: YALE
      ------------------------------------------------------------------
      Building noun group of YALE
         Checking active opinion strategies on YALE
      ------------------------------------------------------------------
         Checking whether to include a personal opinion about YALE
           PRAGS: should say ng stress on YALE in NG-OPINION?
           Rhet goal conflict resolution...
           -->checking rhet goal: RG:PARTIALITY  RG:AGGRESSION
           Working out *UNIV*'s affect for YALE
           ...no
         Searching for head noun of YALE
         Checking active opinion strategies (HEAD-NOUN) on YALE
           No applicable strategy found
         Checking whether to include hearer's opinion about YALE
           PRAGS: mention YALE's role for hearer in NG-ROLE?
           Rhet goal conflict resolution...
           -->checking rhet goal: RG:HEARER-REF  RG:AGGRESSION
           Chosen to satisfy  RG:AGGRESSION
           ...no
         Building up noun group of form (ROLE ART PRE HEAD POST)

      ====>   TO
      ====>   YALE
      ====>   UNIVERSITY
```

At this point, a verb must be selected, because verbs determine the nature of the predicate. As described in chapter 6, the memory network is searched for a pragmatically suitable verb; also, aspects of the topic that may be included in the predicate are tested against the rhetorical goals.

```
----------------------------------------------------------------------
Building predicate with DIVESTED-1
----------------------------------------------------------------------
  Searching for a verb to express DIVESTED-1
  Searching concept hierarchy (against AFFECT):  DIVESTED-1 DIVESTED
  Found verb DIVEST
  Filtering aspects of DIVESTED-1 to build sentence predicate
  (using (VERB (OBJ RECIP FROM) (POST-SENT () (RECIP))))
    PRAGS: can COMPANIES-SA, (the RECIP of DIVESTED-1), be said?
    PRAGS: does affect rule allow COMPANIES-SA?
    (relating affect of COMPANIES-SA to current AFFECT GOAL)
    Working out *SELF*'s affect for COMPANIES-SA
    ...yes
    PRAGS: does interest rule allow COMPANIES-SA?
    Examining hearer KNOWLEDGE
    -->checking rhet goal:  RG:HASTE
    -->checking hearer interest level
    -->checking own interest level
    ...yes
  Now planning to say:
  (<Goal to expand DIVEST using #{Procedure 63 SAY-VERB}
         and instrs (GOOD-GOALS GOOD-RELATIONS COMPL INFINIT)>
   <Goal to expand COMPANIES-SA using #{Procedure 64 SAY-OBJECT}
         and instrs (GOOD-GOALS GOOD-RELATIONS COMPL INFINIT)>
   <Goal to expand DIVESTED-1 using #{Procedure 65 SAY-SENT-END}
         and instrs (GOOD-GOALS GOOD-RELATIONS COMPL INFINIT)>)
```

The syntax goals that realize into the predicate are treated in order:

```
Computing appropriate stress for DIVESTED-1 itself
Checking active opinion strategies (MITIGATING-HAVE-AUX-VERB) on DIVESTED-1
  No applicable strategy found

====>  TO
====>  DIVEST
----------------------------------------------------------------------
Building noun group of COMPANIES-SA
  Checking active opinion strategies on COMPANIES-SA
----------------------------------------------------------------------
  Checking whether to include a personal opinion about COMPANIES-SA
    PRAGS: should say ng stress on COMPANIES-SA in NG-OPINION?
    Working out *UNIV*'s affect for COMPANIES-SA
    ...no
  Searching for head noun of COMPANIES-SA
  Checking active opinion strategies (HEAD-NOUN) on COMPANIES-SA
    No applicable strategy found
  Checking whether to include hearer's opinion about COMPANIES-SA
    PRAGS: mention COMPANIES-SA's role for hearer in NG-ROLE?
    Rhet goal conflict resolution...
    -->checking rhet goal:  RG:HEARER-REF  RG:AGGRESSION
    Chosen to satisfy RG:AGGRESSION
```

```
        ...no
    Building up noun group of form (ROLE ART PRE HEAD POST)

    ====>  FROM
        PRAGS: how many of COMPANIES-SA's 1 aspects to say
        as PRE-NOUN-MODS?
        -->checking rhet goal: RG:HASTE  RG:SIMPLICITY  RG:FORMALITY
        ...will say 1 aspects
        Computing appropriate stress for COMPANIES-SA's filler of NUMBER
      Checking active opinion strategies (ADJECTIVE-NUMBER) on COMPANIES-SA
        No applicable strategy found
    ====>  COMPANIES
    ====>  DOING
    ====>  BUSINESS
    ====>  IN
    ====>  SOUTH
    ====>  AFRICA
```

Next, the run-on sentence is started. As before, PAULINE must check what type
of sentence the active rhetorical goals call for...

```
------------------------------------------------------------------------
Sentence top: setting up CONSTRUCT-1 with modifiers (INITIAL-TOPIC ENHANCE COM
    PRAGS: nominalize CONSTRUCT-1?
    PRAGS: include pre-sentence adverbial clauses?
    Rhet goal conflict resolution...
    -->checking rhet goal: RG:FORMALITY  RG:SIMPLICITY
    Not satisfying any of these goals
    -->checking rhet goal: RG:FLORIDITY
    ... building a normal event sentence
------------------------------------------------------------------------
Setting up words or phrases linking new sentence to previous one

====>  *CMA*
------------------------------------------------------------------------
Building noun group of STUDENTS-1
    Checking active opinion strategies on STUDENTS-1
------------------------------------------------------------------------
    Searching for a subject for sentence about CONSTRUCT-1
    Found sentence subject: STUDENTS-1
    Checking whether to include a personal opinion of STUDENTS-1
    Searching for head noun of STUDENTS-1
    Checking active opinion strategies (HEAD-NOUN) on STUDENTS-1
      No applicable strategy found
    Building up noun group of form (ROLE ART PRE HEAD POST)
    Checking whether to include hearer's opinion about STUDENTS-1
      PRAGS: mention STUDENTS-1's role for hearer in NG-ROLE?
      PRAGS: can PLUR, (the NUMBER of STUDENTS-1), be said?
      ...will say 1 aspects
```

While building the noun group, a (restrictive) strategy of opinion — the strategy
to maximize the number of people performing GOOD actions — fires:

```
   Checking active opinion strategies (ADJECTIVE-NUMBER) on STUDENTS-1
    Running strategy to slant claimed support
    Found MAXIMIZE
====>  A
====>  LARGE
====>  NUMBER
====>  OF
====>  STUDENTS
----------------------------------------------------------------------
Building predicate with CONSTRUCT-1
----------------------------------------------------------------------
   Searching for a verb to express CONSTRUCT-1
   Searching concept hierarchy (against AFFECT):  CONSTRUCT-1 CONSTRUCT
   Found verb CONSTRUCT
   Filtering aspects of CONSTRUCT-1 to build sentence predicate
   Now planning to say:
   (<Goal to expand CONSTRUCT using #{Procedure 63 SAY-VERB}
         and instrs (INITIAL-TOPIC ENHANCE COMPL)>
    <Goal to expand SHANTYTOWN-1 using #{Procedure 64 SAY-OBJECT}
          and instrs (INITIAL-TOPIC ENHANCE COMPL)> (
     <Goal to expand INTO-PLAZA-1 using #{Procedure 66 SAY-INSTR}
           and instrs (INITIAL-TOPIC ENHANCE COMPL)>
     <Goal to expand BEINECKE-PLAZA-1 using #{Procedure 66 SAY-LOC}
          and instrs (INITIAL-TOPIC ENHANCE COMPL)>
     <Goal to expand TIME-1 using #{Procedure 68 SAY-TIME}
          and instrs (INITIAL-TOPIC ENHANCE COMPL)>
     <Goal to expand CONSTRUCT-1 using #{Procedure 65 SAY-SENT-END}
          and instrs (INITIAL-TOPIC ENHANCE COMPL)>))
```

Before saying the verb, the program checks whether any restrictive strategies are applicable; though the strategy to mitigate the verb using "have" could apply, it is not found to be appropriate:

```
   Checking active opinion strategies (MITIGATING-HAVE-AUX-VERB) on CONSTRUCT-1
   No applicable strategy found

====>  CONSTRUCTED
----------------------------------------------------------------------
Building noun group of SHANTYTOWN-1
   Checking active opinion strategies on SHANTYTOWN-1
----------------------------------------------------------------------
   Checking whether to include a personal opinion about SHANTYTOWN-1
    PRAGS: should say ng stress on SHANTYTOWN-1 in NG-OPINION?  ...no
   Checking active opinion strategies (HEAD-NOUN) on SHANTYTOWN-1
    No applicable strategy found
   Checking whether to include hearer's opinion about SHANTYTOWN-1
   Building up noun group of form (ROLE ART PRE HEAD POST)

====>  A
====>  SHANTYTOWN
    PRAGS: say (WINNIE MANDELA CITY), (the NAME of SHANTYTOWN-1)?  ...yes
```

```
====>    ---
====>    NAMED
====>    WINNIE
====>    MANDELA
====>    CITY
====>    ---
====>    ON
====>    BEINECKE
====>    PLAZA
====>    IN
====>    EARLY
====>    APRIL
```

And so the first sentence ends. At this stage, PAULINE has satisfied, to varying degrees, its rhetorical goals; now it gets the opportunity to do so using plans of a more prescriptive nature. More topics must be found. PAULINE still has the two input topics CONSTRUCT-2 and MTRANS-8. As with CONSTRUCT-1, the program finds that the CONVINCE plan is appropriate; when applied to CONSTRUCT-2, it finds the topics GOAL-2, SUPPORT-2 (the local community's outrage at Yale's action), and ARREST-1 (the arrest of the students). For example:

```
----------------------------------------------------------------------
Topic collector considering new topic:  ARREST-1
CONVINCE-PLAN is appropriate
----------------------------------------------------------------------
Now applying *CONVINCE-PLAN*'s steps to ARREST-1
Topic ARREST-1 spawned the following topics: (GOAL-2 SUPPORT-2 ARREST-1)
```

Eventually, when nothing more is found, the topic organization phase is begun. After supervising the reordering of the topics, the paragraph construction plan groups together the topics suited to state and expound a subsequent topic. Then, as before, the presence of rhetorical goals of opinion that suggest the inclusion of sentences with explicit opinions is checked:

```
Starting to organize topics into phrases...

  Reordering input topics
  Final order is: (CONSTRUCT-2 ARREST-1 SUPPORT-2 GOAL-1 GOAL-2)
  ----------------------------------------------------------------------
  Proceeding to next stage of paragraph...
    Grouping together topics suitable for stating and expounding a subsequent to
      -->checking rhet goal:  RG:VERBOSITY
    Using topics (CONSTRUCT-2 ARREST-1 SUPPORT-2)
  ----------------------------------------------------------------------
      PRAGS: is there time to do TOPIC-ORG with CONSTRUCT-2?  ...yes
    Starting to build phrases with CONSTRUCT-2
    Checking active opinion strategies (COMMENT) on CONSTRUCT-2
      No applicable strategy found
```

Following this, PAULINE succeeds in interpreting CONSTRUCT-2 as an instance of someone (Yale) making somebody else (the officials) do their dirty work (the demolishing). This new interpretation is added into memory, and it replaces the original candidate sentence topic:

```
Checking active opinion strategies (INTERPRET) on CONSTRUCT-2
  Found interpretations:

  [<CONFIG-CAUSE-CONCEPT> on CONSTRUCT-2  :
    [ACTOR  :  OFFICIALS (= ?X)]
    [RELATIONS  :  SBG:CONS2-G2]
      [CONC2  :  GOAL-2]
        [ACTOR  :  YALE (= ?Y)]]
  Working out *SELF*'s affect for OFFICIALS
  Working out *SELF*'s affect for INTERP-CAUSE-CONCEPT.585
  Running strategy to interpret as CAUSE-CONCEPT
  Strategy successful


--------------------------------------------------------------------
Found that CAUSE-CONCEPT is a new interpretation of CONSTRUCT-2
    and related concepts
...building new concept INTERP-CAUSE-CONCEPT.585 about it
Indexing INTERP-CAUSE-CONCEPT.585 under high-level concept CAUSE
Adding back-links from CONSTRUCT-2 to <CONFIG-CAUSE-CONCEPT>
--------------------------------------------------------------------

  Starting to work on remindings similar to CONSTRUCT-2
    Found no remindings from ()
  Checking if CONSTRUCT-2 is very similar to other topics  ...not really
  Starting to build affect phrase around CONSTRUCT-2
    Found no suitable other topic
  Starting to cast topic CONSTRUCT-2 into relational phrase
    Searching for another topic from
      - Goals: (GOAL-2)
      - Similar topics: (GOAL-2 ARREST-1 SUPPORT-2)
    Will use ARREST-1 (a SIBLING relation of CONSTRUCT-2) to build a phrase
      -->checking rhet goal:  RG:FORMALITY with phrase <PHRASE %AND1>
  Checking active opinion strategies (COMMENT) on CONSTRUCT-2
    No applicable strategy found

  Finished organizing topic CONSTRUCT-2; built up syntax goals:
    (<Goal to express INTERP-CAUSE-CONCEPT.473
      Nomination: Goal CONVINCE-GOAL activated plan; role is INITIAL-TOPIC
      Derivation: original topic
      Affect: Desired affect is BAD; Goals call for ENHANCE strategy
      Expression: Phrase/verb HAVE
      Followed by
          (<Goal to express ARREST-1
            Nomination: Goal CONVINCE-GOAL activated plan; role is RESULT
            Derivation: Parent INTERP-CAUSE-CONCEPT.473 via relations
                        (GOOD-RELATIONS *CONVINCE-PLAN*)
```

```
            Affect: Desired affect is BAD; Goals call for ENHANCE strategy
            With preceding words (*SEM* ALSO *CMA* AT THAT TIME *CMA*)>)>)
```

Though, under certain circumstances, realization of this goal could begin immediately, the program proceeds with organizing the next candidate topics...

```
        PRAGS: start realization? (checking haste and topic derivation)
        -->checking rhet goal: RG:HASTE
        ...no

Considering SUPPORT-2
Checking active opinion strategies (COMMENT) on SUPPORT-2
  No applicable strategy found
Checking active opinion strategies (INTERPRET) on SUPPORT-2
  as INTERP-CONFRONT-CONCEPT.475: no applicable strategy found
Checking active opinion strategies (COMMENT) on SUPPORT-2
  No applicable strategy found

Finished organizing topic SUPPORT-2; built up syntax goals:
  (<Goal to express SUPPORT-2
    Nomination: Goal CONVINCE-GOAL activated plan; role is RESULT
    Derivation: Parent INTERP-CAUSE-CONCEPT.473 via relations
                (GOOD-RELATIONS *CONVINCE-PLAN*)
    Affect: Desired affect is GOOD; Goals call for () strategy>)
```

At this point, the two syntax goals that derived from CONSTRUCT-2 have been completed, and are sent to the realizer. Still waiting to be handled is the goal to generate MTRANS-8 together with whatever topics can be suitably collected.

```
Generator starting to produce text...

----------------------------------------------------------------------
Sentence top: setting up INTERP-CAUSE-CONCEPT.473 with modifiers (ENHANCE)
... building a normal event sentence
----------------------------------------------------------------------
Setting up words or phrases linking new sentence to previous one
====>  *DOT*
Searching for pre-subject clauses for INTERP-CAUSE-CONCEPT.473
====>  AT
====>  5:30
====>  AM
====>  ON
====>  APRIL
====>  14
====>  *CMA*
Searching for a subject for sentence about INTERP-CAUSE-CONCEPT.473
====>  YALE
Searching for a verb to express INTERP-CAUSE-CONCEPT.473
  Using preselected verb HAVE
  Building a sentence predicate with HAVE
```

```
        Filtering aspects of INTERP-CAUSE-CONCEPT.473 to build predicate
          -->checking hearer's language ability
          -->checking conversational conditions
    ====>  HAD
    ------------------------------------------------------------------
    Sentence top: setting up CONSTRUCT-2 with modifiers (COMPL REPORTED ROOT ENHAN
    ... building a normal event sentence
    ------------------------------------------------------------------
    Setting up words or phrases linking new sentence to previous one
    Searching for a subject for sentence about CONSTRUCT-2
    Searching for head noun of OFFICIALS
    Checking active opinion strategies (HEAD-NOUN) on CONSTRUCT-2
    Checking active opinion strategies (ADJECTIVE-NUMBER) on CONSTRUCT-2
    ====>  OFFICIALS
    Searching for a verb to express CONSTRUCT-2
      Building a sentence predicate with DESTROY
    ====>  DESTROY
      Searching for head noun of SHANTYTOWN-1
    ====>  IT
    ------------------------------------------------------------------
    Sentence top: setting up ARREST-1 with modifiers (GOOD-RELATIONS ENHANCE COMPL)
    ... building a normal event sentence
    ------------------------------------------------------------------
    Setting up words or phrases linking new sentence to previous one
    ====>  *SEM*
    ====>  ALSO
    ====>  *CMA*
    ====>  AT
    ====>  THAT
    ====>  TIME
    ====>  *CMA*
    Searching for a subject for sentence about ARREST-1
      Found sentence subject: POLICE
    ====>  THE
    ====>  POLICE
    Searching for a verb to express ARREST-1
      Building a sentence predicate with ARREST
    ====>  ARRESTED
      Searching for head noun of STUDENTS-2
    ====>  76
    ====>  STUDENTS
    ------------------------------------------------------------------
    Sentence top: setting up SUPPORT-2
    ... building a normal event sentence
    ------------------------------------------------------------------
    Setting up words or phrases linking new sentence to previous one
    ====>  *DOT*
    Searching for pre-subject clauses for SUPPORT-2
    Searching for a subject for sentence about SUPPORT-2
    Checking active opinion strategies (ADJECTIVE-NUMBER) on COMMUNITY-2
      Running strategy to slant claimed support
```

```
   Found  MAXIMIZE
====>  A
====>  LARGE
====>  NUMBER
====>  OF
====>  LOCAL
====>  POLITICIANS
====>  AND
====>  FACULTY
====>  MEMBERS
Searching for a verb to express SUPPORT-2
   Searching for a suitable MTRANS verb
   Building a sentence predicate with EXPRESS
====>  EXPRESSED
   Searching for head noun of CRITICISM
====>  CRITICISM
====>  OF
====>  YALE'S
====>  ACTION
```

Finally, the program gets to the last topic, MTRANS-8. No new additional topics are found, and hence no interpretations or phrasal juxtapositions occur. Realization is straightforward.

```
Topic collector considering new topic:  GOAL-1
Topic GOAL-1 spawned the following topics: (GOAL-2 GOAL-1)
Starting to organize topics into phrases...
Finished organizing topic MTRANS-8; built up goals:
   (<Goal to express MTRANS-8
     Nomination: Goal CONVINCE-GOAL activated plan; role is INITIAL-TOPIC
     Derivation: original topic
     Affect: Desired affect is GOOD;  Goals call for () strategy>)
-------------------------------------------------------------------
Sentence top: setting up MTRANS-8
... building a normal event sentence
-------------------------------------------------------------------
Setting up words or phrases linking new sentence to previous one
====>  *DOT*
====>  FINALLY
====>  *CMA*
====>  THE
====>  UNIVERSITY
Searching for a verb to express MTRANS-8
Searching for a verb to express ALLOW-3
   Building a sentence predicate with GIVE
====>  GAVE
====>  THE
====>  STUDENTS
====>  PERMISSION
Searching for a verb to express CONSTRUCT-3
====>  TO
```

```
====>   REASSEMBLE
====>   IT
```

==

Whole story:

AS A REMINDER TO YALE UNIVERSITY TO DIVEST FROM COMPANIES DOING
BUSINESS IN SOUTH AFRICA, A LARGE NUMBER OF STUDENTS CONSTRUCTED
A SHANTYTOWN --- NAMED WINNIE MANDELA CITY --- ON BEINECKE PLAZA
ON EARLY APRIL. AT 5:30 AM ON APRIL 14, YALE HAD OFFICIALS DESTROY
IT; ALSO, AT THAT TIME, THE POLICE ARRESTED 76 STUDENTS. A LARGE
NUMBER OF LOCAL POLITICIANS AND FACULTY MEMBERS EXPRESSED CRITICISM
OF YALE'S ACTION. FINALLY, THE UNIVERSITY GAVE THE STUDENTS PERMISSION
TO REASSEMBLE IT.

==

At the end, PAULINE displays the final satisfaction statuses of the rhetorical
goals. Note the relatively large number of times the most important goals in this
setting — partiality, timidity, formality, and aggression — are satisfied:

Satisfaction of current rhetorical goals:

FORMALITY:	29	DETAIL:	8
FORCE:	10	HASTE:	34
TIMIDITY:	62	PARTIALITY:	36
SPEAKER-REF:	3	HEARER-REF:	14
COLOR:	4	FLORIDITY:	8
RESPECT:	0	SIMPLICITY:	9
WARMTH:	2	VERBOSITY:	13
AGGRESSION:	20	INCITEMENT:	19

Appendix B

A Phrasal Grammar

As described in chapter 6, PAULINE's grammar is defined as a set of phrases. These phrases are briefly described in this appendix.

The phrases can be arranged in a rough hierarchy depending on how much effect they have on the final text. At the level of largest effect, the phrases control the formation of multi-predicate sentences, such as enhancer and mitigator phrases and relations between topics. At the next level, the phrases determine sentence content and organization to form various types of sentences (questions, imperatives). At lower levels, the content and organization of predicates, adverbial clauses, and noun groups are determined.

- PAULINE's phrasal lexicon contains a large number of multi-predicate patterns. When appropriate, depending on the relationships between the sentence topics, the program's planner casts the topics into these patterns. Multi-predicate patterns are used to express the following:

    - **Slanting phrases:** "Not only X, but Y" and "X, however, Y"
    - **Reminding phrases:** "X, which reminds me of Y"
    - **Goal-relationship phrases:** " X in order to Y" and "X so that Y"
    - **Result-relationship phrases:** "X. As a result, Y" and "Y because X"
    - **Other relationship phrases:** "X is larger than Y" and "After X, Y"

- SAY-SENT-TOP — This specialist determines which type of sentence to make and builds the appropriate syntax goal. The decision is based on the input: objects and states are described by SAY-ATTRIB-SENT, relations between concepts by SAY-RELATION-SENT, and events and state changes by SAY-EVENT-SENT. If implemented in PAULINE, SAY-IMPERATIVE and SAY-QUESTION would be included here.

- SAY-RELATION-SENT — Builds a sentence to express the relation between two concepts. The input is the concept representing the relation, which contains a primary (earlier/antecedent/closer) part and a secondary part. This specialist builds one of the sentence patterns
  - [SAY-PRE-SENT SAY-COMPL SAY-LINK SAY-PRE-SENT SAY-COMPL]
  - [SAY-LINK SAY-COMPL , SAY-COMPL]

  where each COMPL specialist is associated with one part of the relation. From the relation concept, the SAY-LINK specialist can find a suitable relation word. PAULINE's memory contains the following relations between entities:

  1. **Causal:** CAUSE or PRECONDITION (expressed by "because", "since"); RESULT or ENABLE (expressed by "because", "enable")

  2. **Temporal:** AFTER (expressed by "after", "later", "then"); BEFORE ("before", "prior to"); DURING ("while", "during")

  3. **Spatial:** ABOVE ("above", "on top of"); BELOW ("under", "below", "beneath"); PROX ("next to", "beside", "adjoining")

  4. **Comparative:** GREATER (numerical); SMALLER; MUTUALLY-EXCLUSIVE

  5. **Intergoal:** SUBGOAL-TO (an act or a goal serves a goal); SUBSUMING (the inverse relation); OPPOSING (goals with opposite desires)

- SAY-ATTRIB-SENT — This specialist expands into the list of specialists
  - [PRE-SENT SAY-SUBJECT SAY-VERB SAY-ADVERB SAY-ATTRIB
      SAY-POST-SENT]

  after selecting from the input and the rhetorical goals which aspect of the input to describe. If the input is an object, the attribute is an adjective; if an action, an adverb; if a state, a degree; if a state-change, an adverb or a degree. The attribute can be said in various ways:

  - "the bag is red"
  - "the color is red"
  - "the bag's color is red"
  - "the color of the bag is red"
  - "red is the color of the bag"
  - "the bag has a color"
  - "the bag has a red color"

- SAY-EVENT-SENT — This specialist expands into the sequence
  - [SAY-PRE-SENT SAY-SUBJECT SAY-PREDICATE]

  after finding which aspect of the input to make the sentence subject.

To choose the subject, the specialist queries the activated rhetorical goal strategies to find the pragmatically most interesting aspect of the input. If, for example, the goal **RG:haste** has the value *pressured*, no time is wasted on evaluating the affects of various candidates; the ACTOR (or, failing that, the INSTR) aspect is selected directly. Otherwise, the candidates for sentence subject are ordered by affect (sympathetic to the hearer, when not being *aggressive* or *inciting*); by their relation to the central topic; and by the amount of information represented for each one. Strategies of focus, as discussed chapter 6, were implemented in PAULINE.

The choice of the subject is also related to the verb. Some generators always select the verb first, at this stage of the realization process (see, for example, Danlos (1984)), otherwise, the generator may sometimes produce bad text: for example, some pre-sentence clauses may be prohibited by the verb (still to be chosen) or may get from it a non-standard preposition. Thus, verb choice must be able to inspect the exact words that precede it. In addition, of course, verbs have no way of indicating which aspect of the input they prefer as subject. PAULINE usually chooses the verb only when it builds the predicate, because this corresponds to the way people usually speak: we often only choose a verb at 'verb time', after the subject has been said, and any idiosyncratic constraints a verb may have either disqualifies the verb or causes a re-start of the sentence. (Why else does the longest intrasentential pause occur just before the verb? Why else do we so often start the sentence again, using a different subject, at that point?) But, of course, we are able to choose the verb before. (Sometimes we have to. For example, in French, the only way to say "Pete misses Mary" is "Mary manque à Pete"; this selection of a non-ACTOR as subject is required by "manquer". However, PAULINE can choose a verb before starting realization (it does so after the interpretation of topics, as described in chapter 3, for example); in such cases, the only action taken is a check of the the features of the verb in order to ensure a valid subject has been chosen (otherwise, for example, if the verb "beat" has been chosen, and the ACTOR is Kennedy, then the simplistic strategy of choosing the actor would produce "Kennedy beat Kennedy"). These and similar arguments against straightforward left-to-right generation are made in Danlos (1987).

- SAY-COMPL — Builds a sentence without the SAY-PRE-SENT specialist, for use in cases such as "(He said that) they went to New York"; i.e., expands into
  – [SAY-SUBJECT SAY-PREDICATE]

- SAY-REL-CLAUSE — Builds a relative clause. The input marks which aspect is shared by the surrounding syntactic environment; this aspect is associated with the SAY-REL-PRONOUN specialist, and the rest is treated like a sentence

- SAY-PREDICATE — This specialist builds a sentence predicate from its input. Unless a verb has already been chosen by rhetorical planning, it selects a verb.

To get a predicate pattern, it checks the verb; if no idiosyncratic pattern is found, the standard pattern is used:

– [SAY-VERB   SAY-OBJECT   SAY-ADVERB   SAY-POST-SENT]

In the lexicon, the formative pattern associated with a verb is a list of units. Each unit gives the position of its corresponding entity in the predicate. The absence of an aspect in the pattern means that the aspect cannot be said; a required aspect is marked mandatory. This information is used for the *inclusion* decisions. The *ordering* is given in the pattern; when various orders are possible, the pattern itself is written as a specialist function that queries the rhetorical strategies for assistance (for example, the typical adverbial clauses of time, instrument, and location are handled by SAY-POST-SENT). The *casting* function is done by associating specialists and aspects of the input, as prescribed by each unit in the pattern. A unit can consist of singles, pairs, or triplets:

- A single element (or the first one of a pair or triplet) is a keyword that indicates which specialist is to provide the syntactic environment of that entry. If the element is not the name of a specialist function, it is taken to be a literal — part of a frozen phrase — which must be said.

- The second element of a pair or triplet indicates which aspect of the input is to be used by the activated specialist function. For example, the pair (SAY-OBJECT object) indicates that the filler of the OBJECT aspect of the input is to be generated as an accusative case noun phrase.

- The third element of a triplet is the preposition to be used in a preposition group. For example, (SAY-LOC to *to*) indicates that the specialist SAY-LOC is to use the TO aspect filler with the preposition "to".

- The keyword SAY-POST-SENT indicates all the adverbial clauses that can normally be said in an English predicate, each of which has a specialist (SAY-INSTR, SAY-TIME, SAY-LOC, SAY-TO, SAY-FROM, etc.).

- The presence of a literal in the predicate pattern indicates that it must be said. A specialist function keyword indicates its position if it can be included (semantically, if its aspect appears in the input, and pragmatically, if the rhetorical goals allow). Some predicate patterns require the presence of a syntactic environment; this is indicated by a fourth entry in the unit (otherwise, under pragmatic guidance, the generator may produce sentences such as "Kennedy beat in the election"). Sometimes patterns contain parts that may only be said if they differ from the subject, these parts are also appropriately marked (otherwise, the generator may produce "Pete gave the book to John from Pete").

For example, to express the Conceptual Dependency representation primitive MTRANS, PAULINE has more than 20 words. (MTRANS stands for transfer of information; the aspect OBJECT contains the message and the aspect TO the hearer; see Schank (1972, 1975). Some of these words are "tell" (two versions) and "say":

- "tell":
  [SAY-VERB [SAY-OBJECT (aspect TO)] SAY-ADVERB SAY-POST-SENT
  that [SAY-COMPL (aspect OBJECT)]]
  "He told her quietly yesterday that [she should see the film]"

- "tell-1":
  [SAY-VERB [SAY-OBJECT (aspect TO)] SAY-ADVERB SAY-POST-SENT
  [SAY-PRED (aspect OBJECT) infinitive]]
  "He told her quietly yesterday [to see the film]"

- "say":
  [SAY-VERB [SAY-OBJECT (aspect TO) *to*] SAY-POST-SENT *that*
  [SAY-COMPL (aspect OBJECT)]]
  "He said to her yesterday that [she should see the film]"

As discussed before, the verb is chosen when SAY-PREDICATE builds the predicate. Linking into the lexicon from the type of the input concept, PAULINE searches the memory hierarchy until it finds a WORD aspect, which either directly indexes words or provides a discrimination net which indexes other concepts or words. At the top of the hierarchy, elaborate discrimination nets are associated with the conceptual dependency and other primitives to ensure that some verb will always be found.

- SAY-LINK-WORD — This specialist controls the use of words said at the beginning of a sentence to link it to the previous sentence, for example "and", "but", "as a result", "so". The question of when to include SAY-LINK-WORD in the expansion stream illustrates the general problem of where to plan how much of the text.

One argument calls for including SAY-LINK-WORD at a relatively high level — say, before SAY-SENT-TOP. The rationale is that these functions, on or just below the level of the planner, are the only ones with the requisite breadth of view to decide on proper link words, and are therefore in the position to plan for them. For example, in JUDGE example, if the top-level say-function decides to say the final result after the fight itself, it can plan on saying "FINAL-ACTION and finally FINAL-RESULT". There is a problem with this: sometimes FINAL-ACTION and FINAL-RESULT are too different to compare comfortably with "and", for example in "Sam hit Jim. His action was justified, and finally Jim died." The top-level function would have to pre-plan all the way down to the justification to handle this.

The other alternative is to make SAY-LINK-WORD much more intelligent. It must be able to compare the previous and current sentences and decide what link words are appropriate. The simplest version would just say "and" for everything — much as small children do — and a more sophisticated one may still produce sentences such as "She liked the lawn and gardening". This sentence is an example of faulty parallel construction, a topic that receives much attention in stylistic handbooks (this example is from Baker (1966, p. 106)). The fact that people require explicit training in this matter suggests that the decision to make SAY-LINK-WORD do the work is the right one.

PAULINE's construction of an argument and its indication of the relations among parts leaves much to be desired. It does not construct some type of argument graph, as discussed in chapter 6 and in Birnbaum (1985), from which this specialist can choose linking words with which to preface each sentence. In fact, by the time that SAY-LINK-WORD is expanded, most records of the derivation of the situation have vanished and the specialist has to discriminate among its options by whatever residues are left. PAULINE adds some topic collection information (typically, what relation the sentence topic bears to its ancestor in the collection process, as used in the topic collection plans described in chapter 6) to the syntax goal, to enable SAY-LINK-WORD to use phrases such as "one result is" and "a good example is". The work on rhetorical structure theory (Mann & Thompson, 1985) can be extended and used by this specialist.

- SAY-PRE-SENT-CLAUSES — Returns the specialists of all the pre-subject clauses. Check pragmatic strategies to see how many aspects to include, and how many to include before the subject. (As described in chapter 5, the values *complex* for the rhetorical goal **RG:simplicity** and *highfalutin* for **RG:formality** require many clauses in this position)

- SAY-PREPGROUP — Returns [preposition SAY-NOUN-GROUP]

- SAY-SUBJECT, SAY-OBJECT, SAY-POSSESSIVE — Set the case of the syntax goal to *nominative, accusative,* and *genitive,* respectively, and returns
  – SAY-NOUN-GROUP

- SAY-ACT-AS-OBJECT — Builds a noun group of an event or state change (for example, "Sam's shot" if the input has been said before; "John's being shot by Sam", passive for pro-victim affects; "Sam's shooting John" otherwise)

- SAY-NOUN-GROUP — Decides whether to pronominalize or not; if not, selects a head noun and returns
  – [SAY-ART   SAY-PRE-NOUN-MODS   SAY-HEAD-NOUN
      SAY-POST-NOUN-MODS]
  Sets up the context for the noun group: number, case, gender (the latter are used in languages with case and gender declension), etc.

To find a suitable head noun for the input, PAULINE executes a series of tests. If it has just been speaking about the input topic then it can simply say its name or word. It checks the rhetorical goals whether an opinion should be chosen as the head noun (producing "that jerk, Kennedy"). If not, from all the aspects of the input, it excludes those not suitable for the head noun, those that have no defined word, and those that have been said, and then orders them by the rhetorical strategies and uses the preferred aspect. If pragmatics produce no preferences, it uses a predefined default ordering.

PAULINE has four pronominalization strategies:

1. A simple *most-recent* rule, based on the fact that, in English, pronouns carry number and gender information: when PAULINE says a representation element, it stores a triplet — the input, its number, its gender — on a list. The next time PAULINE references an element, it checks whether the most recent entry on the reference list with the same number and gender is the same input element; if so, it pronominalizes. This simple-minded strategy is often described in grammar books. Of course, it doesn't always work: "Pete and John went to the shop. He came back first" — where he is John; or, better: "Pete saw Mike in the store. He..." The "he", according to this strategy, refers to Mike. But in "Pete saw Mike in the store. He told him about Mary", people quite naturally assume subject-subject and object-object correspondence.

2. The obvious *case-correspondence* strategy: if the current sentence subject (object) is the same as the previous sentence subject (object), pronominalize. Then in "Pete saw Mike in the store. He..." "he" refers to Pete. For this strategy, PAULINE obviously also stores case information on the reference list.

3. The conjunction of the above two strategies. This is stricter than either of them: it only allows pronominalization when the input entity corresponds to the most recent match of number, gender, *and* case.

4. The disjunction of the above two strategies. This is less strict than either of them. This strategy gives the most natural text, since it denies pronouns *only* in cases such as "Pete saw Mike in the store. He told Pete about Mary", where the subject and object swop *and* they have the same number and gender.

The most recent strategy is clearly inadequate, and the corresponding-case is better but not yet satisfactory. A better strategy would take into account something like the notion of focus of attention discussed in chapter 6, as worked out in Grosz (1977), Sidner (1979), and McKeown (1982), which allows pronominalization of the input if it is the current focus of attention and has been said. However, to do proper pronominalization, you require unlimited use of the whole inference capability of the system. And that is a big engine to run every time you want to decide whether to say a pronoun or not (see Appelt

(1987) for a formal theory of reference). Though people obviously sometimes do it, we probably often use some shortcut strategy instead. The disjunction strategy is one such shortcut. Since people usually pronominalize as much as possible in normal circumstances, this strategy produces the most natural text.

- The following build parts of noun groups: SAY-ART, SAY-HEAD-NOUN, SAY-PRE-NOUN-MODS, SAY-POST-NOUN-MODS, SAY-PRONOUN, SAY-REL-PRONOUN. Pre- and post-nominal modifiers are selected by the rhetorical strategies from the aspects of the input, and ordered by their affective preference. If none exists, a default order is used. Some modifiers can only appear before or after the head noun; of the rest, PAULINE places equally many in each position, unless required to do otherwise by the strategies described in chapters 3 to 5.

- SAY-VERB — Selects the appropriate tense form and auxiliary verbs and conjugates the selected verb

- SAY-PRE-VERB-MODS — Modify the verb by saying one of [INTENT   ALSO] as in "Mike also hit Jim"; if the action has been represented as intentional, say so; otherwise, STRESS can be said

- SAY-ADVERB — Modify the verb by saying any or all of
  – [PREP-MODIFYING-VERB   STRESS   ADVERB   REPEATER   BACK/AGAIN]
  as in "Jim knocked Mike down very hard again"; for example:

  – INTENT: "purposely", "intentionally", "wilfully", "on purpose", / "accidentally", "unintentionally", "by accident"

  – ALSO: "also"

  – STRESS: "really", "easily", "badly" / "only", "just", "merely", "narrowly"

  – PREPOSITION: any preposition associated with the verb

  – REPEATER: "repeatedly" / "once"

  – BACK/AGAIN: "back" / "again"

  – ADVERB: any adverb

The prepositions "down" and "into" in the sentences
– "Jim knocked Mike down again"
– "Jim bumped into Mike again"
derive from different sources: "down" modifies the verb "knock" — Jim could certainly have knocked Mike over, or to the floor, or under the table. However, "bump into" is a frozen phrase — you cannot change the preposition to "bump to" or "bump over" and retain the meaning. This difference is reflected in the

generator's representation for the two cases. In the former, the specialist SAY-ADVERB finds the semantic equivalent of "down" in the input representation and says "down"; it could just as easily have found "up" or "over". In the latter, the "into" is part of the sentence form for the verb "bump into", and the OBJECT must be said with the preposition.

Most of the specialists listed above correspond to traditional phrase structure symbols such as NOUN GROUP and PREDICATE. But, just as specialists may be used to build multi-predicate sentences, they may be used for other purposes. For example, people talk about money in various highly idiomatic ways. All PAULINE's phrasal knowledge relating to money is grouped together in a single specialist. The phrasal lexicon contains the following specialists:

- SAY-MONEY — Realize the phrases "the measly *$15*" (as head noun); "the *35c* book" (as pre-nominal modifier); and "a green truck *worth 300 bucks*" (as post-nominal modifier). As with all the other variations, options are selected by referring to the relevant pragmatic criteria: for example, "bucks" is not selected when pragmatics call for being very formal.

- The specialists SAY-AMOUNT and SAY-DIFFERENCE express other numerical amounts. The former builds the patterns
  - "a [size] number/amount (of [unit])"
  - "[amount] [unit]"
  - "the most/fewest/X number of [unit]"
  the latter expresses the numerical difference between two amounts.

- The following are adverbial clause specialists: SAY-SOURCE, SAY-RECIPIENT, SAY-TO, SAY-FROM, SAY-TIME, SAY-LOC, SAY-INSTRUMENT, SAY-PRE-INSTR, SAY-MEASURE. Each specialist is able to produce various English forms. For example, depending on the nature of the input it receives, SAY-TIME can produce:
  - "now / today / tomorrow / yesterday": input is a predefined day concept
  - "at 5 o'clock today / yesterday": input is a MEASURE concept
  - "in the future / past": input is the concept FUTURE or PAST
  - "15 hours from now": input is a MEASURE, WHEN aspect is FUTURE or PAST
  - "at 3 o'clock": input is an INSTANCE

- The following specialists are all used to build noun groups: SAY-NAME, SAY-AGE, SAY-GENDER, SAY-NUMBER, SAY-TITLE, SAY-NATION, SAY-RESID, SAY-WEARING, SAY-OCCUP, SAY-DESCRIP, SAY-SIZE, SAY-COLOR, SAY-OWNER, SAY-OPINION, SAY-ROLE, SAY-MONEY. Each specialist must be able to produce various forms, depending on its position. For example, SAY-AGE can produce the following forms:

- *predicate:* "...*is 23 years old*"
- *head-noun:* "the fat but pretty *23-year-old* from Irkutsk"
- *pre-head-noun:* "the *23-year-old* fat woman, Marta"
- *post-head-noun:* "Marta, *a 23-year-old,* ..."

and SAY-GENDER the following:

- *predicate:* "...*is female*"
- *head-noun:* "the green *man* from Mars"
- *pre-head-noun:* "the large *male* dinosaur"
- *post-head-noun:* "the student *who is male...*"

The inclusion and ordering decisions of topic aspects are all made by the rhetorical strategies, as described in chapters 3, 4, and 5.

Bibliography

1. Abelson, R.P., & Rosenberg, M.J. (1958). Symbolic psycho-logic: A model of attitudinal cognition. *Behavioral Science, 4*, 14-25.

2. Allen, J.F., & Perrault, C.R. (1979). Analyzing intentions in dialogues. University of Rochester Technical Report 150.

3. Appelt, D.E. (1981). *Planning natural language utterances to satisfy multiple goals.* Ph.D. dissertation, Stanford University.

4. Appelt, D.E. (1982). Planning natural-language utterances. In *2nd AAAI Conference Proceedings*, Pittsburgh.

5. Appelt, D.E. (1983). Telegram: a Grammar formalism for language planning, In *8th IJCAI Conference Proceedings*, Karlsruhe.

6. Appelt, D.E. (1985). *Planning English sentences.* Cambridge, England: Cambridge University Press.

7. Appelt, D.E. (1987). Towards a plan-based theory of referring actions. In G. Kempen (ed), *Natural language generation: Recent advances in Artificial Intelligence, Psychology, and Linguistics*, (pp. 63-70). Boston, MA: Kluwer Academic Publishers.

8. Atkinson, J.M. (1982). Understanding formality: The categorization and production of 'formal' interaction. *British Journal of Sociology, 33(1)*, 86-117.

9. Bain, W.M. (1985). *Case-based reasoning: A computer model of subjective assessment.* Ph.D. dissertation, Yale University.

10. Bain, W.M. (1986). A case-based reasoning system for subjective assessment. In *5th AAAI Conference Proceedings*, Philadelphia.

11. Baker, S. (1966). *The complete stylist.* New York, NY: Crowell.

12. Becker, J.D. (1975). The phrasal lexicon. Bolt, Beranek and Newman Technical Report 3081.

13. Bienkowski, M.A. (1986). A computational model for extemporaneous elaborations. Princeton University Cognitive Science Laboratory Technical Report 1.

14. Birk, N.P., & Birk, G.B. (1965). *Understanding and using English* (4th ed). New York, NY: Odyssey Press.

15. Birnbaum, L.A. (1985). A functional approach to the representation of arguments. In N. Sharkey (ed), *Advances in cognitive science* (pp. 39-49). Chichester, England: Ellis Horwood.

16. Birnbaum, L.A. (1986). *Integrated processing in planning and understanding.* Ph.D. dissertation, Yale University.

17. Birnbaum, L.A., Flowers, M., & McGuire, R. (1980). Towards an AI model of argumentation. In *1st AAAI conference proceedings*, Stanford.

18. Bloomfield, L. (1914). *An introduction to the study of language.* New York, NY: Holt.

19. Bobrow, D.G., & Winograd, T. (1977). An overview of KRL, a knowledge-representation language. *Cognitive Science, 1(1)*, 3-46.

20. Bock, J.K. (1982). Toward a cognitive psychology of syntax: Information processing contributions to sentence formulation. *Psychological Review, (89)*, 1-47.

21. Bock, J.K. (1987). Exploring levels of processing in sentence production. In G. Kempen (ed), *Natural language generation: Recent advances in Artificial Intelligence, Psychology, and Linguistics* (pp. 351-364). Boston, MA: Kluwer Academic Publishers.

22. Brachman, R.J. (1978). *A structural paradigm for representing knowledge.* Ph.D. dissertation, Harvard University. Also Bolt, Beranek and Newman Technical Report 3605.

23. Broverman, C.A., & Croft, W.B. (1987). Reasoning about exceptions during plan execution monitoring. In *6th AAAI Conference Proceedings*, Seattle.

24. Brown, P., & Levinson, S.C., (1978). Universals in language usage: Politeness phenomena. In E. Goody (ed), *Questions and politeness: Strategies in social interaction* (pp. 56-311). Cambridge, England: Cambridge University Press.

25. Bruce, B., Collins, A., Rubin, A.D., & Gentner, D. (1978). A Cognitive Science approach to writing. Bolt, Beranek and Newman Technical Report 89.

26. Bühler, K. (1934). *Sprachtheorie.* Jena, Germany: Fischer.

27. Carbonell, J.G. (1976). Intentionality and human conversations. In *2nd TINLAP Conference Proceedings*, Urbana.

28. Carnap, R. (1938). Foundations of Logic and Mathematics. In O. Neurath, R. Carnap, & C.W. Morris (eds), *International encyclopedia of unified science* vol 1, (pp. 139-214). Chicago, IL: University of Chicago Press.

29. Carnap, R. (1956). *Meaning and necessity.* Chicago, IL: University of Chicago Press.

30. Carnap, R. (1959). *Introduction to semantics.* Cambridge, MA: Harvard University Press.

31. Charniak, E., & McDermott, D.V. (1985). *Introduction to Artificial Intelligence.* New York, NY: Addison-Wesley.

32. Charniak, E., Riesbeck, C.K., & McDermott, D.V. (1980). *Artificial Intelligence programming,* Hillsdale, NJ: Lawrence Erlbaum Associates.

33. Chomsky, N. (1957). *Syntactic structures,* The Hague, The Netherlands: Mouton.

34. Chomsky, N. (1965). *Aspects of the theory of syntax.* Cambridge, MA: MIT Press.

35. Chomsky, N. (1976). *Reflections on language.* Cambridge, MA: MIT Press.

36. Clark, H.H., & Carlson, T.B. (1981). Context for comprehension. In J. Long & A. Baddeley (eds), *Attention and performance IX* (pp. 313-330). Hillsdale, NJ: Lawrence Erlbaum Associates.

37. Clark, H.H., & Murphy, G.L. (1982). Audience design in meaning and reference. In J.F. Le Ny & W. Kintsch (eds), *Language and comprehension* (pp. 287-299). Amsterdam, The Netherlands: North Holland Publishing Company.

38. Clark, H.H., & Schunk, D. (1980). Polite responses to polite requests. *Cognition, 8,* 111-143.

39. Clippinger, J.H. (1974). *A discourse speaking program as a preliminary theory of discourse behavior and a limited theory of psychoanalytic discourse.* Ph.D. dissertation, University of Pennsylvania.

40. Clippinger, J.H. (1975). Speaking with many tongues: Some problems in modeling speakers of actual discourse. In *1st TINLAP Conference Proceedings.*

41. Cohen, P.R. (1978). *On knowing what to say: Planning speech acts.* Ph.D. dissertation, University of Toronto.

42. Cole, P. (ed). (1980). *Syntax and semantics vol 9: Pragmatics.* New York, NY: Academic Press.

43. Cohen, P.R., & Perrault, C.R. (1979). Elements of a plan-based theory of speech acts. *Cognitive Science, 3(3)*, 177-212.

44. Cohen, P.R., & Levesque, H.J. (1985). Speech acts and rationality. In *23rd ACL Conference Proceedings*, Chicago.

45. Cowan, G., & McPherson, E. (1977). *Plain English rhetoric and reader.* New York, NY: Random House.

46. Cumming, S. (1986a). Design of a master lexicon. USC/Information Sciences Institute Technical Report RR-86-163.

47. Cumming, S. (1986b). The lexicon in text generation. USC/Information Sciences Institute Technical Report RR-86-168.

48. Danks, J.H. (1977). Producing ideas and sentences. In S. Rosenberg (ed), *Sentence production: Developments in research and theory* (pp. 229-258). Hillsdale: Lawrence Erlbaum Associates.

49. Danlos, L. (1983). Some issues in generation from a semantic representation. In *8th IJCAI Conference Proceedings*, Karlsruhe.

50. Danlos, L. (1984). Conceptual and linguistic decisions in generation. In *10th Coling Conference Proceedings*, Stanford.

51. Danlos, L. (1987a). *Génération automatique de texts en langues naturelles.* Ph.D. dissertation, University of Paris (1985). English translation by D. Debize & C. Henderson, *The linguistic basis of text generation.* Cambridge, England: Cambridge University Press.

52. Danlos, L. (1987b). A robust syntactic component in generation. In G. Kempen (ed), *Natural language generation: Recent advances in Artificial Intelligence, Psychology, and Linguistics* (pp. 191-218). Boston, MA: Kluwer Academic Publishers.

53. Davey, A. (1979). *Discourse production.* Edinburgh, Scotland: Edinburgh University Press.

54. De Beaugrande, R. (1984). *Text production.* In series *Advances in discourse processes*, vol XI. Norwood, NJ: ABLEX Publishing Corporation.

55. De Smedt, K., & Kempen, G. (1987). Incremental Sentence Production. In G. Kempen (ed), *Natural language generation: Recent advances in Artificial Intelligence, Psychology, and Linguistics* (pp. 356-370). Boston, MA: Kluwer Academic Publishers.

56. Dik, S.C. (1978). *Functional grammar*. Amsterdam, The Netherlands: North-Holland.

57. Dik, S.C. (1980). *Studies in functional grammar*, New York, NY: Academic Press.

58. Doyle, R.J., Atkinson, D.J., & Doshi, R.S. (1986). Generating perception requests and expectations to verify the execution of plans. In *5th AAAI Conference Proceedings*, Philadelphia.

59. Durfee, E.H., & Lesser, V.R. (1986). Incremental planning to control a blackboard-based problem solver. In *8th Cognitive Science Society Conference Proceedings*, Amherst.

60. Fawcett, R.P. (1980). *Cognitive Linguistics and social interaction*. Heidelberg, Germany: Julius Groos Verlag.

61. Fikes, R.E., Hart, P.E., & Nilsson, N.J. (1972). Learning and executing generalized robot plans. *Artificial Intelligence, 3*, 251-288.

62. Fillmore, C.J. (1968). The Case for Case. In E. Bach & R. Harms (eds), *Universals in Linguistic Theory* (pp. 1-90). New York, NY: Holt, Reinhart & Winston.

63. Fillmore, C.J. (1971). Types of Lexical Information. In D.D. Steinberg & L.A. Jacobovits (eds), *Semantics: an interdisciplinary reader in Philosophy, Linguistics, and Psychology* (pp. 370-392). Cambridge, England: Cambridge University Press.

64. Firby, R.J. (1987). An investigation into reactive planning in complex domains. In *6th AAAI Conference Proceedings*, Seattle.

65. Freud, S. (1935). *A General Introduction to Psychoanalysis* (translated by J. Riviere). New York, NY: Liveright.

66. Garvey, C. (1975). Requests and responses in children's speech. *Journal of Child Language, 2*, 41-64.

67. Garvey, C., & Berninger, G. (1981). Timing and turn-taking in children's conversations. *Discourse Processes, 4*, 27-57.

68. Gasser, M., & Dyer, M.G. (1986). Speak of the devil: Representing deictic and speech act knowledge in an integrated lexical memory. In *8th Cognitive Science Society Conference Proceedings*, Amherst.

69. Gazdar, G., (1979). *Pragmatics: Implicature, presupposition, and logical form*. New York, NY: Academic Press.

70. Gazdar, G. (1980). Pragmatic constraints on linguistic production. In B. Butterworth (ed), *Language production*, vol 1 (pp. 49-68). New York, NY: Academic Press.

71. Gibbs, R. (1979). Contextual effects in understanding indirect requests. *Discourse Processes, 2*, 1-10.

72. Gibbs, R. (1981). Your wish is my command: Convention and context in interpreting indirect requests. *Journal of Verbal Learning and Verbal Behavior, 20*, 431-444.

73. Goldman, N.M. (1973). Sentence paraphrasing from a conceptual base. Stanford University Technical Report.

74. Goldman, N.M. (1975). Conceptual generation. In R.C. Schank (ed), *Conceptual Information Processing* (pp. 289-371). Amsterdam, The Netherlands: North-Holland Publishing Company.

75. Goody, E. (ed). (1978). *Questions and politeness: Strategies in social interaction.* Cambridge, England: Cambridge University Press.

76. Gordon, D., & Lakoff, G. (1975). Conversational postulates. In P. Cole & J.L. Morgan (eds), *Syntax and semantics 9: Pragmatics* (pp. 83-106). New York, NY: Academic Press.

77. Gregory, M. (1982). Towards 'communication' linguistics: a Framework, In J.D. Benson & W.S. Greaves (eds), *Systemic perspectives on discourse* (pp. 45-63). London, England: Edward Arnold Press.

78. Grice, H.P. (1971). Meaning. In D.D. Steinberg & L.A. Jacobovits (eds), *Semantics: an Interdisciplinary reader in Philosophy, Linguistics, and Psychology* (pp. 53-59). Cambridge, England: Cambridge University Press.

79. Grice, H.P. (1975). Logic and conversation. In P. Cole & J.L. Morgan (eds), *Syntax and semantics 9: Pragmatics* (pp. 41-58). New York, NY: Academic Press.

80. Grimes, J.E. (1975). *The thread of discourse.* The Hague, The Netherlands: Mouton.

81. Gross, M. (1979). On the failure of generative grammar. *Language, 55(4)*, 859-885.

82. Gross, M. (1984). Lexicon-grammar and the syntactic analysis of French. In *10th Coling Conference Proceedings*, Stanford.

83. Grosz, B.J. (1977). The representation and use of focus in dialogue understanding. SRI Technical Report 151.

84. Grosz, B.J. (1980). Focusing and description in natural language dialogs. In A. Joshi et al. (eds), *Elements of discourse understanding* (proceedings of a workshop on computational aspects of linguistic structure and discourse setting). Cambridge, England: Cambridge University Press.

85. Grosz, B.J. (1986). A theory of discourse structure. In *8th Cognitive Science Society Conference Proceedings*, Amherst.

86. Grosz, B.J., & Sidner, C.L. (1985). Discourse structure and the proper treatment of interruptions. In *9th IJCAI Conference Proceedings*, Los Angeles.

87. Halliday, M.A.K. (1961). Categories of the theory of grammar. *Word, 17*, 241-292.

88. Halliday, M.A.K. (1976). *Halliday: System and function in language.* (Selected papers, edited by G.R. Kress.) Oxford, Emgland: Oxford University Press.

89. Halliday, M.A.K. (1978). *Language as social semiotic.* London, England: Edward Arnold Publishers.

90. Harada, S.I. (1976). Honorifics. In M. Shibatani (ed), *Syntax and semantics 5: Japanese generative grammar* (pp. 499-561). New York, NY: Academic Press.

91. Herrmann, T., & Laucht, M. (1978). Planung von Aeusserungen als Selektion von Komponenten implikativer Propositionsstrukturen. Universität Mannheim Technical Report 3.

92. Hill, A.S. (1892). *The foundations of rhetoric.* New York, NY: Harper & Brothers.

93. Hobbs, J.R. (1978). Why is discourse coherent? SRI Technical Note 176.

94. Hobbs, J.R. (1979). Coherence and coreference. *Cognitive Science, 3(1)*, 67-90.

95. Householder, F.W. (1971). *Linguistic speculations.* Cambridge, England: Cambridge University Press.

96. Hovy, E.H., & Schank, R.C. (1984). Language generation by computer. In B.G. Bara & G. Guida (eds), *Natural language processing* (pp. 165-196). Amsterdam, The Netherlands: North-Holland Publishing Company.

97. Hovy, E.H. (1985). Integrating text planning and production in generation. In *9th IJCAI Conference Proceedings*, Los Angeles.

98. Hovy, E.H. (1986a). Some pragmatic decision criteria in generation. In G. Kempen (ed), *Natural language generation: Recent results in Artificial Intelligence, Psychology, and Linguistics* (pp. 3-18). Boston, MA: Kluwer Academic Publishers, 1987.

99. Hovy, E.H (1986b). Putting affect into text. In *8th Cognitive Science Society Conference Proceedings*, Amherst.

100. Hovy, E.H. (1987a). *Generating natural language under pragmatic constraints.* Ph.D. dissertation, Yale University.

101. Hovy, E.H. (1987b). Generating language with a phrasal lexicon. In D.D. McDonald & L. Bolc (eds), *Natural language generation systems* (pp. 353-384). New York, NY: Springer-Verlag, 1988.

102. Hovy, E.H. (1987c). Generating natural language under pragmatic constraints. *Journal of Pragmatics, XI(6)*, 689-719.

103. Hovy, E.H. (1987d). Interpretation in generation. In *6th AAAI Conference Proceedings*, Seattle.

104. Hovy, E.H. (1987e). What makes language formal? In *9th Cognitive Science Society Conference Proceedings*, Seattle.

105. Hovy, E.H. (1988a). Two types of planning in language generation. In *26th ACL Conference Proceedings*, Buffalo, 1988, to appear.

106. Hovy, E.H. (1988b). Planning coherent multisentential text. In *26th ACL Conference Proceedings*, Buffalo, 1988, to appear.

107. Irvine, J.T. (1979). Formality and informality of speech events. *American Anthropologist, 81(4)*, 773-790.

108. Jackendoff, R. (1981). On Katz's autonomous semantics. *Language, 57(2)*, 425-435.

109. Jackendoff, R. (1985). *Semantics and cognition.* Cambridge, MA: MIT Press.

110. Jacobs, P.S. (1985a). PHRED: a Generator for natural language interfaces. University of California (Berkeley) Technical Report CSD 85/198.

111. Jacobs, P.S. (1985b). *A knowledge-based approach to language production.* Ph.D. dissertation, University of California (Berkeley).

112. Jakobson, R. (1960). Linguistics and poetics. In T. Sebeok (ed), *Style in language* (pp. 350-377). Cambridge, MA: MIT Press.

113. Jameson, A. (1987). How to appear to be conforming to the 'maxims' even if you prefer to violate them. In G. Kempen (ed), *Natural language generation: Recent advances in Artificial Intelligence, Psychology, and Linguistics* (pp. 19-42). Boston, MA: Kluwer Academic Publishers.

114. Johnson, P.N., & Robertson, S.P. (1981). MAGPIE: A goal-based model of conversation. Yale University Technical Report 206.

115. Joncas, E. (1972). *Action expectations in social situations.* Ph.D. dissertation, Yale University.

116. Joshi, A.K. (1987a). Tree adjoining grammars and their relevance to generation. In G. Kempen (ed), *Natural language generation: Recent advances in Artificial Intelligence, Psychology, and Linguistics* (pp. 233-252). Boston, MA: Kluwer Academic Publishers.

117. Joshi, A.K., (1987b).
Word-order variation in natural language generation. In *6th AAAI Conference Proceedings*, Seattle.

118. Kamp, H. (1981).
A theory of truth and semantic representation. In J.A.G. Groenendijk, Th.M.V. Janssen, & M.B.J. Stokhof (eds), *Formal methods in the study of language* (pp. 25-37). Amsterdam, The Netherlands: Mathematisch Centrum Tracts 135.

119. Katz, J.J. (1977). *Propositional structure and illocutionary force.* New York, NY: Crowell.

120. Katz, J.J. (1980).
Chomsky on meaning. *Language, 56(1)*, 1-41.

121. Kay, M. (1979). Functional grammar. In *5th Berkely Linguistics Society Meeting Proceedings*.

122. Kay, M. (1984). Functional unification grammar: a Formalism for machine translation. In *10th Coling Conference Proceedings*, Stanford.

123. Keenan, J.M., MacWhinney, B., & Mayhew, D. (1982). Pragmatics in memory: a Study of natural conversation. In U. Neisser (ed), *Memory Observed* (pp. 315-324). San Francisco, CA: William Freeman Press.

124. Kempen, G. (1976). Directions for building a sentence generator which is psychologically plausible. Unpublished paper, Yale University.

125. Kempen, G. (1977). Conceptualizing and formulating in sentence production. In S. Rosenberg (ed), *Sentence production: Developments in research and theory* (pp. 259-274). Hillsdale, NJ: Lawrence Erlbaum Associates.

126. Kempen, G., & Hoenkamp, E. (1978). A procedural grammar for sentence production. University of Nijmegen Technical Report.

127. Kroch, A., & Joshi, A.K. (1986). Analyzing extraposition in a tree adjoining grammar. In G. Huck & A. Ojeda (eds), *Syntax and semantics (discontinuous constituents)* (pp. 56-70). New York, NY: Academic Press.

128. Kukich, K. (1983a). Design of a knowledge-based report generator. In *21st ACL Conference Proceedings*, Cambridge.

129. Kukich, K. (1983b). *Knowledge-based report generation: a Knowledge-engineering approach*. Ph.D. dissertation, University Of Pittsburgh.

130. Kuno, S. (1973). *The structure of the Japanese language*. Cambridge, MA: Harvard University Press.

131. Lakoff, R. (1970). Language in context. Manuscript, University of Michigan.

132. Lakoff, R. (1977). Politeness, pragmatics, and performatives. In *Performatives, Presuppositions, and Implicatures Conference Proceedings*, Texas.

133. Laucht, M., & Herrmann, T. (1978). Zur Direktheit von Direktiva. Universität Mannheim Technical Report 1.

134. Lehnert, W.G. (1978). *The process of question answering*. Hillsdale, NJ: Lawrence Erlbaum Associates.

135. Lehnert, W.G. (1982). Plot units: a Narrative summarization strategy. In W.G. Lehnert & M.H. Ringle (eds), *Strategies for natural language processing* (pp. 375-412). Hillsdale, NJ: Lawrence Erlbaum Associates.

136. Levelt, W.J.M., & Schriefers, H. (1987). Stages of lexical access. In G. Kempen (ed), *Natural language generation: Recent advances in Artificial Intelligence, Psychology, and Linguistics* (pp. 395-404). Boston, MA: Kluwer Academic Publishers.

137. Levinson, S.C. (1983). *Pragmatics*. Cambridge, England: Cambridge University Press.

138. Levin, J.A., & Moore, J.A. (1977). Dialogue-games: Metacommunication structures for natural language interaction. *Cognitive Science, 1(4)*, 395-420.

139. Litman, D.J., & Allen, J.F. (1984). A plan recognition model for subdialogues in conversations. University of Rochester Technical Report 141.

140. Loomis, R.S, Hull, H.R., & Robinson, M.L. (1936). *The art of writing prose.* New York, NY: Farrar & Rinehart.

141. Lytinen, S.L. (1984). *The organization of knowledge in a multi-lingual, integrated parser.* Ph.D. dissertation, Yale University.

142. Mann, W.C. (1982). The anatomy of a systemic choice. USC/Information Sciences Institute Technical Report RR-82-104.

143. Mann, W.C. (1983a). An overview of the Nigel text generation grammar. USC/Information Sciences Institute Technical Report RR-83-113.

144. Mann, W.C. (1983b). An overview of the Penman text generation system. USC/Information Sciences Institute Technical Report RR-83-114.

145. Mann, W.C. (1984). Discourse structures for text generation, USC/Information Sciences Institute Technical Report RR-84-127.

146. Mann, W.C., & Matthiessen, C.M.I.M. (1983). Nigel: a Systemic grammar for text generation. USC/Information Sciences Institute Technical Report RR-83-105.

147. Mann, W.C., & Thompson, S.A. (1983). Relational Propositions in Discourse. USC/Information Sciences Institute Technical Report RR-83-115.

148. Mann, W.C., & Thompson, S.A. (1987). Rhetorical structure theory: description and construction of text structures. In G. Kempen (ed), *Natural language generation: Recent advances in Artificial Intelligence, Psychology, and Linguistics* (pp. 85-96). Boston, MA: Kluwer Academic Publishers.

149. Matthiessen, C.M.I.M. (1984). Systemic grammar in computation: the Nigel case. USC/Information Sciences Institute Technical Report RR-84-121.

150. McCawley, J.D. (1978). Conversational implicature and the lexicon. In P. Cole (ed), *Syntax and Semantics Vol 9: Pragmatics* (pp. 245-259). New York, NY: Academic Press.

151. McCoy, K.F. (1985). The role of perspective in responding to property misconceptions. In *9th IJCAI Conference Proceedings*, Los Angeles.

152. McCoy, K.F. (1987). Contextual effects on responses to misconceptions. In G. Kempen (ed), *Natural language generation: Recent advances in Artificial Intelligence, Psychology, and Linguistics* (pp. 43-54). Boston, MA: Kluwer Academic Publishers.

153. McDermott, D.V. (1978). Planning and acting. *Cognitive Science, 2(2)*, 71-109.

154. McDermott, D.V. (1981). Artificial Intelligence meets natural stupidity. In J. Haugeland (ed), *Mind design*, Cambridge, MA: MIT Press.

155. McDonald, D.D. (1980). *Natural language production as a process of decision making under constraint*. Ph.D. dissertation, Massachusetts Institute of Technology.

156. McDonald, D.D. (1981). Natural language generation as a computational problem: an Introduction. University of Massachusetts (Amherst) Technical Report 81-33.

157. McDonald, D.D., & Pustejovsky, J.D. (1985). Description-Directed Natural Language Generation. In *9th IJCAI Conference Proceedings*, Los Angeles.

158. McDonald, D.D. (1986). Description-directed control: Its implications for natural language generation. In B. Grosz, K. Sparck Jones & B. Webber (eds), *Readings in natural language processing* (pp. 12-35). San Francisco, CA: Morgan Kaufman.

159. McDonald, D.D., Vaughan, M.M., & Pustejovsky, J.D. (1987). Factors contributing to efficiency in natural language generation. In G. Kempen (ed), *Natural language generation: Recent advances in Artificial Intelligence, Psychology, and Linguistics* (pp. 159-182). Boston, MA: Kluwer Academic Publishers.

160. McGuire, R. (1975). Political primaries and words of pain. Unpublished manuscript, Yale University.

161. McKeown, K.R. (1982). *Generating natural language text in response to questions about database queries*. Ph.D. dissertation, University of Pennsylvania.

162. McKeown, K.R. (1985). *Text generation: Using discourse strategies and focus constraints to generate natural language text*. Cambridge, England: Cambridge University Press.

163. Miller, D.P. (1985). *Planning by search through simulations*. Ph.D. dissertation, Yale University.

164. Montague, R. (1974). Universal grammar. In R.H. Thomason (ed), *Formal Philosophy: Selected papers* (pp. 222-246). New Haven, CT: Yale University Press.

165. Moore, J.D. (1988). Enhanced explanations in expert and advice-giving systems. USC/Information Sciences Institute Technical Report, forthcoming.

166. Morris, C.W. (1938). Foundations of the theory of signs. In O. Neurath, R. Carna, & C.W. Morris (eds), *International encyclopedia of unified science* (vol 1), (pp. 77-138). Chicago, IL: University of Chicago Press.

167. Novak, H-J. (1984). A relational matching strategy for temporal event recognition. In J. Laubsch (ed), *Proceedings of GWAI-84*. Berlin, Germany: Springer Verlag.

168. Novak, H-J. (1987). Strategies for generating coherent descriptions of object motions in time-varying imagery. In G. Kempen (ed), *Natural language generation: Recent advances in Artificial Intelligence, Psychology, and Linguistics* (pp. 117-132). Boston, MA: Kluwer Academic Publishers.

169. Osgood, C.E. (1957). A behavioristic analysis of perception and language as cognitive phenomena. In J. Bruner (ed), *Contemporary approaches to cognition* (pp. 45-76). Cambridge, MA: Harvard University Press.

170. Osgood, C.E., & Bock, J.K. (1977). Salience and sentencing: some production principles. In S. Rosenberg (ed), *Sentence production: Developments in research and theory* (pp. 89-140). Hillsdale, NJ: Lawrence Erlbaum Associates.

171. Osgood, C.E., May, W.H., & Miron, M. (1975). *Cross-cultural universals of affective meaning*. Urbana, IL: University of Illinois Press.

172. Paris, C.L. (1985). Descriptions strategies for naive and expert users. In *23rd ACL Conference Proceedings*, Chicago.

173. Paris, C.L. (1987). *The use of explicit user models in text generation: tailoring to a user's level of expertise*. Ph.D. dissertation, Columbia University.

174. Paris, C.L., & McKeown, K.R. (1987). Discourse strategies for descriptions of complex physical objects. In G. Kempen (ed), *Natural language generation: Recent advances in Artificial Intelligence, Psychology, and Linguistics* (pp. 97-116). Boston, MA: Kluwer Academic Publishers.

175. Patten, T. (1986). *Interpreting systemic grammar as a computational representation: a Problem-solving approach to text generation*. Ph.D. dissertation, University of Edinburgh.

176. Patten, T., & Ritchie, G. (1987). A formal model of systemic grammar. In G. Kempen (ed), *Natural language generation: Recent advances in Artificial Intelligence, Psychology, and Linguistics* (pp. 279-300). Boston, MA: Kluwer Academic Publishers.

177. Payne, L.V. (1969). *The lively art of writing*. Chicago, IL: Follett (Mentor Books).

178. Piaget, J. (1955). *The language and thought of the child.* New York, NY: New American Library Inc. (Meridian Books).

179. Reichman, R. (1985). *Getting computers to talk like you and me.* Cambridge, MA: MIT Press.

180. Reithinger, N. (1984). *Antwortgenerierung für das Erlanger Spracherkennungssystem.* Master's degree dissertation, University of Erlangen-Nürnberg.

181. Reithinger, N. (1987). Generating referring expressions and pointing gestures. In G. Kempen (ed), *Natural language generation: Recent advances in Artificial Intelligence, Psychology, and Linguistics* (pp. 71-82). Boston, MA: Kluwer Academic Publishers.

182. Rich, E.A. (1979). User modeling via stereotypes. *Cognitive Science, 3(4),* 329-354.

183. Riesbeck, C.K., & Martin, C.E. (1985). Direct memory access parsing. Yale University Technical Report 354.

184. Rombauer, I.S., & Becker, M.R. (1975). *The joy of cooking.* New York, NY: Bobbs-Merrill.

185. Rosenberg, S. (1977). Semantic constraints on sentence production: an Experimental approach. In S. Rosenberg (ed), *Sentence Production: Developments in Research and Theory* (pp. 195-228). Hillsdale, NJ: Lawrence Erlbaum Associates.

186. Rösner, D. (1986). *Ein System zur Generierung von Deutschen Texten aus Semantischen Repräsentationen.* Ph.D. dissertation, Universität Stuttgart.

187. Rösner, D. (1987). The automated news agency SEMTEX — a Text generator for German. In G. Kempen (ed), *Natural language generation: Recent advances in Artificial Intelligence, Psychology, and Linguistics* (pp. 133-148). Boston, MA: Kluwer Academic Publishers.

188. Sacerdoti, E. (1977). *A structure for plans and behavior.* Amsterdam, The Netherlands: North-Holland Publishing Company.

189. Sacks, H., Schegloff, E.A., & Jefferson, G. (1974). A simplest systematics for the organization of turn-taking for conversation. *Language, 50(4),* 696-735.

190. Sanford, D.L., & Roach, J.W. (1987). Parsing and generating the pragmatics of natural language utterances using metacommunication. In *9th Cognitive Science Society Conference Proceedings,* Seattle.

191. Schank, R.C. (1972). 'Semantics' in conceptual analysis. *Lingua, 30(2)*, 101-139. Amsterdam, The Netherlands: North-Holland Publishing Company.

192. Schank, R.C. (1975). *Conceptual information processing.* Amsterdam, The Netherlands: North-Holland Publishing Company.

193. Schank, R.C. (1977). Rules and topics in conversation. *Cognitive Science, 1(4)*, 421-442.

194. Schank, R.C. (1979). Interestingness: Controlling inferences. *Artificial Intelligence, 12(3)*, 273-297.

195. Schank, R.C. (1982). *Dynamic memory: a Theory of reminding and learning in computers and people,* Cambridge, England: Cambridge University Press, 1982.

196. Schank, R.C., & Abelson, R.P. (1977). *Scripts, plans, goals and understanding.* Hillsdale, NJ: Lawrence Erlbaum Associates.

197. Schank, R.C., & Birnbaum, L.A. (1983). Memory, meaning, and syntax. In T.G. Bever, J.M. Carroll, & L.A. Miller (eds), *Talking minds: Studies in the cognitive sciences* (pp. 209-251). Cambridge, MA: MIT Press.

198. Schank, R.C., Collins, G.C., Davis, E., Johnson, P.N., Lytinen, S.L., & Reiser, B.J. (1981). What's the point? Yale University Technical Report 205.

199. Schank, R.C., & Lehnert, W.G. (1979). The conceptual content of conversation. Yale University Technical Report 160.

200. Schegloff, E.A., Jefferson, G., & Sacks, H. (1977). The preference for self-correction in the organization and repair of conversation. *Language, 53(2)*, 361-382.

201. Searle, J.R. (1969). *Speech acts.* Cambridge, England: Cambridge University Press.

202. Searle, J.R. (1975). Indirect speech acts. In P. Cole & J.L. Morgan (eds), *Syntax and semantics 3: speech acts* (pp. 59-82). New York, NY: Academic Press.

203. Searle, J.R. (1979). *Expression and meaning.* Cambridge, England: Cambridge University Press.

204. Sidner, C.L. (1979). Toward a computational theory of definite anaphora comprehension in English. Massachusetts Institute of Technology Technical Report AI-TR-537.

205. Simmons, R.F., & Slocum, J. (1972). Generating English discourse from semantic networks. *Communications of the ACM, 15(10)*, 891-905.

206. Stefik, M., & Bobrow, D.G. (1986). Object-oriented programming: Themes and variations. *AI Magazine, 6(4)*, 50-55.

207. Stockwell, R.P., Schachter, P., & Partee, B.P. (1972). *The major syntactic structures of English.* New York, NY: Holt, Reinhart and Winston.

208. Straker, D.Y. (1980). Situational variables in language use. University of Illinois (Urbana) Technical Report 167.

209. Strunk, W. jr, & White, E.B. (1959). *The elements of style.* New York, NY: Macmillan.

210. Swartout, W.R. (1981). Producing explanations and justifications of expert consulting programs. Massachusetts Institute of Technology Technical Report LCS-TR-251.

211. Sycara-Cyranski, K. (1985a). Persuasive argumentation in resolution of collective bargaining impasses. In *7th Cognitive Science Conference Proceedings*, Irvine.

212. Sycara-Cyranski, K. (1985b). Arguments of persuasion in labour mediation. In *9th IJCAI Conference Proceedings*, Los Angeles.

213. Sycara-Cyranski, K. (1987). *Resolving adversarial conflicts: an Approach integrating case-based and analytical methods.* Ph.D. dissertation, Georgia Institute of Technology.

214. Tjoe-Liong, K. (1987). A computer model of functional grammar. In G. Kempen (ed), *Natural language generation: Recent advances in Artificial Intelligence, Psychology, and Linguistics* (pp. 315-332). Boston, MA: Kluwer Academic Publishers.

215. Van Dijk, T. (1985). *Studies in the pragmatics of discourse.* The Hague, The Netherlands: Mouton.

216. Watzlawick, P., Beavin, J.H., & Jackson, D.D. (1967). *Pragmatics of human communication.* New York, NY: Norton.

217. Weathers, W., & Winchester, O. (1978). *The new strategy of style.* New York, NY: McGraw-Hill.

218. Wilensky, R. (1981). A knowledge-based approach to natural language processing: a Progress report. In *7th IJCAI Conference Proceedings*, Vancouver.

219. Wilensky, R. (1984). KODIAK — a knowledge representation language. In *6th Cognitive Science Conference Proceedings*, Boulder.

220. Willis, H. (1969). *Structure, style, and usage (the rhetoric of exposition)* (2nd ed). New York, NY: Holt, Rinehart & Winston.

221. Wish, X., Deutsch, Y., & Kaplan, Z. (1976). Perceived dimensions of interpersonal relations. *Journal of Personal and Social Psychology, 33(4)*, 101-145.

222. Wodehouse, P.G. (1979). *Carry on, Jeeves*. New York, NY: Penguin.

223. Wong, H.K.T. (1975). *Generating English sentences from semantic structures*. M.S. thesis, University of Toronto Technical Report 84.

224. Woolf, B.P. (1984). *Context dependent planning in a machine tutor*. Ph.D. dissertation, University of Massachusetts (Amherst).

225. Woolf, B.P., & McDonald, D.D. (1984). Context-dependent transitions in tutoring discourse. In *4th AAAI Conference Proceedings*, Austin.

226. Zernik, U. & Dyer, M.G. (1986). Disambiguation and acquisition using the phrasal lexicon. In *11th Coling Conference Proceedings*, Bonn.

Name Index

Topic Index